"This excellent guidebook is a winning com~~~ ~~~ ~~~ ~~~try experience, biblical insight, and a broad understanding of how people ~~~ ~~~ ~~~ ~~~ in today's world. I have read most of the classic manuals on pastoral work and written a few of my own, but *Pastoral Ministry in the Real World* has elements that are superior to them all. You will especially appreciate the section on Christ's handling of the conflicts He encountered."

Warren W. Wiersbe, author and former pastor, Moody Church, Chicago

"Being a pastor is hard work—it's a maze of urgent and sometimes conflicting challenges and opportunities, and young pastors need guides to help them. Dr. Wilson's book *Pastoral Ministry in the Real World* is a guidebook for maneuvering that ministry maze, drawn on years of his own pastoral experience. Wilson deals with issues like pastoral care, teaching, and leadership, and he brings practical insights to each. I look forward to using this book with my own students."

Michael Duduit, Executive Editor of *Preaching* magazine;
Dean and Professor of Christian Ministry,
Clamp Divinity School of Anderson University, Anderson, SC

"In his new work, *Pastoral Ministry in the Real World,* Dr. Wilson has given us a book that is biblical, thoughtful, and rooted in years of experience. By consistently integrating Scriptural truth with some of the latest insights from psychology, sociology and organizational management, it provides practical help to all those called to shepherd Christ's church. This is a book I can recommend to any student, new pastor, or seasoned leader in the church world of twentieth-century America."

Scott Wenig, Professor of Applied Theology, Denver Seminary

"The best books derive from hard-won experience on the ground. This is such a book. Jim Wilson is a pastor who knows his way around. The practice of your ministry will be enhanced by the opportunity to reflect on Wilson's experience. Pastoral ministry requires knowledge, skill, and character. This book offers all three."

Kenton C. Anderson, President of Northwest Baptist Seminary; Professor of
Homiletics, ACTS Seminaries of Trinity Western University, Langley, BC

"Crisp, engaging, and helpful, this volume orients ministry students and pastors to ministry in the real world—its questions, concerns, responsibilities, skills, pains, and privileges. It covers the content well, strikes the right tone, interweaves research with pastoral experience, and is outlined quite clearly. There is much wisdom in this book."

Christopher W. Morgan, Dean and Professor of Theology, School of Christian
Ministries, California Baptist University, Riverside

"Wilson's *Pastoral Ministry in the Real World* is true to its title. That alone would be sufficient reason for recommending the book to anyone training for or already slugging it out in the trenches. But there's much more. Along with being honest about the difficulties of pastoral ministry, Wilson is biblical, balanced, and full of wise counsel. This is an excellent book for anyone called by God to be a soul-watcher."

Randal Pelton, Senior Pastor, Calvary Bible Church, Mount Joy, PA

"Becoming a pastor is an intimidating step into a significant spiritual leadership role. *Pastoral Ministry in the Real World* paves the way forward by summarizing and explaining, in a down-to-earth fashion, the key roles and responsibilities pastors fulfill. We need more men to answer God's call to spiritual service as pastors. This book is a helpful guide to those who embark on this lifelong journey."

Jeff Iorg, President, Golden Gate Seminary

"Because people are complicated and messy, ministry often feels complicated and messy. Dr. Wilson knows that world, but his knowledge of the soul and skills of pastoring points us to clarity, focusing on loving well, teaching well, and leading well."

Marshall Shelley, Editor, *Leadership Journal*

"Dr. Wilson has written a pastoral ministry book that will help every minister of the gospel to grow on every practical level of ministry from 'good ministry' into 'great ministry.' I highly recommend that you get a copy of *Pastoral Ministry in the Real World* for you and everyone sharing ministry with you!"

Walt Kallestad, Lead Pastor, Community Church of Joy, Glendale, AZ

"As a seminary professor I found it frustrating to find a suitable textbook for my Pastoral Ministry class since there is a real dearth of resources in this area. I am glad to see a book written from an experienced pastor who speaks practically and biblically to this subject. I believe it will be helpful to students who are new to pastoral ministry as well as those who have served for years as pastors. I highly recommend Dr. Wilson's book!"

David W. Johnson, Executive Director, Arizona Southern Baptist Convention

"*Pastoral Ministry in the Real World* is an easy read filled with practical content. Dr. Wilson models an approach of introspection and transparency that all pastors would be wise to follow. It clarified and affirmed my own calling and practice."

Tom Jones, President, Williams Baptist College, Walnut Ridge, AR

"In his book *Pastoral Ministry in the Real World*, Dr. Wilson provides the theoretical principles of ministry through practical advice and real life examples. The book helps pastors understand that they all face similar struggles, and provides the tools to over-come them. Although written in a USA context, its content transcends many cultural boundaries. I hope to see the book translated to Spanish soon."

Robert Carter, Rector, Seminario Teologico Bautista Santiago, Chile

"Dr. Jim Wilson has written a brilliant work on the practical aspects of pastoral lead-ership. From walking well in the midst of pain to leading with courageous conviction, this book is as helpful as they come."

Eric Herrstrom, Lead Pastor, Lake Arlington Baptist Church, Lake Arlington, TX

"While there is great joy in serving the living God, serving God's people as a pastor has never been easy. The rapid rate of cultural change in the twenty-first century has meant that each day seems to surface new issues. In times like these, it is good that every pastor be reminded that his work is described and detailed in the Scriptures. From the first to the last, Dr. Wilson's book is Scripture-saturated and laced with the wisdom of a long-time practitioner. It addresses every major facet of a pastor's work, with biblical truth and teaching on every page. Pastors at all stages of life and ministry will benefit from this book."

Randy Adams, Executive Director-Treasurer Northwest Baptist Convention

"*Pastoral Ministry in the Real World* is a good book full of practical wisdom for pastors. I wish I could have read this book before my first pastorate thirty years ago!"

Benny Wong, Senior Pastor First Chinese Baptist Church Los Angeles, CA

"Pastoral ministry is difficult to do well in today's world. Dr. Wilson's book *Pastoral Ministry in the Real World,* lays a solid biblical foundation to guide pastors in building healthy churches. His honest stories of painful ministry encounters are refreshing and add a needed reality check to idealized pastoral ministry. I appreciated the balance of loving people with the need to lead them in spite of the challenges involved. I will be recommending this book to aspiring pastors for years to come."

Steve Davidson, Founding Pastor of Clovis Hills Community Church

"Finally, a book that lists practical steps for pastors including bonafide research and illustrative material to help avoid common pitfalls and heartaches that comes with ministry. *Pastoral Ministry in the Real World* would have saved me so much struggle 30 years ago. This resource is a must read for all of my staff and every young minister that I have the opportunity to mentor."

David Miracle, Lead Pastor, Watershed San Antonio, TX

"Being the pastor of a local church is not only a great privilege, but also a great responsibility. Dr. Wilson has not only been a pastor, but now as a professor has a desire to help other pastors fulfill their calling. This book is real, down to earth, and can be a great help to not only a new pastor but also a seasoned one. God has used the author, and reading his book will make any pastor better."

Rob Zinn, Pastor, Immanuel Baptist, Highland, CA

"Healthy churches are led by healthy ministers. *Pastoral Ministry in the Real World* is both a learning guide and a field manual for a healthy minister written by one who has mined wisdom from the Scriptures and forged it in the fire that only comes by serving God's people in the best and worst of times. The author's use of the systems approach to leading during times of conflict has been useful to me personally and will revolutionize your ability to achieve victory in times when many become a victim. Every person serving in ministry would benefit from reading this book."

Randy McWhorter, Healthy Church Group Leader,
California Southern Baptist Convention

"Dr. Wilson has shown a bright and refreshing light onto the current ministry scene in a way that will serve every pastor well. Combining practical wisdom with helpful, engaging real-life examples, Wilson calls ministers to excel in the essential tasks of ministry."

Bob Royall, Director of Coaching, Blackaby Ministries International

"Thorough and practical, Dr. Wilson's book describes in a new way what church members need in pastoral care. Because it is well-organized, biblical, and relevant, the book makes a great manual for every pastor or church leader who wants to carry out pastoral care in a compassionate manner. Pastoral Ministry in the Real World is highly recommended as a textbook in seminaries and Bible institutes. I pray that we have it soon in Spanish."

Daniel Jiménez, Director, Seminario Teológico Bautista Mexicano

PASTORAL MINISTRY
in the Real World

Loving, Teaching, and Leading God's People

Jim L. Wilson

WEAVER BOOK
COMPANY
WOOSTER, OHIO

Pastoral Ministry in the Real World: Loving, Teaching, and Leading God's People
© 2015 by Jim L. Wilson

First edition published by
Weaver Book Company
1190 Summerset Dr.
Wooster, OH 44691
Visit us at weaverbookcompany.com

Scripture quotations unless otherwise indicated are from the Holman Christian Standard Bible®. Copyright © 1999, 2000, 2002, 2003 by Holman Bible Publishers. Used by permission.

Scripture quotations marked NASB are from the New American Standard Bible®. Copyright © 1960, 1962, 1963, 1968, 1971, 1972, 1973, 1975, 1977 by The Lockman Foundation. Used by permission. www.Lockman.org.

Scripture quotations marked NIV are from the Holy Bible, New International Version®, NIV®. Copyright © 1973, 1978, 1984, 2011 by Biblica, Inc.™ Used by permission of Zondervan. All rights reserved worldwide. www.zondervan.com

Scripture quotations marked AMP are from the Amplified Bible, Copyright © 1954, 1958, 1962, 1964, 1965, 1987 by The Lockman Foundation. Used by permission. www.Lockman.org.

Scripture quotations marked NLT are from the Holy Bible, New Living Translation, copyright © 1996, 2004, 2007 by Tyndale House Foundation. Used by permission of Tyndale House Publishers, Inc., Carol Stream, Illinois 60188. All rights reserved.

Cover: Frank Gutbrod
Interior design and typesetting: { In a Word }
Editing: Line for Line

Print: 978-1-941337-46-2
EPUB: 978-1-941337-47-9

Library of Congress Cataloging-in-Publication Data

Wilson, Jim L.
    Pastoral ministry in the real world : loving, teaching, and leading God's people / Jim L. Wilson. — First edition.
        pages   cm
    Includes bibliographical references and index.
    ISBN 978-1-941337-46-2
    1. Pastoral theology. I. Title.
    BV4011.3.W484 2015
    253—dc23

                                2015031899

Printed in the United States of America

15 16 17 18 19 / 5 4 3 2 1

*I dedicate this book to the pastor
who keeps watch over my soul,*

*my pastor,
Dr. Dale Garland*

Contents

Part IV   LEADING GOD'S PEOPLE

Foreword

Our world and our churches are crying out for leadership. I have the privilege of consulting with pastor search teams, and the three traits that surface when I ask them to describe what they are searching for are these: "someone to love us, someone to preach the Word of God to us, and someone to lead us."

Dr. Wilson has woven together these three cords that help us achieve that mission of leader by reminding us to care for the flock, which builds trust that releases them to follow us as their leaders. These three traits are foundational as they reflect the heart of God. I don't know of any pastor with significant kingdom of God impact that was not marked by these unbreakable marks: love for the people, consistent preaching of the Bible, and the willingness to lead.

This book is one of those I wish I had in my earlier days of ministry. I had my fair share of stepping on ministry land mines that could have been avoided had I been exposed to the wisdom and experience Dr. Wilson brings to the table. It's been my privilege to be in his classes as an adjunct professor and listen to him unfold timeless diamonds of truth and muttering under my breath "Why didn't someone tell me this?" or "How could I have missed that?" or "Wow, what an insight!"

The material on conflict in chapters 9 and 10 are with the price of the book. Wish I had that in my first pastorate when a man I considered a friend, rose up in a business meeting and wanted me fired.

This book is the carefully constructed work, not of a thesis, but the expressions of a lifetime sketched from the frontlines of congregation and classroom. I add this book as one of the best go-to resources. You will find yourself drinking from this fountain of wise counsel often, dog-earing its pages, and wearing out your Sharpie as you mine the nuggets of ministry gold. I have only one regret after reading this book — I wish I had it fifty years ago!

Jim Henry, Pastor Emeritus, First Baptist Church, Orlando, FL
President, Southern Baptist Convention 1994-1995

Preface

On the evening of my ordination, I sat on the steps of Brotherhood Hall at Wayland Baptist College in Plainview, Texas, and let the full impact of the evening soak in. Though still a teenager, the members of College Heights Baptist Church had just set me apart for the gospel ministry after Northfield Baptist Church, a small, half-time church called me to be their pastor. At that moment, I began to feel the weight of the responsibilities of pastoring. I was scared to death, but I trusted in God for strength to *love, teach, and lead* His people. Today, I feel that same weight.

For most of my ministry, I served as a local church pastor. In 2006, I transitioned and became a professor. Though I am a professor now, I continue to serve as an interim or transitional pastor as opportunities present themselves. Though my title has changed from pastor to professor, my heart remains firmly in the local church. I hope you will feel my respect for the office as you read this book.

As you read, please look at the footnotes for the research or rational that supports the positions I take in the text. In an attempt to make the book more readable, I placed the bulk of any quotations or research recommendations in the footnotes. Because of this approach, there will be some pages with more space dedicated to footnotes than text.

May God bless you as you grow in your calling to love, teach, and lead God's people.

Jim L. Wilson
Hemet, CA
May 8, 2015

Acknowledgements

Thank you to President Jeff Iorg, Dean Michael Martin, and the Board of Trustees of Golden Gate Baptist Theological Seminary for the sabbatical leave to research and write this book.

My thanks also to Don Beall and the professors of the "P" Department who encouraged me to write the book to fill a pressing need for Contextualized Leadership Development students. Thanks also to the many colleagues who read early versions of the manuscript and made suggestions for improvements, and to Christian Wilder, my research assistant, whose eye for detail provided balance to my big-picture-thinking proclivities.

Many of the ministry illustrations in the book were previously published in books or articles I've written for Parakaleo Ministries, *Christianity Today*, FreshMinistry.org, LifeWay, Leadership Network, and Focus on the Family. Some of my current thinking has also been sharpened by interaction with faculty members with whom I've taught or D.Min. candidates with whom I've interacted in seminars. I am thankful for what I've learned from those editors, faculty members, and students.

I take full responsibility for any errors this book contains, but must share the credit for any helpful insights it contains with all those mentioned above. It is my joy and honor to serve with them in ministry.

PART ONE

INVITATION TO PASTORAL MINISTRY

Chapter 1   Who Is a Pastor?

God gave pastors to the first century church to love, teach, and lead His people. The New Testament writers used three words to refer to pastors: *poimén* (shepherd), *presbuteros* (elder), and *episkopos* (overseer). Some may see these as three separate offices, but there is evidence they are synonymous[1] and refer to the single office of pastor.[2]

Poimén (shepherd) and its subsequent forms appear eighteen times in the New Testament, referring usually to the literal vocation of tending sheep (Luke 2:18) or, metaphorically, to Jesus' care of His people (John 10:11). In Ephesians 4:11, Paul uses *poimén* to refer to a church leader, "And He personally gave some to be apostles, some prophets, some evangelists, some pastors[3] and teachers." In this passage, Paul was not introducing a new concept by referring to a spiritual leader as shepherd. Jeremiah referred to spiritual leaders as shepherds, "I will give you shepherds who are loyal to Me, and they will shepherd you with knowledge and skill" (3:15); and in John 21:15-17, Jesus asked Peter to shepherd His sheep.

By using a word that most commonly referred to those who had responsibility for sheep in a pasture to denote one who cares for people in a congregation, the biblical writers drew an analogy between the two professions that speaks to the devotion and character of congregational leaders and the nature of their work. While shepherds were not always respected (Gen. 46:34), they were responsible for protecting and caring for their sheep at all costs and without regard to their own safety or comfort (1 Sam. 17:34-35). Pastors have a similar duty. They are to love the people they serve (1 Tim. 4:11-12) and keep watch over their souls (Heb. 13:17).

Jesus drew on the shepherd analogy to reveal a bit about his core identi-

---

1   Peter refers to the same office with all three words in 1 Peter 5:1-2.

2   Paschall, "The Pastor as Overseer," 319: "In the New Testament it is clear that the appellations bishop, elder, and pastor designate the same office and order of persons (Acts 20:17, 28; Phil. 1:1; 1 Tim. 3:1, 8; Titus 1:5, 7; 1 Peter 5:1, 2)."

3   Ποιμένας is the Greek word.

ty:[4] "I am the good shepherd. The good shepherd lays down his life for the sheep" (John 10:11). Pastors, like shepherds, are to devote themselves to the well-being of those under their care, without regard for personal benefit or enrichment (John 10:12). Pastors are to love their people.

Presbuteros (elder) in its various forms appears sixty-six times in the New Testament and is used to refer to an older person (Acts 2:17), or more commonly a Jewish official (Matt. 16:21). The biblical authors also use the term to refer to heavenly elders (Rev. 4:4), a governing body (Acts 21:17–26), and on a few occasions, church leaders (Titus 1:5–7).

Their use of elder for the role of congregational leader communicates two important concepts: (1) pastors have leadership responsibilities, and (2) they require personal gravitas[5] to fulfill their responsibilities. Furthermore, in 1 Timothy 3:6, Paul warns against allowing a novice to serve and requires those selected be "above reproach" (1 Tim. 3:2). Pastors are to be respected leaders.

Episkopos (overseer) is the only term New Testament writers used exclusively to refer to church leaders.[6] In the five times it appears in the New Testament,[7] it has the meaning of a person who is keeping watch over a congregation. On three of the five occasions, it is paired with elder or shepherd. Of those three times, overseer is paired with elder once in Titus 1:5–7: "The reason I left you in Crete was to set right what was left undone and, as I directed you, to appoint elders[8] in every town: someone who is blameless, the husband of one wife, having faithful children not accused of wildness or rebellion. For an overseer,[9] as God's administrator, must be blameless, not arrogant, not hot-tempered, not addicted to wine, not a bully, not greedy for money. Notice that the same leader referred to as an elder in verse 5 is called an overseer in verse 7.

Biblical writers also paired overseer with shepherd on two occasions. The first is found in Acts 20:28: "Be on guard for yourselves and for all the

---

4 John affirms Jesus' divinity with this "I am" statement (one of seven in the Gospel of John) revealing something about who Jesus is (Exod. 3:14).

5 Shepherds, in the ancient world, were synonymous to rulers (Matt. 2:6) Ancient royal documents reveal that kings compared their responsibilities to that of a shepherd.

6 The word is sometimes translated "bishop," but it can mislead contemporary readers because of some denominations using the term for those who supervise local church pastors.

7 This word is used a sixth time as a verb in Hebrews 12:15, which is a command to look for something with diligence rather than referring to an overseer.

8 Πρεσβύτερος.

9 Ἐπίσκοπος.

flock that the Holy Spirit has appointed you to as overseers,[10] to shepherd[11] the church of God, which He purchased with His own blood." This pairing is not contrasting the work, showing the roles to be unique and distinct, but demonstrating the overseer functioning as a shepherd.

The second pairing is found in 1 Peter 5:2: "Shepherd[12] God's flock among you, not overseeing[13] out of compulsion but freely, according to God's [will]; not for the money but eagerly." Again, the terms likely refer to the same person, making them interchangeable.[14] Therefore, using overseer to refer to the office of pastor reinforces the expectation that pastors are leaders. Clearly, the Ephesians 4:11 listing are different offices — an evangelist and a prophet are different. Bishop and elder are notably absent from the list. This absence is likely due to these terms referencing the same pastoral office and leadership role, rather than separate roles.[15]

Poimén (shepherd), *presbuteros* (elder), and *episkopos* (overseer) therefore all refer to a single leadership role in a congregation, but the nuance of each word provides a depth and richness in understanding the person and work of the pastor. *Poimén* emphasizes the loving and caring for the people, and Paul uses it alongside teacher in Ephesians 4:11 to underscore that teaching is that one of the ways shepherds show love to their people. *Presbuteros* adds a sense of gravitas to the pastoral role. And *episkopos* identifies pastors as serving in a leadership role. Therefore, pastors are *influential and respected leaders who watch over God's people by loving, teaching, and leading them — without regard for personal enrichment.*

Paul provides two almost identical lists[16] describing qualifications of *episkopoi* (overseers, 1 Tim. 3:2–7) and *presbuteroi* (elders, Titus 1:6–9). These lists lend credence to the argument that Paul is writing to those occupying the same pastoral office.[17] According to these passages, pastors must have a stable lifestyle, character that is above reproach, and necessary skills to do their work.

---

10   Ἐπισκόπους.

11   Ποιμαίνειν.

12   Ποιμένα.

13   Ἐπίσκοπον.

14   Grissom, "Elder," 473.

15   Carson et al., eds., *New Bible Commentary*, 1238.

16   When comparing the lists, I grouped similar concepts together, for instance, I saw "not hot-tempered" as a subset of self-controlled. I also saw blameless, righteous, holy from the Titus passage as substantially the same as respectable and good reputation among outsiders from the Timothy listing (see table 1 for my grouping).

17   Towner, *Letters*, 249.

Biblical Qualifications for Pastor: Stable Lifestyle

Paul describes a solid family man in 1 Timothy 3:2-7 and Titus 1:6-9. He has only one wife,[18] is able to control his children, and is not addicted to wine. Most would agree that these passages prohibit a polygamous person from serving. After that clear prohibition, it gets complicated. Can a single man serve?[19] If God calls a man to be a pastor and his wife dies, is he disqualified and must he then resign?[20] What about those who were divorced before becoming Christians, and then convert, grow in their faith, and are called by God to pastoral ministry — can they become pastors?[21] What about a woman?[22] These are all fair questions, but likely are not Paul's point in this passage. This is not a "pilot's checklist"[23] to go through prior to takeoff, it is a general description of the Pastor's lifestyle. It is descriptive language.

The pastor must have control over his children. Though not a pastor, Eli was an Old Testament priest who was criticized for the wickedness of his sons (1 Sam. 2:12-36). That example stands as an extreme end of a spectrum, and perhaps a pastor with a teenager struggling with depression, who attempts suicide, is on the other. The truth is, no father has complete control over the choices his children make, but he still has responsibility to supervise his children and guide them into adulthood. What is clear from this text is that while they are in his household, the pastor must have control over his children.[24]

---

18 Lea and Griffin, *1, 2 Timothy, Titus*, 109-10.

19 Likely, this was not Paul's intent, especially since it would disqualify him from serving (1 Cor. 7:7-8). Like the rest of this passage, it refers to a character trait, not a marital status.

20 In other places, Paul allows those whose spouses die to remarry (1 Cor. 7:39-40).

21 Those who allow a divorced man to serve as a pastor should exercise caution. A distant divorce while an unbeliever is one thing, but a recent divorce while serving as a pastor is another, and as a general rule, the circumstance would warrant stepping down as pastor, especially if the pastor was the "offending party" (Matt. 5:31-32; Matt. 19:3-12 and Mark 10:2-12).

22 My position is that phrase "husband of one wife" restricts the senior pastor's gender. However, I also acknowledge that this passage is more descriptive than prescriptive and there are legitimate grounds for a person to take a counter position.

23 Mounce, *Pastoral Epistles*, 158: "But the list is not a checklist requiring, for example, that all church leaders be married and have more than one child."

24 MacArthur, *Pastoral Ministry*, 72-73. MacArthur makes the case that this is

The pastor should not be under the control of an intoxicant. Of course, Paul allows for the use of medicine (1 Tim. 5:23), but he also underscores the need for sobriety among the pastorate. The Spirit of God, not alcohol, should control all believers (Eph. 5:18), including pastors. No credible interpretation would argue that a pastor could be a substance abuser, but where to draw the line on the other end is open to debate. Some pastors see responsible drinking as a reasonable response to this passage,[25] while others, including myself,[26] make a personal choice to be teetotalers.[27]

---

referring to a pastor with grown children, since elders were usually older men and their children will be older and Paul used the general Greek word for children, not one that denotes a baby or small child. I take a different position on this text. Notice that the statement about keeping children under control follows a statement about the necessity of managing his household well (1 Tim. 3:4). If a grown child remains in a pastor's home, the pastor has responsibility for his or her conduct. If they do not, the children are responsible for their own conduct. The emphasis here is on how well a pastor manages his household, not whether his children have made mistakes. One meaning of the Greek word τέκνον is inhabitants and would imply that the children are living in the pastor's home. The church generally shows admiration and respect for the father in the parable of the prodigal son (Luke 15:11–32), even drawing analogies between his love for his sons and God's love for us. Yet at the same time, they can have doubts about a pastor, who has a wayward adult child. While Proverbs 22:6 is general wisdom, not a promise, it does give guidance about how a child should respond in old age to proper training, but it says nothing about young adulthood.

25   Driscoll, *Radical Reformission*, 139–53.

26   My own practice is total abstinence and I encourage others to make the same choice. I've chosen a sober lifestyle, in large part due to my conservative faith tradition, upbringing, and not wanting to be a poor example (Rom. 14:21), but those aren't the only reasons. As a matter of practicality, a sober lifestyle demonstrates wisdom (Prov. 23:29–35) and is a necessary approach to being ready to minister at all times. The FAA prohibits pilots from reporting to work when they have consumed alcohol within the past 8 hours, or have other impairment (see http://www.alpa.org/portals/alpa/magazine/2003/April2003_AlcoholProhibitions.htm [accessed 8, 2014]). While there may be times a pastor can't respond to a crisis for medical reasons or because of medications they are taking under a doctor's order, they should be ready at all times to teach (2 Tim. 4:2). Total abstinence insures that they will not have to opt out of ministering to a need because they are impaired.

27   Reinke, "A Beer with Jesus?"

Biblical Qualifications for Pastors: Above Reproach

While many are ready to draw disqualifying red lines over lifestyle issues like divorce or drinking,[28] fewer are ready to disqualify a pastor from serving who is quarrelsome or a bully. Ironically, those who draw the former lifestyle lines with the boldest strokes often display the later traits in the way they express their views on a pastor's lifestyle. Paul, however, requires a pastor to be "above reproach."[29]

The lists of virtues that Paul provides in table 1 illustrate what it means to be above reproach.[30] Many of these virtues align with the fruit of the Spirit (Gal. 5:22–23), while some others align with Paul's listings of things that should occupy a believer's mind (Phil. 4:8). Still others, like hospitable, sensible, not greedy, and not arrogant have particular significance for those in pastoral ministry.

Table 1: Above Reproach Virtues

1 Timothy 3:2–7	Titus 1:6–9
respectable	righteous
good reputation among outsiders	holy
	self-controlled
self-controlled	not hot-tempered
sensible	sensible
hospitable	hospitable
not a bully but gentle	not a bully
not quarrelsome	not greedy for money
not greedy	not arrogant
	loving what is good

Some contend that the list does not go far enough and that there is

---

28   The preferred approach to these texts is to see them as descriptive of the kind of person that should be a pastor, not as a disqualifying checklist.

29   Lea and Griffin, *1, 2 Timothy, Titus*, 109: "To be 'above reproach' demanded that the overseer be a man of blameless character. The same word (*anepilēmpton*) is used of widows in 5:7 and of Timothy in 6:14. It may serve as a general, covering term for the following list of virtues that should distinguish a church leader."

30   Paul uses the word "blameless" in Titus1:6–9.

nothing uniquely Christian about it.[31] That may be true in cultures that align themselves with Aristotle's "unity of virtues."[32] They would expect their leaders to conduct themselves with prudence, virtue, and integrity in private and in public; but that is not the reality of the twenty-first century Western world. These biblical teachings are counter to the widely accepted contemporary notions that people can be effective public leaders while making questionable choices in their private life.[33] These lists are a timeless reminder that church leaders must meet high standards for leadership. For pastors, their private lives matter[34] in their ability to love, teach, and lead God's people. Nothing on this list is unimportant.

While most would acknowledge that committing adultery, a crime, or teaching heresy would bring reproach upon a pastor and would necessitate stepping down from service, others would minimize the equal importance of having a domineering spirit, being prideful, or expressing anger in an inappropriate way.[35] The entire list is important—and rather daunting. Good pastors reflecting on it likely will be challenged by the standard it represents; if they are not, they might be exhibiting arrogance, which is a not an "above reproach" trait (Titus 1:7). In reality, apart from the grace of God and the work of the Holy Spirit (Gal. 5:22–23), no person's life would always be characterized by these character traits.

---

31   Lea and Griffin, *1, 2 Timothy, Titus*, 108.

32   For Aristotle, character was an all-or-nothing proposition. A person's "ethos" is what made him or her believable and persuasive. He considered it the "most effective means of persuasion he possesses." People will interpret these matters out of their own culture. It is not that the meaning of the text will ever change, but out of different cultures, people will find different applications of the text significant or insignificant. See Aristotle, *Rhetoric*, 6.

33   One argument President Clinton's supporters made in the midst of the Clinton-Lewinsky scandal was that what he did in his private life was his personal business as long as it did not affect his ability to govern.

34   Towner, *1–2 Timothy and Titus*, 85: "What one does or is in one's private life has consequences for the church."

35   Bailey, "Exclusive." Mark Driscoll resigned as pastor of Mars Hill Fellowship on October 14, 2014. In the letter, he reported that the elders, who investigated charges against him, said to him, "I had not disqualified myself from ministry." He also wrote, "I readily acknowledge I am an imperfect messenger of the gospel of Jesus Christ. There are many things I have confessed and repented of, privately and publicly, as you are well aware. Specifically, I have confessed to past pride, anger, and a domineering spirit."

While the lists are almost identical,[36] they are not. In the 1 Timothy passage, Paul writes that the pastor should not be a new convert (1 Tim. 5:22) and in the Titus passage he mentions that the pastor should not be arrogant and should love what is good. The two lists are complementary, even though they are not "copy-and-paste" identical. They have an authoritative unity. The fact that they are not identical lends credence to the assessment that they are not exhaustive prescriptive lists; rather, they are descriptive traits that illustrate what it means to be "above reproach," which is the same terminology Paul used to describe widows that could be on the church's list for financial support (1 Tim. 5:7).

BIBLICAL QUALIFICATIONS FOR PASTORS: ABLE TO TEACH

These lists also include a necessary skill set: able to teach. In one of Paul's lists, the pastor is to be "an able teacher" (1Tim. 3:2), and the other "holding to the faithful message as taught so that he will be able both to encourage with sound teaching and to refute those who contradict it" (Titus 1:9).

Further, in Ephesians 4:11, Paul lists the words pastors[37] and teachers[38] together without a definite article before the word "teachers." Most likely, they refer to the same role rather than two separate offices.[39] One way to express the idea of the text is to hyphenate the office as pastor-teacher. While New Testament writers use *episkopoi* (overseers) and *presbuteroi* (elders) more commonly to refer to a pastor, this is the only place they use *poimén* (shepherd) as a title for a pastor. It is significant that in the only place New Testament writers use pastor as a title, it has another title — teacher — as a modifier. It is impossible to separate pastor from teacher. That is because a formal sermon is not the only venue that a pastor teaches.

Pastors teach when they do the following: speak God's word (Heb. 13:7a), live their lives before the people (Heb. 13:7b; 1 Peter 5:3), "rebuke,

---

36   1 Timothy 3:2–7 and Titus 1:6–9.

37   Ποιμενας.

38   Διδασκαλους.

39   Patzia, *Ephesians, Colossians, Philemon*, 240–41: "The absence of the article before teachers (*tous de poimenas kai didaskalous*) leads one to suspect that these words express two aspects of the same office — an office that has a pedagogical and pastoral ministry."

correct, and encourage" (2 Tim. 4:2), and even when ministering in the midst of church or personal conflict (2 Tim. 2:25). Part 3 of this book will explore the pastoral role of teaching.

Like other types of ministry, pastoral ministry involves *doing* ministry. It has some things in common with other types of ministry, but it also has some differences.

Chapter 2   What Is Pastoral Ministry?

Before exploring the core functions of pastoral ministry – loving (part 2), teaching (part 3), and leading (part 4)–it is important to clarify what ministry is and what distinguishes pastoral ministry from other ministries. *Diakonia*, the Greek word for service/ministry,[1] and its various forms occur thirty-four times in the New Testament. It refers to many types of service: Moses giving the Ten Commandments (2 Cor. 3:7), Paul's evangelism among the Gentiles (Rom. 11:13), and Martha preparing a meal (Luke 10:40). Some of these people were in leadership positions, while some were not.

Pastoral ministry is unique because of its calling and specific responsibilities, but at its core, it is ministry. From a New Testament perspective, ministry is *participating with God and cooperating with His people in serving others to meet their needs, fulfill our calling, and bring glory to God.*

This definition begins and ends with God and has at its core the needs of others. Believers do not perform a ministry task because it interests them or because they want prestige that comes with service. Rather, they minister because of the needs around them (serving others to meet their needs) in response to what God is doing (participating with God) with the ultimate goal of bringing Him glory (bring glory to God). This approach surrounds the needs of the human condition with God's activity and His glory.

Participating with God

*Ministry is **participating with God** and cooperating with His people in serving others to meet their needs, fulfill our calling, and bring glory to God.*

---

1   Διάκονος is the word used for the title servant or minister. In this section, I am not focusing on the use of the word in the noun form as a title, which appears twenty-nine times in the New Testament, but rather διακονία, as an act of service.

Paul's writings depict ministers as "co-workers" with God (1 Cor. 3:9; 1 Thess. 3:2). In this instance, the word "co-workers" does not imply equality. Believers work on God's agenda, not theirs.[2]

In their ministries, believers are participating with God, who is working through them (Acts 21:19) and in their situation (2 Sam. 14:14) to accomplish His will (Ps. 138:7–8). Apart from God, they can accomplish nothing (John 15:5), but can endure much (Phil. 4:13) in participation with Him.

Pastoral ministry requires keen spiritual insight to see beyond surface issues to the core needs (Acts 3:6) and to see the spiritual forces at work (2 Kings 6:17). It requires an ability to receive God's vision (Col. 3:2), then influence and equip others (Eph. 4:12) to accomplish that vision.[3]

COOPERATING WITH HIS PEOPLE

Ministry is participating with God and **cooperating with His people** *in serving others to meet their needs, fulfill our calling, and bring glory to God.*

While ministry can be one-on-one, all ministries occur with the support of a Christian community, which equips, encourages, and blesses the ministers. Ministry is always cooperative. Even Judas, whose later betrayal demonstrated his unworthiness for the disciple's work, *shared* in the ministry (Acts 1:17).

The believers formed a collective priesthood (1 Peter 2:9) in the first-century church with a spirit of cooperation existing between those who led and those who served. In the second century, however, the church separated clergy for holy lifestyles, which they believed an average person was not capable of following. This resulted in a fissure between clergy and laity.[4] With the clergy's elevated status, came special privileges like interpreting God's word, a greater access to God and a higher spiritual status, which diluted the priesthood of all believers, resulting in a clergy-laity divide. This separation discouraged the laity from ministry and pursuing a holy lifestyle,[5] which resulted in a shift of spiritual responsibility and

---

2 Blackaby, et al., *Experiencing God*, 101–18.
3 Blackaby et al., *Spiritual Leadership*, 20.
4 Latourette, *History, vol. 1*, 133.
5 Walker and Handy, *History*, 95.

transferred control of the church to the clergy.[6] Unfortunately, even after
the Reformation, the clergy-laity divide remains in the church, deteriorat-
ing the cooperative nature of ministry.[7]

This divide is not solely the result of clergy ordination – it is much
bigger than that. Baptists have some history of not requiring ordination of pastors.[8] In 1746 a query came to the Philadelphia Association
asking "whether it be lawful or regular for any person to preach the
gospel publicly without ordination?" The Association answered thus:
"That which we have both rule and precedent for in the word of God,
is, and must be, both lawful and regular."[9] Of course, in the Baptist
church, standards for filling a pulpit are set at the local church level,
so requirements vary, but evidence exists that in the eighteenth century
a convening body declared it "both lawful and regular" for someone to
preach without ordination.

The clergy-laity divide continues when there is a perception that the
pastor has greater access to God, has the final word on biblical interpretation, is holier, and is *the* minister. While the perception might exist, none
of these things accurately reflects the biblical ideal.

The Pastor Does Not Have Greater Access to God

The pastor is not equivalent to the Old Testament priest. Jesus completed
that role (Heb. 4:15) and is the sole mediator between people and God
(1 Tim. 2:5). Sinful people can approach a holy God with confidence and
boldness because of Christ has finished his work (Heb. 4:16). From the
beginning, God intended people to have direct access to Him (Exod. 19:6),
and because of Christ's work of reconciliation, all God's people – not just
pastors – have direct access to God (Rev. 1:6).

The Pastor Does Not Have the Final Word on Biblical Interpretation

The pastor is not the official Bible interpreter with the final word on its
meaning and significance. All believers must read and apply the word
of God to their lives (Josh. 1:8; Ps. 1:2). The believer does not need an

---

6   Chadwick, *The Early Church*, 51.

7   Cooper, "The Need," 6.

8   Latourette, *History, vol. 2*, 959–60.

9   Gillette, *Minutes*, 50–51.

interpretative edict from clergy to understand God's will as revealed in Scripture.[10] While the Lord may speak through pastors, God gives understanding to the people (2 Tim. 2:7; 1 Cor. 2:6-16).

The Pastor Is Not the Proxy Holy Man

Pastors, whether called overseers (1 Tim. 3:2-7) or elders (Titus 1:6-9), are required to live holy lives, but so are deacons (1 Tim. 3:8-13) and all believers (1 Peter 1:16). Pastoral ministry cooperates with other believers to help them grow in their relationship with God.

The Pastor Is *a* Minister, not *the* Minister

As previously noted, the clergy-laity divide developed after the New Testament era. The English word "clergy" is derived from the Greek word *kleeros*, signifying "lot." In 1 Peter 5:2-3, it refers to a specific lot of church members, not professional ministers.[11] "Laity" comes from the word *laikoi*, but the New Testament writers never used it.[12] Clement, an early church father uses *laikoi* in a sentence that contrasts three classes: presbyters, deacons, and the laity.[13] The problem, however, is that the people of God are not *laikoi*, contrasting clergy (qualified) with laity (unqualified); they are not uninitiated, inept, or unqualified to minister. They are His *laos*, which denotes the people of God, the Christian community.[14]

A Pastor Is a Minister among Ministers

Pastoral ministry requires the ability to cooperate with other ministers. During the uprising of the Hellenistic Jewish widows against the Hebraic Jewish widows, there was an urgent need to settle the dispute. So the leaders instructed the congregation to select seven qualified men to devote

---

10   Hobbs, "Baptist Faith and Message," 9-10.
11   Kistemaker, *Exposition of Hebrews*, 193: "In early ecclesiastical Latin, the expression 'clerus' signified a congregation and pointed to a group of unordained members. In later years, however, the Latin term 'clericus' became the designation for an ordained person; the rest of the people were called *laity*."
12   Stevens and Collins, *Equipping Pastor*, 138.
13   Clement, *On Marriage*, 82.
14   Strathmann, "λαός," 54.

themselves to resolving the conflict, while they continued to devote themselves to "prayer and the ministry of the word" (Acts 6:1-7). [15]

This pastoral ministry was cooperative — the leaders trusted the congregation to make good choices in the selection of the seven and they trusted those chosen to settle the conflict. The leaders set parameters, both to guide the congregation's decision,[16] and the tasks the seven ministers would perform.[17] Showing wisdom and competence, the congregation chose seven men with Greek names to assure leaders did not neglect the Hellenistic Jews in the food distribution. The apostles did not micromanage the men, but empowered them to fulfill their ministry,[18] while they concentrated on their ministry of prayer and the Word. Because of this cooperative ministry, the dispute did not hinder the spreading of the gospel. In other words, the leaders kept the congregation on God's agenda with their leadership, while empowering others to become the solution to the problem. They blessed others to be ministers. The seven were neither an audience nor assistants, but ministers in their own right fully supported by their leaders who called for their selection and the congregation who chose them.

Pastors can view God's people in one of three ways. The people can "watch" pastors minister, "help" pastors minister, or to "be" ministers themselves (see table 2). In Ephesians 4:11-12 — the one New Testament passage that uses *poimén* (shepherd) to refer to the office of pastor — Paul writes that pastoral ministry involves equipping believers to be ministers. This is another way that pastoral ministry is cooperative — it equips others to do the work of ministry. Pastoral ministry is not recruiting others to watch or help, but is equipping others to be ministers.

---

15   Luke used *diakonia* in verse four to describe the work of the apostles, διακονια του λογου (ministry of the word) and in verse two, διακονειν τραπεζαις (ministry to tables). Luke did not choose a different word to describe what the apostles and what the seven men were doing — both were ministry. It is not that one was more important, (when conflict is happening, little takes precedence over resolving it), it was they were different.

16   Seven men full of wisdom and the Spirit.

17   Supervise the food distribution.

18   Selecting the seven, and the seven supervising the food distribution.

Table 2. Lay Ministry Models

	Watch Model	Help Model	Be Model
Who ministers?	Preacher	Overworked few	Everyone
Obligation	Watch and play	Sacrifice and serve	Minister as gifted
Competition	Preacher vs. preacher	People vs. people	Church vs. Satan
Burn-out potential	Preacher	People	

Watch-the-Minister Model

Pastors who follow the Watch-the-Minister model view themselves as *the* minister, which sets up an unhealthy competition between them and other pastors. Since the members' primary obligation is to watch the minister, they are selective in whom they choose to watch. If one pastor's sermons are not as entertaining or interesting as his competition, he will likely lose some members to another church. The preacher in this model has a high probability of burnout.[19] If he loses enough members, the church may decide to ask him to move along. Since the people are relegated to observing, and do not participate in ministry or decision-making, their only recourse for feedback is to leave or ask the pastor to leave. Members, however, do have obligations in this model—attend and tithe.

By its nature, this model creates a distance between pastor and people because it either elevates or denigrates the pastor. If the people elevate a pastor, their myopic view blurs their common sense that a pastor is subject to the same human frailties and sin as the congregation. Therefore, they elevate a pastor's holiness beyond theirs and place him on a pedestal. Members of a Watch-the-Minister church can also denigrate a pastor by picking at his faults. The pastor and his family, therefore, exist in a fishbowl with every action subject to scrutiny.

Help-the-Minister Model

Pastors following the Help-the-Minister model still have pressure to perform every Sunday, but they know that they cannot do everything. Therefore, they recruit some of the members to help. Under this model, the pastors are still the minister, but they need some people to do some things

---

19   Rumford, "Untitled Speech": "Pastors burn out when they minister out of people's expectations instead of who they are."

that they do not have time to do themselves. The pastors need others to do ordinary work so they can devote themselves to the demands of their "spiritual work." There is a competitive spirit between helping members for the more prestigious titles of position.

The people have a high probability of burnout in this church. Their "church work" is demanding and time consuming. They get some satisfaction from God's blessing on their work, but often feel unappreciated by others in the church and that the church takes them for granted. They are not performing their ministry; they are helping others to do theirs.

Pastors can become benevolent dictators in the *Help Church*. Members assist them in their ministry, but the members have no personal ownership. Pastors give personal direction to all the church's ministry and control the activity of the lay ministers.

Be-the-Minister Model

When pastors follow the Be-the-Minister model and embrace the equipping role of Ephesians 4:11–12, they view themselves as a minister among other ministers. The pastors strive to assist and equip the members in their ministries. They do not try to do everything, nor do they attempt to get others to help them. The pastors' goal is for the members to discover God's call and gifts for their lives and to grow spiritually as they minister. One of the benefits of this approach is the contribution it makes to church health. Healthy churches have 90 plus percent of their membership active in ministry, whereas unhealthy churches can go as low as 11 percent.[20]

The members' perspective changes from doing church work to ministering in Jesus' name. People are not answering a plea to help or do their part. They are not asking the question, "What does the church need me to do?" Rather, they ask, "Who does God want me to be?" In Acts 8:1, Luke describes a major turning point in the history of the early church when the persecution of the church began. Luke states, "Saul agreed with putting him to death. On that day a severe persecution broke out against the church in Jerusalem, *and all except the apostles* were scattered throughout the land of Judea and Samaria" (emphasis added). In God's strategy to spread the gospel, everyone except the key leaders went out. As the church dispersed, people spread the gospel everywhere they went. The *laos*, God's people, went out and ministered — and the gospel was unhindered.

---

20   Ford, *Transforming Church*, 8.

When people are co-workers with God (see first part of the ministry definition), they are doing God's ministry, gain a sense of being a part of the team,[21] and become willing to participate in the decision-making process.[22] People hesitate to give themselves fully to another person's agenda, but when they own the decisions and the ministry, they lose their reluctance. This participatory decision-making process was evident in practice of the early church.

The church handled decision-making in a variety of ways throughout the book of Acts. At times, the apostles made unilateral decisions, as when they cast lots and chose a replacement apostle (Acts 1:23-26) or approved of Saul of Tarsus (Acts 9:27-28). Other times, the apostles also shared the decision-making authority with the elders in settling disputes (Acts 15:2; 15:6). On other occasions, other leadership groups made decisions like when prophets and teachers in Antioch sent out Barnabas and Saul (Acts 13:1-3), who in turn appointed elders in every church (Acts 14:23). Yet there are still other occasions where the church leaders shared the decision-making process with the people. The people, with the leadership's blessing, selected the seven men to minister to the widows (Acts 6:3-6), approved of the baptism of Gentiles (Acts 10: 46-47) sent out Barnabas (Acts 11:22), received a report of missionary efforts (Acts 14:27-28) and selected men to send to Antioch (Acts 15:22, 25; 16:4).

Pastors following the Be-the-Minister model encourage this ownership by allowing genuine participation in ministry and decision-making. The shared ministry concept motivates workers in their ministries.[23] This cooperation means being in harmony with other ministers (Rom. 12:16), and helping others grow through their ministry and giving ministry away. Pastors are "first among equals."[24] They do not claim any superiority over the

---

21 McDonough, *Working with Volunteer Leaders*, 59: "For a person to feel that he is a significant member of the team is important. Each member of the team has a job to perform. Teamwork gives each person a sense of belonging."

22 Callahan, *Twelve Keys*, 56: "The decision-making process is participatory whenever there is a high degree of ownership both for the process and for the decisions reached."

23 Jackson, *Doing the Impossible*, 91: "To be successful at motivation, you need to employ other people's minds and ask them for ideas, for feelings, and for input."

24 Greenleaf and Spears, *Servant Leadership*, 75. Greenleaf suggests leaders can structure an organization using a "primus"—a first among equals, instead of a chief who leads subordinates. This is a good point of view for pastors who follow the Be-the-Minister model.

lay ministers; however, their unique role and calling is to be a lead minister. To be successful, pastors must minister according to their gifts and lead others to minister according to their gifts. When this happens, the church benefits like it did in Acts 6.

SERVING OTHERS

*Ministry is participating with God and cooperating with His people in **serving others** to meet their needs, fulfill our calling and bring glory to God.*

At the center of this definition is *serving others*, just as people are at the center of every act of true ministry. One of the great mysteries of ministry is that ultimately, our ministry to others is ministry to God (Matt. 25:40–45), but it begins as a service to others. Ministers therefore serve to meet another person's needs, not because serving fulfills an internal need. If pastors preach because they have a need to be on the stage and thrive on the adrenalin rush of being in front of a crowd, their preaching is not pastoral ministry – it is a quest for self-fulfillment. If counselors listen to other people's problems, because of the ego boost they get when others are dependent upon their advice, their counseling is not pastoral ministry – it is a quest for self-fulfillment. Ministers must direct their ministry toward other people. Unfortunately, that is not always the case.

In his book *Servant Leadership* Robert Greenleaf writes,

> Twelve ministers and theologians of all faiths and twelve psychiatrists of all faiths had convened for a two-day, off-the-record seminar on the one-word theme of healing. The chairman, a psychiatrist, opened the seminar with this question: "We are all healers, whether we are ministers or doctors. Why are we in this business? What is our motivation?" There followed only ten minutes of intense discussion before they were all agreed, doctors and ministers, Catholics, Jews, and Protestants. "For our own healing," they said.[25]

While the very act of ministry benefits ministers, it is not the focus of ministry – other people are. Without any attempt to disparage those in the healing seminar cited above, they generated a significant insight: those who minister benefit from the service they give. While the driving factor

---

25   Ibid., 49.

behind doing ministry is not the benefits derived, it is nonetheless true that ministers derive benefit from serving.[26] This makes keeping *others* in the heart of ministry even more important. No doubt some ministers do what they do for the wrong reasons (Phil. 1:15), and many even minister without having a genuine relationship with God (Matt. 7:22-23), but it is also true that well-intentioned ministers can be sidetracked by making their needs central to the neglect of other people's needs. Why, then, should believers minister? The last part of the ministry definition suggests three reasons.

MEETING NEEDS

*Ministry is participating with God and cooperating with His people in serving others to **meet their needs**, fulfill our calling, and bring glory to God.*

Ministry begins with an accurate diagnosis of the underlying core need, not just the presenting need. When Jesus encountered the paralytic man in Capernaum (Mark 2:1-12), He immediately addressed his core need—forgiveness of sin (Mark 2:5). The scribes were thinking that Jesus committed blasphemy by forgiving the paralyzed man's sins, so Jesus addressed their unspoken objection by providing visible evidence of His divine power and healed him of paralysis. Ultimately, as the final part of this definition *bring glory to God* indicates, God received glory (Mark 2:12), but the man's presenting need was also met—he walked out of the room, carrying the pallet that had been carrying him.

Rarely is the presenting need the only need. Usually there is something much deeper than the surface issue. While the presenting need may be very basic, like the need for food or shelter, the core need might be gaining self-control by surrendering to the Holy Spirit (Gal. 5:23) so the person can hold down a job, stop doing drugs, and provide for herself. It is not sufficient to address the presenting need without diagnosing and addressing the core need.

This diagnostic process takes time, energy, and a willingness to listen. It requires wisdom and the help of the Holy Spirit to know what to say and do.

---

26   Swenson, *Margin*, 88: "Medical studies reveal that service is health enhancing. One of the best ways to heal your own emotional pain is to focus instead on meeting the needs of others. It works, powerfully."

This is why *participating with God* is such a vital part of true ministry. While most will have the ability or resources to give someone food, water, or shelter, only Spirit-led people who are participating with God can discern the deeper core need. Failure to do so will place ministers in a whirlwind of activity, leaving them without adequate time or resources to address the core need.

The four men who lowered the paralyzed man to through the roof spent time, energy, and resources to get this man to Jesus.[27] However, after Jesus addressed his presenting and core needs, they no longer had to carry the man — the man could carry his own pallet.

Complications can arise when meeting the presenting need accentuates the core need. It is possible to hurt someone by attempting to help, yet pastors must "do no harm."[28] People commonly refer to saying no as tough love, but really love never needs a modifier. There are times when no is the right ministry response. If a person requests benevolence money at the first of every month to pay his electric bill, there is a chance that giving him money is enabling poor money management. These complicating issues make meeting people's needs impossible without the first part of the definition of ministry: *participating with God and cooperating with His people.* God's direction and counsel of other ministers is necessary to know what the core needs are.

Fulfill a Call

*Ministry is participating with God and cooperating with His people in serving others to meet their needs, **fulfill our calling**, and bring glory to God.*

Ministry does more than meet the needs of others; it also fulfills the calling of God's people. The church uses the word "call" in different ways. Every believer has a call to minister that comes with salvation and has responsibility to minister according to his or her spiritual gifts and God's purposes.[29] The

---

27   Did they have to pay for repairs?

28   American Counseling Association, *Code of Ethics*, A.4.a: "Counselors act to avoid harming their clients, trainees, and research participants and to minimize or to remedy unavoidable or unanticipated harm." Pastors share a similar responsibility; they must avoid doing harm, even in the attempt to help.

29   Hobbs, "The Baptist Faith and Message," 42: "Every Christian is set apart to serve God in whatever capacity he/she is gifted to serve."

laos are God-called ministers and on mission for God,[30] and their call to salvation and ministry is the highest and most important calling, resulting in believers, saved by grace, doing the good works God ordained them to accomplish (Eph. 2:8–10).

However, some have an additional calling to pastoral ministry. Jeff Iorg identifies this calling as a "general call to ministry leadership."[31] It is a call to be someone (chap. 1) and to love, teach, and lead God's people (parts 2–4). Paul expressed gratitude to Jesus for this call to pastoral ministry (1 Tim. 1:12) and was determined to complete it to the end (Acts 20:14). He also encouraged Timothy to fulfill such a call even while enduring hardship (2 Tim. 4:5).

Both the universal call to ministry and the call to pastoral ministry are irrevocable,[32] but there is also a call that changes—the call to specific assignments or locations for those involved in pastoral ministry.

One of the most difficult decisions pastors face is when to leave one ministry assignment to take another one. Sometimes that means changing locations, but essentially doing the same work, like when a pastor moves from one town to another to pastor a church. Other times it means changing work, like moving from leading a church to becoming a hospital chaplain. There are four principles that help interpret God's call to a specific assignment or location.

The open door principle (Acts 16:6–10). God will not call pastors to a place where He has not opened the door for them to serve. Paul learned this principle when he was trying to go to Asia, but Jesus wanted him in Macedonia. This principle is the most important of all: if God is not directing and opening the door for service, do not go. Beating down a door God closed is never a good idea.

The singing heart principle (Ps. 16:9). God prepares pastors for roles and prepares roles for pastors. Usually the assignment will make a pastor's heart sing. A person who despises administration likely would not thrive as a minister of education, nor would a person likely do well as a youth

---

30   Edge, *Doctrine of the Laity*, 24: "The uniqueness of God's people is they are a people who have been called to a mission—God's mission!"

31   Iorg, *Is God Calling Me?*, 22.

32   Pastors may have to step down from service due to moral failure and will suffer the consequences of living under an unfulfilled call, but that does not mean God's call is nullified, just that they wasted their opportunity to fulfill God their call to pastoral ministry.

pastor if that person did not enjoy spending time with adolescents. While there is something in every assignment that a pastor might not enjoy, that something should be minor, not the assignment's core function.

The blessing principle (Acts 13). If God is in it, likely others will bless pastors as they accept the assignment. Those who know the pastors well may be able to see whether an assignment is a good fit for them, sometimes better than they can. These counselors have an emotional distance that is not plagued by second-guessing, mixed motives, and self-doubt. God often moves through others to bless pastors in the direction He wants them to go.

Inner-peace principle (John 16:33). Does God provide an inner peace? God is not a God of chaos and confusion; He brings peace in the midst of storms (Mark 4:39) and order out of chaos (Isa. 45:18). At times, His message comes via a still small voice (1 Kings 19:12). God will ultimately give pastors peace about what ministry assignments they should take.

Ministry is fulfilling for those called to serve. Whether it is the universal call, a call to pastoral ministry, or a call to a specific assignment or location, when believers answer God's call they find fulfillment but that should not be the ultimate reason they minister.

Bring Glory to God

Bringing glory to God is a believers' ultimate purpose in life, according to the Westminster Catechism.[33] Moreover, it is written in Scripture that God is worthy to receive glory (Rev. 4:11) and His righteous people bring Him such glory (Isa. 60:21) in all they do (1 Cor. 6:20; 10:31). Ministers also bring God glory in all they do (1 Cor. 10:3), when they are filled with the fruits of righteousness (Phil. 1:9–11), and when they minister to others (2 Cor. 9:13). While the one reason for ministering is meeting people's needs, and another is fulfilling a calling, the ultimate reason for ministering is to bring glory to God.

While all ministry *is participating with God and cooperating with His people in serving others to meet their needs, fulfill our calling, and bring glory to God,* pastoral ministry is unique because of the God-given call and responsibility to shepherd God's people and oversee His church. Not everyone can

---

33   Schaff and Schaff, *History, vol. 7*, 557. According to the Westminster Catechism, "man's chief end is to glorify God, and to enjoy Him forever."

be pastors — only those called by God and invited by a local church to serve are pastors. They *are influential, respected leaders who watch over God's people, by loving, teaching, and leading them, without regard for personal enrichment* (chap. 1). With this foundational understanding, the remaining three parts of this book explore the core duties in detail and examine them in a twenty-first century ministry context.

Pastoral Ministry: Loving God's People

The New Testament word *poimén* (shepherd) emphasizes the pastoral role of loving and caring for the people (Heb. 13:17).[34] Pastors, like shepherds, devote themselves to the well-being of those under their care, without regard for personal benefit or enrichment (John 10:12). Pastors love their people. Paul commanded Timothy to be an example of love to the people he served (1 Tim. 4:11–12). Part 2 explains and illustrates what healthy pastoral love looks like when caring for the hurting, the hurtful, and in conflict situations.

Pastoral Ministry: Teaching God's People

When Paul placed the two words *poimén* (shepherd) and teacher together (Eph. 4:11) he underscored the role of the pastor as teacher. Paul encouraged Timothy to teach God's Word to His people (2 Tim. 2:15) and the apostles devoted themselves to this work (Acts 6:2–4.) This part will give guidance about teaching in formal and informal settings.

Pastoral Ministry: Leading God's People

When the New Testament writers used the words *presbuteros* (elder), they were emphasizing that the pastor had gravitas; and when they used *episkopos* (overseer) they were underscoring that pastors are leaders (1 Thess. 5:12).[35] Part 4 explores how to be a strategic leader against a strong headwind, with or without power and effect positive change in the organization.

---

34   Part 2 explores the theme of loving God's people.
35   Part 4 explores the theme of leading God's people.

As far as pastoral ministry goes, core functions are dependent on one another. These divisions should not imply hard boundaries between the words. Pastoral ministry is greater than the sum of its parts (loving, teaching, and leading).[36] One part cannot function without the other. It is not possible to teach without love (1 Cor. 13:1-2). Part of leading is informing, which is a teaching function. Pastors use formal teaching opportunities to cast a vision, which is a leadership function. One of the greatest ways pastors show their love for their congregations is to preach well-prepared sermons that are faithful to the text. Please do not see these categories as stand-alone core functions. Faithful pastoral ministry includes the sophisticated blending of the core functions together as pastors *participate with God and cooperate with His people to serve others, to meet their needs, fulfill their calling, and bring glory to God.*

---

36   Certainly, in a *Gestalt* sense, any whole is greater than the sum of its parts. But more than that, these words systematize understanding for the core functions of pastoral ministry.

PART TWO

LOVING GOD'S PEOPLE

.

Chapter 3   *Caring for the Hurting*

On the door in big red letters was the warning INFECTIOUS DISEASE PRECAUTIONS. In smaller letters the words WEAR GLOVES AND A MASK. At the time, Acquired Immune Deficiency Syndrome was just beginning to make the headlines. Before then, AIDS meant people who helped teachers, not a disease. Inside lay a fragile man, covered with sores. He habitually licked his lips and spoke with a soft, cracking voice.

Though I did not know much about AIDS at the time, I knew that of the three common ways to contract it, my faith tradition considered two of them immoral. I never asked "Roy" how he contracted AIDS. The question seemed inappropriate and irrelevant. He complained about the sores in his mouth and the pain—it was with him constantly. He knew he would die sooner or later. He preferred it to be sooner.

I listened to him, read Scripture, prayed, and gave him my card. As I was leaving, I kissed him on his forehead and assured him of my continued prayer. The visit took only a few minutes, yet its impact remains with me today. This man allowed me to enter into his suffering. I felt the presence of the Lord in that room.

HOSPITAL VISITATION

The first rule of effective hospital visitation is to go. In mega-churches, the pastoral ministry team may not be able to visit every hospitalized church member, but someone from the church can. In most churches, a member of the pastoral ministry team can visit members in the hospital. Those whom they visit benefit from the caring touch of their pastors, but the pastors also benefit from their time in the hospital because they are better able to connect with their people.[1] It promotes con-

---

1   Hughes, "Going to Your Left," 225-26.

gregational exegesis,[2] which is a necessary step to an effective pastoral teaching ministry.

The ministry of presence gains significance from the incarnation of Jesus. God came and dwelt among man. He did not send a messenger. He came (John 1:1–14). There is no higher priority than loving God's people – it is a core function of pastoral ministry. This is not to say that the amount of love equals the amount of time a pastor spends in a hospital, but rather that overseeing the congregation to insure that a member of the pastoral ministry team or someone else shows up is crucial.

Be Aware of Where You Are

Once pastors arrive, they need to remember where they are. Bedrooms are normally private places. Most people do not invite visitors to tour their bedroom when they visit their homes, and they definitely do not entertain visitors when they are in bed. The one exception to this rule is their hospital room.

Before entering a hospital room, sanitize your hands and freshen your breath. Also, check with the nurses' desk to see if it is a good time for you to pay a short visit. If not, hand the nurse your card and ask him to give it to the patient. If the nurse is not available, knock on the door and ask if it is all right to enter. Remember, even if the patient is sharing a room with another patient, it is a private place.

When making a visit in a hospital, pastors are walking into a private place that is void of most bastions of privacy. For the most part, hospital patients are unable to keep up with routine hygiene and grooming needs. They are wearing hospital gowns that likely do not close in the back. Patients have little control over who walks in and disturbs them. Some must use bedpans and endure sponge baths, losing what little dignity their disease or injury has not taken from them.

Because of the vulnerability of a hospital room, it is best to limit touch to the shoulder or hand after seeking permission of the patient. Also, avoid standing at the foot of the bed or sitting on the bed.

Then why did I kiss the AIDS patient's forehead? I do not think kissing a person with AIDS is prudent medically or ordinary pastoral care. I have

---

2 Just as preachers must exegete the Bible to prepare a solid sermon, they must also come to understand their congregation if they will rightly apply the biblical message to the people's needs.

never kissed a patient's forehead before or since and do not recommend it. In retrospect, I think I kissed his forehead in response to the sign on the door. It was my way of acknowledging his humanity. I don't know how he received it; my hope is that he felt the same way as the leper did when Jesus touched him (Matt. 8:3). I never spoke to him again. A few weeks later, his parents sent me a note. They found my card in his belongings after he died and they wrote to thank me for ministering to him.

Be Considerate of the Patient's Circumstances

Hospital patients face the fears of the unknown, the hassles of institutional living, and mental anguish and boredom. Doctors use twenty syllable words most people do not understand. It is easy to lose patience while being a patient. "Under the doctor's orders," nurses wake patients up to take vital signs. Sometimes, they even have to wake a patient up to give her a sleeping pill.

Then there are administrative hassles. Did you know that a family deductible of $400 does not mean that the family has paid the first $400 of a bill? One member of the family can only pay $200 toward the family deductible under some plans.

Did you know that calling an insurance company to tell them you are going into the hospital does not mean the visit is pre certified? To pre-certify, you have to call a number on the West Coast. To find out if a hospital is on your plan, you call a number on the East Coast. If you call the East Coast instead of the West Cost, you are out of luck. Since the left coast does not know what the right coast is doing—you have to pay 30 percent of the bill, instead of 10 percent. At least that was one patient's experience.

Sometimes seniors are limited on the amount of rehabilitation time they can have after surgery, even if it is not adequate. Bureaucrats can get in the way of doctors' care for their patients. While the medical issues are the most pressing problems most patients face, it is not their only problems.

Listen

Whenever patients share details of their condition or situation, it is easy to tell a corresponding story from when you or someone else you know was dealing with a similar problem. Please do not. Instead, use active listening skills to focus on what the patient is saying. When appropriate, maintain eye contact, assure the patient you are listening, and avoid giving unsolicited advice.

Words flow freely in most visits, but what do you say when the need is so great that you do not know what to say? Saying nothing is better than saying the wrong thing. The most effective ministry of Job's friends was sitting with him in silence. They did not blow it until they started talking. Immersed in the frustration of their poor ministry, Job said to them, "Hear diligently my speech, and let this be your consolations" (Job 21:2). When the patient is finished speaking, you can offer hope, but without making medical promises. Discover if there is something practical, you or the church can do to help during this time. Offer to pray and read a familiar selection of Scripture like Psalm 23, Jeremiah 30:17, or Romans 8:38-39.

The Banality of the Routine

Routine is a good word to describe life in a hospital. Meals come around the same time every day and taste the same despite the menu choice. Doctors make their rounds every day. Nurses come faithfully to take vital signs and dispense meds. And there the patient lies at the mercy of others, awaiting the next interruption.

In the midst of all this frustration, confusion, and pain you walk into the patient's room. You do more than provide needed relief from the boredom, loneliness, hopelessness, uncertainty, and agony. You are a symbol of something much greater, in that moment you are God's representative and His compassion for His people.

You visit, you pray, you listen, you show compassion, and when you do, you become the hand of Christ touching others who hurt. When you put your hand on the patient's shoulder, she may not feel the nail scars of Jesus' hand, but regardless, she feels a divine touch. As you feel her shoulder in your hand, you are not touching mere flesh and blood, but the shoulder of Jesus. He said it Himself, "Inasmuch as ye have done it unto one of the least of these my brethren, ye have done it unto me" (Matt. 25:40b). In human frailty, you touch human frailty, and when you do, something divine takes place – the body of Christ ministers to the body of Christ.

On second thought, routine is not a good word to describe hospital ministry at all. It is anything but routine. It is one way that pastors love their people.

GRIEF MINISTRY

I was a green pastor about to make my first grief counseling call. The person I visited was a daughter-in-law of a church member's neighbor. She was in her early twenties, about my age at the time, when her new husband died in a motorcycle accident. I had absolutely no training or experience in what I was about to do. However, I was the pastor, so off I went with my pocket New Testament in hand.

Her tears made me feel uncomfortable. I did not know whether just to sit there and watch her cry or to say something. Her grief paralyzed her and she was in no emotional condition to carry a conversation. Small talk seemed inappropriate, and I knew it was my place to initiate any conversation.

Intuitively, I knew I needed to comfort her. But how? I wanted to say something like, "Well at least your husband is in heaven," but I did not know him or her. After about two or three hour-long minutes, I dove in: "Ma'am, was your husband a Christian?"

"Well . . . no, he wasn't."

Now what? What could I possibly say?

Have you ever watched a young baby learning to hold a cup? That is how I felt. Without any ministerial dexterity I responded, "I'm sorry, I guess I have no comfort to bring you."

At the time, I thought I was being bold when I talked to her about heaven and hell and gave her the plan of salvation. Today as I look back on that inaugural pastoral care visit, I know that I was cold, insensitive, and rude.

Over thirty years and countless pastoral care visits have passed since that day. In retrospect, I wish I had done a better job of ministering. If I could turn back the hands of time, I would return to her side, sit quietly, and weep with her. Today all I can do is pray that her memory is not as good as mine and determine never to behave like that again.

Grieving Spectrum

Perhaps the greatest pain people suffer is losing a loved one. The pain is so great that those grieving cannot process the loss instantaneously; instead, they do their best to adapt and cope with their new reality through grief stages. Elisabeth Kübler-Ross lists the stages of grief as denial, anger, bargaining, depression, and acceptance.[3]

Some have misunderstood these stages as graduated steps, as if it were possible, once leaving the anger stage, never to be angry about the loss again. In reaction to this misunderstanding, others question the value of Kübler-Ross' stages of grief.[4] A grief spectrum is an alternative way to understand grief.[5] The spectrum runs from denying the loss on one end to accepting its reality on the other. Those grieving a loss will experience Kübler-Ross' stages, but not necessarily in a pre-defined order. Grieving people will progress and regress through the spectrum over a period of years until they settle into a state of accepting the loss.[6]

The gradations in the grieving spectrum can be adaptive strategies, which enable grieving people to cope with their losses in healthy ways. Upon hearing that a loved one is chronically ill or died, the initial response will likely be shock or denial. Sometimes, it may be a conscious choice not to believe the news, but more times than not, denial is an adaptive strategy beneath the surface to appropriate the burden of the news over time.[7] The news is so weighty that a grieving person cannot bear all the weight in a single moment. The human spirit takes time to process losses and so people vacillate between knowing and not knowing the veracity of the news.

Along the journey to acceptance, grieving people often process their growing reality of the loss with anger. As a secondary emotion, anger gives a momentary relief from the pain of the loss and becomes an outlet to "unload" the pain on others.[8] Just the stress of the event is enough to leave a grieving person short-tempered. However, at a deeper level, the perceived injustice of the loss exacerbates the pain and intensifies the emotional outburst. Anger can be free flowing, but it will find a target.[9] Sometimes the anger strikes a medical professional, a family member, a pastor, or even God. The recipient of the anger is not usually the point. Anger, like

---

3   Kübler-Ross and Byock, *On Death and Dying*, 10.

4   Konigsberg, *Truth about Grief*, 37: "'Stages' implies that there are escalating steps to grief that somehow chart our recovery."

5   Katz and Chochinov, "Spectrum of Grief," 295.

6   Wright, *Helping Those in Grief*, 221.

7   Vos, *Denial and Quality*, 26.

8   Feindler, *Anger-Related Disorders*, xxi.

9   Potter-Efron, *Handbook of Anger Management*, 175.

denial, can be an adaptive strategy to cope with the pain.[10] The point is
that grieving people often get angry as they process their losses.

The tendency to bargain takes on intensified significance for those with
religious backgrounds who understand that God loves them (1 John 4:8)
and that He can do miraculous things like raise the dead (Ezek. 37:13; Luke
7:11–17; Acts 20:7–12; Acts 3:15).[11] The Scripture is clear about what God
can do. What grieving people are often unclear about is what He will do
in their circumstance. In a grieving state, many attempt to bargain with
God to alleviate their suffering by appealing to His love for them and His
power to do the impossible.[12] What makes it bargaining instead of faith is
that they offer something in return for God's favor.

In the 1978 motion picture "The End," Burt Reynolds plays a character
who finds himself in a life-threatening situation — off shore without enough
energy to swim to safety. As he swims, he prays. He offers many things to
God in exchange for the strength to swim all the way to shore, including
promises to be a better father, obey all the Ten Commandments, and be a
generous giver. However, as he got closer to shore, he lessened what he was
willing to do for salvation, knowing he was going to make it.[13] This scene
is a light-hearted look at the bargaining stage. Bargaining, however, is no
laughing matter. It is one of the adaptive strategies grieving people use in
the grief spectrum to cope with their losses.

As grieving people progress along the spectrum, denial loses potency
and the reality that God is not going to intervene intensifies. Hope fades
and depression sets in. Some view depression as anger turned inward.[14] It
is a season of adjustment to the current reality and processing the weight
of the pain. Fear that life will never be the same and a sense of dread
overshadow everything.

Acceptance does not mean life returns to normal. It is an adaption to
the new reality. Loss remains, but hope returns. What the Doppler Effect

---

10   Tangney and Dearing, *Shame and Guilt*, 111.

11   Koenig, Mccullough, and Larson, *Handbook of Religion*, 310.

12   In John 11 Jesus raised Lazarus from the dead. While it is true that He loved
Lazarus' sisters Mary and Martha (John 11:35), that love was not the reason He raised
Lazarus from the dead. He raised Lazarus to bring glory to God and the observers to
faith (John 11:40–41).

13   Reynolds, "Negotiating with God." The scene is currently available on You-
Tube: https://www.youtube.com/watch?v=wzqbqDW9z6E.

14   DiGiuseppe and Tafrate, *Understanding Anger Disorders*, 186.

is to sound, acceptance is to loss — the intensity of the pain becomes fainter over time, until it is a memory for most people.[15]

When ministering to those suffering a loss, pay attention to the grief spectrum — whether the loss is health, death, finances, or status isn't the point since every loss triggers a reaction. The comments of those you visit may reflect their relative position in the grief spectrum, not their faith condition.

As already stated, people suffering a loss may express anger at God. If they come from an unhealthy religious background, this could be spiritual distress. They may be thinking they are getting what they deserve because they see God as a vengeful tyrant and they are fighting back. Or it could be that they are simply processing the life-altering event by grieving. In either case, the pastoral ministry response is to listen and help them process, rather than trying to defend God.

Besides, the statement "Why are you doing this to me, God?" is not so much a question as it is an expression of grief and a statement of faith. People do not expect an answer when they ask, "What did I ever do to deserve this?" They want a listening ear.

Could they ask "Why God?" if they did not believe God existed? The question is a profound expression of a belief in the existence of God. It also presupposes a loving God who cares. If they thought God was distant and uninvolved, they could never ask why God allowed something bad to happen to them. The question also affirms that God is all-powerful and sovereign. If they did not think God is in charge, they would not question what He is doing. The initial moments of grief are not the time to wax eloquent about the philosophical proofs of the existence of God or to feel the need to defend Him. Instead of arguing with grieving people about their pain, enter into it. Show your love in word and deed.

I wonder how Mary felt when Jesus asked the question, "My God, my God, Why hast thou forsaken me?" Did she want to correct Jesus? Or did she want to hold Him tight?

Listen — and Don't Repeat Clichés

"She's in a better place" or "At least she isn't suffering anymore" are common clichés people say when they do not know what else to say. While

---

15 Romanoff, "Acceptance and Commitment," 133: "However, approximately 10 percent of bereaved individuals develop complicated or prolonged grief reactions; continual rumination over the circumstances of the loss, prolonged yearning and searching, or avoidance of painful affect leave them unable to rebuild a 'life worth living.'"

theologically correct, these words do not help the pain. People do not grieve because they do not know where their loved ones are; they grieve because of where they are not—with them. The thought of heaven is comforting at the acceptance end of the grieving spectrum, but when a person is numb, in denial, or angry with God, they cannot even think those thoughts.

When people are hurting, clichés do not help. These words form a barrier between the minister and the hurting person. Perhaps the reason pastors say them is to keep from entering into the person's pain. The cliché provides insulation from the brutal cold of suffering.

Instead of a cliché, why not just say, "I love you and I'm so sorry that this happened. How can I help you get through the next few days?"

Funerals

Ministering to the grieving can involve preaching a funeral service. Some funerals have the tone of celebrating the life of a saint who lived to a ripe old age; others involve circumstances that are more tragic. Perhaps the most difficult funerals to preach involve someone who commits suicide or the death of an infant.

Suicide

"I think you knew my father," he said. "His name was Bill Brooks."

"Bill Brooks—sure, I baptized him about a year ago, but haven't seen him in a while. Is he okay?"

"No," his son said. "That's why I'm here. He killed himself yesterday."

After I baptized Bill, he came to the office a couple of times to visit. He was experiencing deep guilt over something that he could not seem to shake. I did the best I could to encourage him but never really connected with him. He slipped away from the church and I never reached out to him as I wish I would have.

"We're here to see if you would be willing to hold a funeral service for him if the rest of the family agrees to let you preach. You see, most of the family are not Christians and do not have much use for the church. Nevertheless, we are Christians and know that Dad thought highly of you."

Planning a funeral service is not preparing for a ministry to come—it is ministry. On this occasion, I got a rather cool reception when I paid a visit on the family the next day, but I treated them the same way I would have treated any family. I listened. After they agreed to hold the service at our church, I asked them for input into the funeral service. Were there any passages of Scripture they wanted me to read or familiar songs they wanted us to sing? I was careful not to overstay my welcome. I gathered the information that I needed and led the family in a prayer for strength.

After the service, I had a private moment with the widow. "I'm so sorry about Bill's death. You know he came to see me a couple of times."

"Yes, I knew he did." She responded.

"I always liked him, even though I didn't know him very well. I just don't understand why such a good, decent man would take his own life."

"We don't understand it either," she said as she hugged me. "Thank you for standing beside our family."

We both wiped away our tears and walked away with many unanswered questions. I did not know why a well-respected person like Bill would swallow the barrel of his hunting rifle, or why a good God would allow it to happen. Instead of trying to answer the unanswerable, I articulated the frustration and pain and shared the burden of the family. To do otherwise would have pushed them further away from church and God. Instead, three generations of the family that never attended our church before the funeral began attending.

Death of an Infant

A few days after Bill's funeral, a church member called to see if I would be willing to do a funeral for the nephew of his wife's sister. He said the baby died of SIDS (Sudden Infant Death Syndrome) and the funeral home was waiving its fee. However, the family did not have money for a minister. I agreed to minister to the family, without honorarium, and committed the church to send some money to help pay for the cemetery plot.

I was still numb from Bill's funeral and was not in any shape for another ministry. I scanned a funeral sermon from a minister's manual into my word processor and used it as a starting point to develop a sermon for the funeral. My plan was to preach from the manuscript because I feared that in my emotional condition, I could not preach an extemporaneous sermon. I felt depleted and would do the best I could do, but was afraid my best would not be good enough.

The morning of the funeral, I was sipping a cup of hot tea in a room at the funeral home when the director knocked on the door. She had just received a fax from the coroner's office. The baby did not die of SIDS; he died of suffocation. The father laid the baby down on a waterbed to sleep.

During the nap, he rolled over and trapped himself between the mattress and the side of the bed.

"Does the family know?"

"Yes," she said, "They do. I thought you would want to know too."

During the service, the father gripped his wife's hand, and with his head down, nervously rocked back and forth. Beneath the sound of my calculated voice was his muffled weeping. My finger moved down the manuscript as I preached, but my eyes kept escaping from the carefully prepared text to watch the father. There was a car wreck right before my eyes and I could not resist rubber necking.

Back and forth, he rocked, and as he did, memories flooded my mind. I remembered a late night phone call from my mother telling me that my little sister just died; my surgeon telling me that he thought he got all the cancer but that I might never be able to speak again; and Bill's son telling me that his father killed himself the day before. The scab was gone. My soul began bleeding.

I left my text and began to weep. "I can't begin to know your pain right now. I don't even pretend to know the depth of your hurt. But I do know that when I've sat where you're sitting, I doubted God's presence. I asked, 'Where are you, God?'"

The father looked up.

"In the distance, if you will listen, you will hear a voice. Go to the voice. It is saying, 'Come unto me all who are weary and heavy laden, and I will give you rest.' Go to the voice. God is in the voice."

Others began to weep.

At the graveside service, the father carried his baby in the small casket, put it on the stand and took his seat. I read the Shepherd's Psalm, prayed, and dismissed the service. I did not promise them that the pain would ever go away or that there was a reason for this suffering. All I promised was that God was there and that He cared.

Our tears often bring hope to hurting people. I wonder how Mary and Martha felt when Jesus wept at Lazarus's tomb?

Pastoral ministry does not end after the funeral. It is good to schedule a grief visit a few weeks after the funeral service to minister to the grieving family. By then, most of the visiting relatives have cleared out of town and people have stopped bringing casseroles by the house. At this visit, I usually talk about the grief spectrum and assure the family there is no rush to "get on with their lives." I encourage them to grieve at their own pace and in their own way.

It is also a good idea to put the date of their loved one's death on your calendar and remember to send a note, text, email, or make a phone call on the anniversary, assuring the family of your continued prayer. Over the years, many widows gave me one of their husband's favorite ties. I would always wear that tie a Sunday near the anniversary date of his death. The widow would usually comment and say, "You know, it was three years ago this week that my husband, passed away." I'd just smile, and say, "I know, I miss him. Thank you again for sharing this tie with me — it is a great reminder to me of what a great man he was, and it was my joy to wear it in his honor today."

Crisis Ministry

Some people are hurting because of illness or grieving the loss of a loved one, but those are not the only times people need ministry. In late spring, a faulty wire in a porch light started a fire in Lois' trailer. She escaped her burning home with nothing but the nightclothes she was wearing and her little dog in her arms. Lois was sixty-nine years old. Everything she owned went up in that blaze. All she had to live on was her meager Social Security benefit, which was not enough for her to start over at her age.

Though she had only attended a few times, her Sunday school class went to work to help her, giving her emergency money for her immediate needs. Her teacher set up a trust fund for her at a local bank and mobilized the community to help through the Community Center.

The local newspaper ran the story, publicizing the need. The community's response was overwhelming. Because of the organizational skills of a Sunday school teacher and the compassion of a community, Lois was able to move into her new apartment completely furnished with donations from the community.

Divorce, job loss, or coping with a troubled teen are crises that often escape our notice. Traditionally, the church copes well with catastrophes, deaths, and illnesses, but not with more embarrassing problems like teenage pregnancy, divorce, or bankruptcy.

"Bruce" and "Tammy" made a calculated choice to declare bankruptcy. They did not ask my opinion and I did not offer it. However, when the news hit the newspaper, we invited them over to our home. After dinner, Bruce and I took a walk together. "Do you want to talk?" I asked. That is all I had to say. His comments were not limited to the financial problems, but this crisis opened the floodgate and he poured out his soul to me. I did not judge him. For that matter, I did not say much at all. I listened.

Later that week I was visiting in the home of another family when the wife whispered, "Did you read about Bruce and Tammy?" Why was she whispering?

Sometimes we fear that we are endorsing a sin if we minister to a sinner. So we do not have a baby shower for an unwed mother and we stop inviting a divorcee to dinner. We shun those in bankruptcy and feel uncomfortable around those fired from their jobs. Why? We should minister to them just as we do to those who lost a loved one or someone whose house just burned down.

The sad reality of life is people get sick, and sometimes they die. People have life-altering accidents, declare bankruptcy, have their homes foreclosed, or get divorced. When these moments of transitions occur, they are experiencing deep needs that require ministers of reconciliation (2 Cor. 5:11–21) to come beside them and meet their needs.

Chapter 4   Ministry to Hurtful People

M y eight-year-old son was in the backyard of our parsonage playing with our dogs when he saw a couple of church members looking over the fence and whispering. "Why are they looking over our fence?" he asked his Mom. Susan did not know what to tell him, but I did. It was our delivery from "The Conflict-of-the-Month Club." Our dogs were digging up the backyard and the "church owners" did not like it.

The constant conflict was wearing me down. By now, I could not remember why I ever came to this church and was beginning to question whether I belonged in the ministry at all.

After ten years at my first full-time church, a larger church showed some interest in me so I accepted an invitation to come for an interview. Though red lights were flashing all over the room during the interview, I wanted to go to a bigger church so I accepted their call. What I did not know was that a subscription to The Conflict-of-the-Month Club came with the pulpit.

The first delivery came the first day on the job. The pastor's study did not have enough bookcases for my library and the finance committee would not allocate money for them like the pulpit committee promised. In response, I moved some shelving from our garage into the pastor's study and unpacked my boxes of books. I did not want to argue with anyone the first day of work, so I gave in. I did not know what lay ahead.

The church experienced rapid growth, so we had to increase the number of bulletins we printed for Sunday morning.[1] The church treasurer checked the counter on the copier and kept a total of how many copies we ran every week. She surprised me during a finance committee meeting by pointing out that the office was spending too much money on copier paper and

---

1   Rainer, *Effective Evangelistic Churches*. This book is a study of the most evangelistic churches in the Southern Baptist Convention as defined by baptizing over 25 with baptismal ratio of 20:1 members to baptism. The church I served was one of the 576 churches Rainer studied for this book.

toner. I prepared a cost analysis of the ratio of worshipers to copy expense that covered the last five years and showed that we were spending less per worshiper than before. That analysis did not settle the matter. In the church office, the finance committee kept a thick three-ring binder with the words "Budget Bible" on the spine. The book contained all the church financial policies, including one that did not allow for overspending a line item without their approval. The finance committee would allow the overage, but required ongoing proof that the office was not being wasteful, so they required the logging of every copy we made in the office and the filing of a report with the finance committee on a monthly basis, which, in an ironic twist, required running off more copies.

Instead of confronting the problem, I just worked harder. The church continued to baptize people and grow so I thought that eventually my critics would come around as the church enjoyed success. I tried to turn my critics into coaches and learned from what they said. If they said I did not visit enough, I would extend my workday and make a few more visits. When they said I did not care about them, I would spend my recreation time to take them golfing, fishing, or out to eat. All I did was work.

Anytime I could find a work around to the problem instead of confronting it, I did. That is what I did with the dogs and the backyard. Lady was a black German shepherd mix; Tramp was a brown mutt with elephant ears. Lady and the Tramp were good-natured dogs and our whole family loved these pets. However, with the pressure building from the constant conflict, I snapped. I could not bear to hear another person complain about the backyard, so I asked Susan to take the dogs to the pound while the kids were at school, which she reluctantly did. I listened to my boys cry themselves to sleep that night.

Loving People Is Never Optional,
Especially When They Are Hurtful

I regret that I never confronted the power group with how reaching people takes precedence over their three-ring binder, or that our mission, not policies, should drive us. I regret that I did not confront them about the ugly way they were treating my family and me. (I will not go into further details, but it was not pretty.) While I never confronted them, one of their key players, the treasurer, did confront me. She was not mad. Actually, she was very kind, even vulnerable when she came to see me. She had something she wanted to know, "Why don't you like me?" she asked.

I was stunned and left speechless, but that did not keep me from talking. To this day, I regret what I said. What came out of my mouth was, "We don't have to like each other. We just have to work together." What I was thinking was, *Are you kidding me? You oppose every idea I have. You put up administrative roadblocks, hoping we will fail. You take new members out to dinner, right after I baptize them to tell them to "watch out for the pastor" and you want to know why I don't like you?*

I missed an opportunity to minister to her that day, and I missed it because she was a hurtful person. At the time, I did not understand that hurtful people are not the way they are because they do not like me—it is because they are hurting. I do not know if ministering to her would have changed her opposition or not, but that is not the issue. She was opening herself up for ministry and I passed.

What would have happened if, in a diplomatic way, I confronted her with my thoughts? What if, deep down in my heart, I would have loved her as pastors are supposed to love the people they serve, even hurtful people—especially hurtful people? What if I would have attempted to meet her needs (chap. 2)? Without excusing her actions, I must take responsibility for mine. I was not a good pastor to her. Being a good pastor for the church is never a substitute for being a good pastor to church members and loving them enough to minister to them, even when they are hurtful.

Conflict Is an Occasion to Minister

Conflict, first and foremost, is an opportunity to minister. Pastors minister the Word with hurtful people in a longsuffering manner by reproving, rebuking, and exhorting (2 Tim. 4:2). Those three words, "reprove, rebuke, and exhort" imply the conversation is in the midst of conflict.

If we avoid conflict, we are avoiding ministry. In retrospect, I know my avoidance was more of a problem than the conflict itself. Why did I cave in and put my books on shelving with oil stains? After all, the pulpit committee promised my new bookcases. Why did I ever agree to keep a log of every copy we made in the office? This extra work was demeaning and adversely affected office productivity and morale. Why did I push my workweek beyond sixty hours to try to please my critics? The work drained me of my energy, absorbed all my free time, put me on edge, and contributed to my spending less time with my family than they needed.

I thought if I avoided the conflict, it would go away. Therefore, I ignored the hurtful people I encountered (actually, that statement is not accurate since they owned me and they consumed my every thought). More accurately, I avoided confronting those driving the conflict and avoided working to solve the issues driving the conflict.

Hurtful People Want Ministry

"Bruce" was upset again and boycotted church. He told his wife, "Be sure and have the house clean. Pastor Jim will come by to see us this Tuesday night." I did not go.

The next Sunday he did not come, and the next Tuesday I did not go. The same happened the third week, and by the fourth week, I began to think something was wrong. I called him to find out if there was illness in the family.

He told me why he was upset. He also told me how they had prepared for my visit for three weeks, but I did not come. He wanted to know why. My answer? I did not know he wanted to see me.

I learned something that day: even my critics want me to minister to them. This gentleman told me I had never preached a good sermon in my life; yet, he wanted me to visit him. Why? People want contact from pastors, even when they are mad at them. He wanted a conflict visit.

Members want to know we love them even when they are angry. The church was large enough that I did not notice his absence at first. I did not miss him, but think about the phrase "I did not miss him" from his point of view. I wonder what it is like to be absent for three weeks and not be missed? The size of the church was an issue, and I am not beating myself up for not noticing. But looking at it from his point of view, I get it. He wanted to know that he mattered to me. He wanted me to come after him. In short, he wanted me to value him.

I had an opportunity but failed to learn this lesson at the previous church I had served, which was mostly a peaceful place. "Helen" was a new member of the church whose family had recently moved to California from Missouri. Within a month of joining our church, she came into my office with a list of needed changes in the nursery. Her suggestions seemed reasonable and I was appreciative of her bringing the deficiencies to my attention. We made the changes and I thought that was the end of the matter. What I did not know at the time was that she boasted to the nursery workers about how fast she was able to get things done. The workers resented the implication that she was able to do what they could not do for themselves. Her gloating caused major discontentment among the nursery employees. Because of the conflict, one nursery worker resigned.

The next week, the church secretary transferred a call to me with this introduction, "Helen is very upset about a decision the church council made last night, and she says we don't care about missions because we are not properly promoting the Easter offering. She wants to talk to you." A flash of anger seized me. I thought, *who does she think she is to question the council. She has no right!* I was beginning to understand that she wanted our church to fit the mold of her last church, but what I did not notice at the time was the reason she was trying to get us to be like them.

When I got on the phone, I did not hear a word she was saying. I was defensive and outraged at her suggestion that the church council is not sensitive to missions. I perceived that she would be at my office door with a new challenge each week. I felt overwhelmed.

The conflict escalated until it encompassed the entire church. She was vocal about her discontent. She complained to whoever would listen. She whispered in the halls and spoke forcefully in the congregational business meetings. She became the focal point of the church. If I was not listening to her complain about the church, I was listening to church leaders complain about her. Finally, her husband asked to have a meeting with me to talk about the problem.

Her husband was a very reasonable man who acknowledged his wife was acting inappropriately and that he felt the best thing for them and the church was for them to leave. Then he asked me a question that helped me understand the needs of hurtful people, "What does a person have to do around here to get a visit from a deacon?" He went on to explain that if the church had disciplined his wife before she ruined her reputation, perhaps they could have stayed. By listening to him, I learned that her misbehavior was grief-driven. She missed her home church and was trying to remake her new church into its image, not for malicious reasons, but because she was not doing well emotionally.[2] The more she complained the more I distanced her, so she complained more to get my attention. It became a death spiral.

If I could do it all over again, I would have spent time helping her process her grief (chap. 3), but also let her know that the culture in California

---

2   Shelley, *Well-Intentioned Dragons*, 94: "According to the National Institute of Mental Health, more than 25 percent of Americans ages 18 and older suffer from a diagnosable mental disorder in a given year."

churches is different than the culture in Missouri churches and that it would be much easier for her to adapt than to try to change everyone else. How did this happen? I failed to understand that everybody has a story that drives his or her behavior.[3] I was so caught up in my story—defending a church culture that was being berated by someone who didn't understand it—that I missed her story, that is, being a "new kid in class" and trying to find her place in a place she really didn't want to be. I now regret that I fought with her out of my insecurity instead of ministering to her out of love. She did not need a sparring partner. She needed a pastor.

The Best Time Is Now

Eventually I learned to stop postponing ministering to hurtful people. One of the deacons at a subsequent church I pastored was upset about a change we were making while remodeling the auditorium. In a congregational business meeting, he let me have it, reminiscent of the way Helen had approached disagreement in public. Calmly, I answered every question he asked me and assured him of my desire to come to a solution to the problem.

While closing the meeting, I asked him to remain behind for a few minutes. When the room was empty, I said, "I don't mind your disagreeing with me, but I do mind you raising your voice at me in public. I am your pastor and your friend and I believe you owe me more respect than you showed me tonight. In the future, I'd appreciate you expressing your opinions to me in private, when possible, and to do so in a friendly tone. That's the way friends treat one another." He apologized and eventually we worked out the disagreement. Our relationship remained amiable until eventually I presided over his wife's funeral and later his. There was never a repeat of the boorish behavior.

He was a good man—a good friend who had shown genuine affection for my family through the years. He just got emotional one night because he thought the use of technology in the auditorium would take away from the worshipful atmosphere. He had a bad night and spoke in a disrespectful manner to his pastor. My comments to him reminded him of the importance of following the scriptural admonition to be kind to one another (Eph. 4:32). I did not stew. I did not take offense. I did not avoid the

---

3   DeGroat, *Toughest People to Love*, 14–15.

confrontation; instead, I ministered to an older man in a respectful manner (1 Tim. 5:1) and it de-escalated the conflict.

DE-ESCALATING CONFLICT

Maintain Proper Pastoral Boundaries

While it is healthy not to take oneself too seriously, it is not helpful to ignore disrespectful forms of communication. When I spoke to the upset deacon after the meeting, I reminded him of the importance of communicating with his pastor (and his friend) in appropriate ways. He immediately acknowledged his error and apologized. He calmed down. I did not embarrass him publicly; instead, I waited for a private moment to minister to him.

I also reassured him that he would get a fair hearing of his complaints in a private setting. Sometimes people go public with a problem because the public forum gives them advantage, forcing the pastor to answer the questions. However, this works against problem solving because it requires off-the-top-of-the-head thinking, instead of serious contemplative consideration. If reasonable people know their concerns are important to their pastor, they may be willing to air them in a less threatening environment.

What about unreasonable people? Antagonists are a different story and require a different approach (chap. 10), but not all hurtful people are unbalanced or antagonistic. Most are good, decent people who need ministry.

De-escalation Requires Proper Pastoral Decorum

It is inappropriate for pastors to enter into shouting matches. Doing so increases the scope of the disagreement and escalates the intensity of the conflict. Besides, pastors are supposed to be gentle and self-controlled, not hot-tempered and not a bully (1 Tim. 3:2–7; Titus 1:6–9). Those are needed qualities because there are times in ministry when others act inappropriately and need guidance from a Spirit-filled pastor to help them. One way to de-escalate conflict is to help upset people calm down. Instead of raising your voice to match the level of theirs, speak one level quieter than normal and be gentle in your answers (Prov. 15:1).

De-escalation also Means That Pastors Work
to Decrease the Intensity of the Conflict

Just as there is a spectrum of grief (chap. 3), there is an intensity-of-conflict scale.[4] Some intensities are healthy and some of them quite destructive. In his scale, George Bullard places the first three of seven intensities in the healthy range:

1. Individuals engaged in task-oriented disagreements between individuals about how or when to do something.
2. Individuals engaged in personality-oriented conflicts that cloud the issues and make it difficult to work out task-oriented conflicts.
3. Groups involved in either task-driven or personality-driven conflicts.

The conflict can still be healthy at all of these stages because of the personal growth potential for all involved as they gain better understanding of the issues, of one another, and of the best means to accomplish the mission together. In de-escalating the conflict, the pastor attempts to move it down an intensity level, if possible before solving the problem. If the conflict is at the intensity level 3, he might say something like, "Is it possible for us to work through this disagreement in private instead of making it a public matter?" Really, my ministry with the deacon in the story above began by de-escalating the conflict from intensity 3 to intensity 1 by reminding him that we could solve the issue in private and that we were friends who cared for one another. My posture was we are on the same side but we do have a disagreement about what we should do. At intensity level 1, we found a solution—we installed the screen, but put a cover over it when not in use so that it did not take away from the ascetics of the building. When we needed video projection, we had it. But when we did not, the screen did not detract from his worship experience.[5] If it would have remained in intensity 3, we may not have found a solution and people could have been hurt needlessly.

If the conflict is at the intensity level 2, pastors might say, "Let's see if

---

4   Bullard, *Every Congregation*.

5   This was in the 90s, long before flat screen TVs or inexpensive video projectors. We were installing a cathode tube TV above a storeroom door at the front of the auditorium. He was right—it would not have looked good without a door that matched the woodwork. In this case, his opposition was reasonable and the compromise was better than my original proposal.

we can set the personal issues aside for a moment to see if we can work together to solve the problem. After we do that, then we can deal with the personality conflict we are experiencing, would that be okay?" Problems are easier to solve at lower intensities, so de-escalating them provides a better atmosphere to solve the problem and minister to those who are upset.

The remaining four intensities of Bullard's model are helpful while leading during anxious times (chaps. 10–11), so I'll describe them in a footnote for future reference,[6] but these three are a helpful diagnostic tool for pastors wanting to de-escalate the early stages in conflict.

Maintain Self-control

It will be impossible to de-escalate conflict without maintaining self-control. Pastors must stay in control of themselves.[7]

Whenever people feel threatened, the fight-or-flight response kicks in, involving the release of adrenalin and an increased heart and respiratory rate.[8] Blood flow then diverts from the brain to the large muscles in the legs and arms to allow for either a fight or flight.[9] Perhaps you have expe-

---

6   Bullard's next intensity level is transitional in nature, meaning it can either be healthy or unhealthy and will likely require outside help to address the problems involved. Level 4: Conflict has gone congregation wide and will require a vote of the people to resolve. It doesn't appear that it can be resolved by a smaller group and in the end; someone will lose the battle and will likely leave. At this level, it is likely that de-escalating the conflict means bringing in a third party who has no self-interest in the outcome of the vote to work to calm the people down so they can make a wise decision. Perhaps it can be returned to a small group to decide, moving the conflict to an intensity three level. The next three levels are all unhealthy with there are no winners. They require outside help to resolve the conflict – an arbitrator, attorney or the police. Level 5: The congregation was unable to solve the issues with a vote and the conflict is viral, demanding everyone takes sides. If not de-escalated, it will result in a church split. Level 6: People have left by now, but their departure did not solve the problem. The conflict continues. At this intensity, the battle goes into the courts for people to address their grievances and exact their revenge. Level 7: People threaten violence or become violent.

7   Leas, *Leadership and Conflict*, 99: "Of course, you cannot control the behavior of others. They will do what they will do. But you can control yourself and contribute to an environment that invites the other into fair and reasonable discourse."

8   Kollack-Walker, et al., "Central Stress Neurocircuits," 344.

9   Patterson, *Crucial Conversations*, 5: "Your brain then diverts blood from

rienced a flush feeling that comes in these high-anxiety moments as the blood rushes from the brain to the arms and legs. Unfortunately, whenever a person feels threatened, the blood rushes away from the part of the brain where clear thought and theological reflection reside,[10] leaving a pastor ill equipped to demonstrate love and care.

In moments when there is a genuine threat of bodily harm (like an attempted mugging in a parking lot), the biological automatic reaction might prove to be life-saving. However, those moments are few in pastoral ministry. Unfortunately, the same biological reactions occur when an irate church member raises his voice at the pastor in a congregational business meeting. In that situation, running away or taking a swing at the church member is not an appropriate reaction. The situation requires a higher brain function. Reactivity, as in our fight-or-flight response, is a lower brain function. Responsiveness, by way of comparison, is an upper brain function requiring the engagement of the full brain. That is not to say that pastors should ignore the emotions they experience when feeling threatened; rather, it means they should not be controlled by them. They should respond with emotional intelligence by identifying, using, understanding, and managing their emotions.[11]

Paul McClain's triune brain is helpful to explain the biological brain structures where different levels of cognition, from reacting emotionally (lower brain function) to responding intelligently (upper brain function) reside. While on faculty at Yale, McClain developed a theory that the brain has three regions: the brain stem, the limbic system, and the neocortex.[12]

---

activities it deems nonessential to high-priority tasks such as hitting and running. Unfortunately, as the large muscles of the arms and legs get more blood, the higher-level reasoning sections of your brain get less. As a result, you end up facing challenging conversations with the same equipment available to a rhesus monkey."

10   Goleman, *Working with Emotional Intelligence*, 74: "When the mind is calm, working memory functions at its best. But when there is an emergency, the brain shifts into a self-protection mode, stealing resources from working memory and shunting them to other brain sites in order to keep the senses hyperalert — a mental stance tailored to survival."

11   Caruso and Salovey, *Emotionally Intelligent Manager*, x.

12   LeDoux, *Emotional Brain*, 101. LeDoux critiques the triune brain model with a conclusion that the limbic system does not exist; nevertheless, he sees it as "useful anatomical shorthand." Since my purpose to illustrate the difference between higher and lower brain function, this anatomical shorthand is useful, even though it does not enjoy universal acceptance among medical personnel.

He ultimately published his findings in a book in 1990.[13] The brain stem controls autonomic functions and handles the reactive processes for the brain.[14] It is also known as the *reptilian brain* because it is similar to the cognitive capacities of a snake or lizard. The limbic system[15] in the middle of the brain processes emotions, bonding, and the like, and is known as the *mammalian brain*. It is equivalent to the brain other mammals have. The neocortex[16] is the outer part of the brain and is unique to humans. It is also known as the *thinking cap* because of its capacity for advanced reasoning.

However, in reactive states, people will likely use their snake (brainstem) or their pit-bull (limbic system) brain to react, rather than exercising self-control and responding in a reasonable way while using their full brain. The flush feeling is a warning that the snake brain (brainstem) or pit bulldog brain (limbic system) is about to take over—in that brief moment, pastors must get in control of themselves before reacting.

Retrain Your Brain

Research is affirming the plasticity of the brain, that is, the neocortex is capable of reorganizing.[17] This is significant in this discussion, because it is possible to preprogram a response into your brain[18] to react in stressful situations in an acceptable manner. Or to use biblical language, it is possible to "renew your mind" (Rom. 12:1-2). In other words, you can train your brain to remain calm and in control during stressful moments at church by practicing the behavior at home. Never let your guard down. Never excuse boorish personal behavior anywhere. Remain disciplined

---

13   Maclean, *Triune Brain*.

14   "Brainstem," About.com, accessed September 29, 2014, http://biology.about.com/od/anatomy/p/Brainstem.htm.

15   "Limbic System," About.com, accessed September 29, 2014, http://biology.about.com/od/anatomy/a/aa042205a.htm.

16   "Definition of NeoCortex," MedicineNet.Com, accessed September 29, 2014, http://www.medterms.com/script/main/art.asp?articlekey=25283.

17   Steven and Blakemore, "Cortical Plasticity," 1243.

18   Grossman and Christensen, *On Combat*, 74: "Dr. Artwohl's research found that 74 percent of the officers involved in a deadly force encounter acted on automatic pilot. In other words, the actions of three out of four officers in combat were done without conscious thought." Just as those in combat situations can learn to preprogram their responses prior to the conflict, pastors can learn to preprogram kind, thoughtful responses before they are in conflict situations.

in stressful situations in your personal life—at home, on the golf course, at a sporting event, and you will be better equipped to handle them in ministry situations.

Ask Questions

Because advanced cognition is necessary to answer a question, you can engage the upper brain by asking yourself questions like, "Why am I feeling afraid, angry, or threatened?" Or, "I wonder what has this person so upset?"[19]

Take a deep breath. There is no rush to respond (notice I did not say react) when encountering a hurtful person who is upset. Take your time—think. If you feel bombarded by emotions, ask for a chance to regroup. Say something like, "Though I'm sure it is not your intention, I am feeling a bit defensive right now and I wouldn't want to say the wrong thing, can we take a moment, sit down over a cup of coffee, and think this through together?" This will result in attacking the problem, not the hurtful person.[20]

Negative Sentiment Override

John Gottman, of the University of Washington, is a world-renowned psychologist who can predict with 91 percent accuracy whether a marriage will last based on whether the couple engages in positive or negative sentiment override.[21] In positive sentiment override, the person's overall positive emotion towards the other person keeps him or her from becoming overly upset when wronged. If a husband snaps at the wife after a long day,

---

19   Patterson, *Crucial Conversations*, 44: "When we present our brain with a demanding question, our body sends precious blood to the parts of our brain that help us think, and away from the parts of our body that help us take flight or begin a fight."

20   Leas, *Leadership and Conflict*, 113: "Invite the other (even a person who is attacking you) to join you in a common search to identify what the problems are, stay with the other in order to work through the differences, look for alternatives that you both can agree have merit and value for each of you."

21   Gottman, *Seven Principles*, 2–3: "In their day-to-day lives, they have hit upon a dynamic that keeps their negative thoughts and feelings about each other (which all couples have) from overwhelming their positive ones. They have what I call an emotionally intelligent marriage."

in positive sentiment override, she overlooks the irritability. Her overall positive feelings about him override the isolated negative action.

Negative sentiment override does the opposite. The negative emotion overrides positive overtures. Gottman explains, "In the negative sentiment override state, people draw lasting conclusions about each other. If their spouse does something positive, it is a selfish person doing a positive thing. It's really hard to change those states, and those states determine whether when one party tries to repair things, the other party sees that as repair or hostile manipulation."[22] Have you ever had the feeling that you cannot do anything right in someone else's eyes? This is a perception that someone else is in negative sentiment override with you. However, the issue is not so much their attitude toward you (that is something you have no control over) but your attitude towards them, over which you do have control.

In *Preaching*, Fred B. Craddock writes,

> Once a minister becomes suspicious of the love and trust of the parishioners, a negative interpretation of every facial expression, every whisper, every motion appears. In such a frame of mind a preacher looks out upon frowns of disproval not intense listeners, upon critical mumbling not soft amens, upon mutinous huddles not groups planning for the minister's fifth anniversary. When a person leaves the sanctuary during the sermon of one minister, it is assumed that he or she has to catch a plane or was suddenly ill. When a person leaves the sanctuary during the sermon of another minister, it is assumed the person is upset at something said, is angry, stomping out never to return. Those two scenes, worlds apart, are both creations of the preacher's attitude toward the listeners.[23]

When pastors are in negative sentiment override, they misinterpret the motives of hurtful people and are at a disadvantage to provide them with the nurture and care they need. Hurtful people are usually hurting people and need help adapting, growing, and reaching their potential. Pastors must have the ability to help others without hurting themselves so that they can be spiritually and emotionally healthy, which is required to minister to hurtful people.

---

22   Gladwell, *Blink*, 29–30.
23   Craddock, *Preaching*, 217.

Chapter 5   *Helping Others without Hurting Yourself*

As he rounded the corner and pulled into his driveway, Pastor "Bruce" officially ended his summer vacation. In years past, he dreaded getting back to the grind, but not this time. *Funny thing,* he thought, *I'm really looking forward to getting back to work.* The first five years at Grace Community Church had not been very gracious. But things were changing.

"Peggy," Bruce's wife, took the children inside and Bruce started unloading the car when one of his most supportive church members parked next to Bruce's car. Bruce saw the expression on "Brian's" face, and immediately knew something was wrong. His stomach tightened as Brian put his hand on his pastor's shoulder and said, "Pastor, I don't know if you heard or not, but 'Chester' is at it again. He made an announcement after this morning's service that the elders are calling a special congregational meeting to relieve you of the pulpit."

The nightmare was not over. In many ways, it was just beginning.

Bruce had a solid ministry for four years at his first full-time church out of seminary. To say Bruce was excited when Grace Church first contacted him is an understatement. Really, he felt honored that a large church would pursue him. There was only one issue – their last pastor had multiple affairs with women in the church. However, that was over two years ago. The church had put it behind them and were ready to go forward, or so the pastoral search committee told him.

The weekend he spent with them as a candidate for the pulpit went smoothly, but something did not feel quite right. There was an unexplainable ominous feel in the air. When he met in private with the leaders, he told them, "I know the church has some healing to do, and I just want to tell you that if you're depending on me to fix things for you that you'll be disappointed. I can't do it. However, I believe that Jesus can."

Over the first few years, his optimism faded. The environment had a constant antagonistic overtone, especially surrounding the annual congregational business meetings. The meetings always had a spirit of contention. It was not overt or nasty – it was more like steady undercurrent, a faint throbbing, or dark storm cloud.

"Pastor Bruce," Chester said in an elder's meeting during Bruce's fifth year, "a number of families are beginning to doubt your ability to lead the church."

"What families?" Bruce asked.

The chair showed him a list of fifteen families.

"What are their complaints?"

"They just don't have confidence in you anymore," Chester said. "They're saying things like you don't visit enough, that you are too controlling, and that you're not preaching like you used to."

There must be some misunderstanding, Bruce thought, *I need to talk to these folks and we can straighten things out.* "Could you get a meeting together with the families?" Bruce asked. This was not how they did things in Grace Church. Usually, the elders fought the member's battles with the pastor; they never spoke for themselves. Reluctantly, the elders called the families together to have them confront the pastor. At the meeting, the members with grievances set in a semi-circle, the elders sat behind tables off to the side—like a panel of judges. Bruce sat by himself across from the members. One by one, the members fired their complaints. Bruce listened. After everyone was done, the pastor agreed to take to heart what he had heard and asked to have private meeting with everyone who aired complaints. In doing so, he demonstrated true humility and a desire to listen so he could grow as a pastor and be a better minister to them.

None of them took him up on his offer.

Bruce did not understand what was happening. He had a heart to minister to people, even when the people were acting in a hurtful way, but if they would not meet with him, how could he minister to them? He tossed and turned at night and could not find any relief from the pain. The constant conflict robbed him of his physical, emotional, and spiritual vitality. He could not help but internalize the complaints and began to doubt whether he was fit for the ministry. His relationships became more distant—even his relationship with Peggy. It was as if he was never home.

Eventually all fifteen families left the church, but the dark cloud did not. Bruce not only dreaded every congregational business meeting, he also dreaded every elder board meeting. Before the meetings, Bruce felt like a boy preparing to face the school bully. The elder body did not have unity. Some felt he should leave; others supported him. To find the underlying cause of the problem, the elders all made a list of areas where they thought he could improve. Chester's list was ten pages long.

With great patience and humility, Bruce worked through the list with the elders. Everyone has areas of possible improvement, and Bruce wanted desperately to be effective in ministry. He listened. He second-guessed himself and he redoubled his efforts. He stopped playing golf. When he was with his family, his mind was back at the church. If you subtracted the time that he spent in sermon preparation and praying for the pain to stop from the total amount of time he spent in the Bible and prayer, he spent very little time with God.[1]

The dark cloud that used to hover over the church now hovered over him. He had absorbed the pain. He had become the pain. He was passing the pain on to those he loved the most. He was becoming a hurtful person himself. Finally, Bruce had enough and decided he had to fight back. One elder's meeting the chair brought a possible solution to Bruce, "From now on, do not do anything without our approval," he said. "Pass everything through us."

"You mean everything?" Bruce asked. "Everything," the chair responded. His rationale was that Bruce would have cover from the elder body and they would share the responsibility—essentially, it would be leading by committee. Bruce polled the elders and asked each man if they agreed that he should take the chair's advice. Half supported the idea, the other half did not.

Bruce said no. He was not about to become a teenager on restriction who had to ask "Mommy may I?" before doing anything. By now, he knew trust was the big issue. The church did not trust him to lead because of the broken trust resulting from the previous pastor's multiple affairs with women in the church, which included one of the members of the pastor search committee.

THE STORM

Bruce began to lose his motivation and grip on reality. Something was wrong. He was not functioning well anymore. He was shutting down. Bruce took a two-week leave of absence and checked himself into a clinic

---

1   Krejcir, "Statistics on Pastors." A survey of 1,050 pastors conducted by the Francis A. Schaeffer Institute of Church Leadership Development discovered that only 26 percent of the pastors they surveyed have personal devotionals and feel they are spiritually fed.

to get help from his mounting depression.[2] The first week was an intensive inpatient treatment; the second one was on an outpatient basis. When he left the facility, he had a positive attitude. They *can have my hide*, Bruce thought, *but not my heart.*

Bruce was feeling much better after the first week so he decided to go to the scheduled elder's meeting. It was an important meeting since they were electing a new chair. He was supposed to stay home and rest. Just like patients who stop taking the full course of prescribed medication because they feel better, Pastor Bruce decided he did not need the rest. He began to feel like he could leap tall buildings in a single bound, outrun a locomotive, and outwit his enemies with one hand tied behind his back. So he reengaged before the doctor said he should.

Bruce was surprised to see "Dave" at the elder board meeting. He had not been attending church at all; really, he should not still be an elder. When it came time for nominations for chair, someone nominated "Ted," an outspoken opponent of the Pastor. Pastor Bruce spoke against the nomination, so they withdrew it. The next nomination was for Dave. Bruce spoke against it too, because the elder chair ought to attend church. After a time of silence, "Hector" spoke up. "I don't know how you will interpret this," he said, "but I feel God calling me to the job." Hector was a humble, quiet spoken man who had not been involved in the battle. The men elected him.

Over the next few months, Hector worked hard to help the pastor and the elders find unity, but he was unsuccessful. One evening the meeting went especially long. Upstairs the worship service began, the congregation singing a song reminiscent of their church name— "Amazing Grace"— when one of the elders finally made the motion, "I move we ask the pastor to resign."

The pastor could hear the singing upstairs, "When we've been there ten thousand years" as the men discussed the motion to fire him. It was surreal. The singing continued, but the discussion stopped. Everyone just looked at each other. "Men," Bruce spoke into the silence, "you need to decide what you are going to do so I can decide what I'm going to do."

More silence.

"Okay," Bruce said, "I'll tell you what I'm going to do. I'm going upstairs and take to pulpit and tell the congregation that we've come to an impasse — that we can't find unity and turn this over to them."

---

2   Lehr, *Clergy Burnout*, 5. Half of pastors say they are either currently depressed (10 percent) or are battle with depression or chronic fatigue (40 percent).

And that's exactly what he did.

One of the members asked the elders, "What's the problem? Why is the church's leadership divided?" But none of them could answer. The tide was turning and Bruce's support was building. He thought it was over—over, that is, until Brian pulled into his driveway as he was unloading his car from his summer vacation.

When Brian, the pastor's friend, saw Chester go forward during the invitation to talk to the youth pastor, he was relieved. *Thank you for moving in Chester's heart.* He prayed. Then Chester went to the microphone to read the notice for the special called congregational meeting. He did not go forward to make a decision; he went forward to tell the youth pastor he needed to address the congregation.

"That was not an official word," the youth pastor said after Chester read the announcement. "Pastor Bruce will be back from vacation today and we'll sort everything out; right now, I think we should just close in prayer and go home." He began to pray, "Lord, thank you for being in this place today, and help us . . ."

Chester and another elder rushed the platform. "Who do you think you are?" The elder yelled. "You're nobody! You're not an elder. You're not a pastor. You're nobody!"

The service was bedlam.

This event solidified those who were on the fence to take sides. No matter what had gone on before, it was clear to the congregation that what these elders were doing was not of God.

BITTER VICTORY

That evening Pastor Bruce addressed the congregation. In the coming weeks, they had a special congregational meeting to vote to enter into conflict resolution. After the meeting, the elders had a secret meeting with their supporters and fired Bruce. When Bruce got their letter, he called Chester and told him he was not going anywhere.

Shortly after the meeting, the church entered into conflict resolution. Chester and his group left. The church began a multi-year process of healing, dreaming, and an era of productive ministry. For more than ten years, he had fought the good fight—and he won. The divisive power brokers left in defeat. Bruce could now lead Grace Church into their future.

However, the constant fighting took a toll on Pastor Bruce's spiritual life. In his weakened state, he failed to take care of his own soul. While devoting all of his energy to gaining leadership control, he lost his self-control. One of the women in the church began to give Bruce personal attention. She listened to him. She admired him. They spent a few minutes here and a few hours there and before long, their relationship crossed a line.

After twelve years of ministry at Grace Church, Bruce resigned due to an inappropriate relationship.[3] Though he claimed it was not sexual in nature, like his predecessor's downfall, he did admit that it was inappropriate so he stepped down.

Bruce stayed through difficult times. All along the way, he put his ministry first and did everything he could to be a good pastor to the people, even the hurtful people. He survived the storm, but the sacrifices and compromises he made along the way finally defeated him. His enemies did not defeat him; his wounds were self-inflicted.

Is it possible that the sacrifices pastors make in the name of serving God and His people can actually destroy their ministry and devastate their walk with God? Some would look at Bruce's story and dismiss it merely as moral failure without understanding how burnout can contribute,[4] cause,[5] or be correlated[6] to the failure. Certainly, he was no longer "above reproach," but there are times that poor moral choices stem from poor soul hygiene[7] and a loss of appropriate boundaries.

Good intentions can have a dark side when taken to an unhealthy

---

3   *Leadership Journal*, "Pastoral Indiscretion," 12. A *Leadership Journal* survey of pastors indicates that 23 percent of the pastors they surveyed have done something they considered was "sexually inappropriate" with someone, while they've served in ministry. Another 12 percent admitted having "sexual intercourse" with someone other than their spouse while in ministry.

4   Iorg, *Character of Leadership*, 44: "I know of several ministry leaders who have had some major failure of integrity — often a moral failure. In almost every case, burnout was part of the problem."

5   Colson and Vaughn, *Being the Body*, 332: "Many of these moral failures are the result of burnout."

6   London and Wiseman, *Shepherd's Covenant*, 159: "We believe there's a direct correlation between fatiguing burnout and moral failure among pastors."

7   Binford Gilbert, *Pastoral Care of Depression*, 93: "Many of them become naively involved because they are empty, hungry, and lonely." I do not use the term "soul hygiene" as Socrates did. And I am not implying that we should mix science and psychotherapy. I am simply saying that spiritual maintenance and practicing the spiritual disciplines is important.

extreme; they can hurt pastors who are trying to help others. Just as a nurse who treats an Ebola patient has some risk of exposure to the disease, pastors who are driven with success or wanting to be helpful to others can experience spiritual, emotional, and physical shutdown, even though they have good intentions.

No doubt, pastors with the "whatever it takes" or "I feel your pain" approach may have good motives. With good soul hygiene and with the proper boundaries in place, those with these attitudes can experience ministry resiliency.[8] However, when taken to extremes, these approaches can result in burnout or empathy fatigue.

UNDERSTANDING THE FATIGUE SYNDROMES

Of the terms that describe fatigue syndromes, burnout is the most commonly used and understood word. Often people use it as a generic term, regardless of the causes, for those who lose their drive or desire to continue to serve. However, there are distinctions between burnout, compassion fatigue, and empathy fatigue.

Burnout results from unbridled, maladapted ambition.[9] A desire to achieve goals is not bad. It is necessary for leaders to accomplish anything. At its best, that desire uses a person's strength, time, and ingenuity to succeed in life and to accomplish goals. However, the dark side of that desire can drive leaders to run over other people, lose their self-control, and become frustrated, resulting in exhaustion, no longer caring, and burnout.[10]

Compassion fatigue[11] results from unrestrained, maladaptive caring when empathizing with someone who has experienced one or more traumatic events.[12] A desire to help others is not bad—it is central to ministry (see chap. 2). Like ambition, a desire to help can be maladapted to allow other people's pain to overtake caregivers until they experience the pain

---

8   Hopkins, *Pursuing Pastoral Excellence*, 55: "Psychologists talk about resilience as the capacity to 'bounce back' from difficult experiences, as well as the ability to endure challenging circumstances."

9   Valent, "Diagnosis and Treatment," 22.

10   London, *Refresh, Renew, Revive*, 7.

11   Figley, *Compassion Fatigue*, 15: "Joinson first used the term in print, in 1992, in discussing burnout among nurses."

12   Valent, "Diagnosis and Treatment," 22.

vicariously[13] and begin to show the same[14] or even greater[15] pain level and immobilization as the traumatized person.

Empathy fatigue results from empathizing with other people's pain from common stressors over an extended period. It is cumulative in nature.[16] What it shares with compassion fatigue is that empathy is the transmitter of the other person's pain to the caregiver. It differs from compassion fatigue in that it results from working with a number of people with non-traumatic incidents instead of someone who has experienced one or more traumatic incidents. In other words, caregivers are at risk of experiencing compassion fatigue when they work with those who have experienced traumatic events like war or a terrorist attack. They are at risk for empathy fatigue when they are working with people who have not experienced acute trauma.

Those who minister with an ambitious "whatever it takes" attitude run a risk of experiencing burnout, and those who minister out of an empathetic "I feel your pain" posture are susceptible to empathy fatigue.

WHATEVER IT TAKES

For some, the "whatever it takes" drive focuses on leading the organization and accomplishing goals; for others, it is a drive to help someone regardless of the costs. While personal sacrifice (Luke 18:28–30) and dedication (Matt. 6:24) are admirable traits, they can become destructive to self, family, and ministry if not seen in context with healthy boundaries and human limitations.

William Carey is famous for his "whatever it takes" attitude in his mission venture to India, so much so that he is widely accepted as the father of the modern mission movement. However, he is infamous in his neglect of his family.[17]

---

13 Vachon, "Reflections on Compassion," 323.

14 Valent, "Diagnosis and Treatment," 19.

15 Hoffman, *Empathy and Moral Development*, 199.

16 Stebnicki, *Empathy Fatigue*, 23: "Empathy fatigue can be acquired by professionals who approach their work empathically and deal with a variety of clients/consumers who have been exposed to everything from daily hassles (e.g., school, work, relationship problems) and life adjustments (e.g., divorce, job loss, major grief) to traumatic stress-related issues (e.g., exposure to death, rape, homicide)."

17 Dunagan, *Mission-Minded Family*, 57.

In the early days, Bill Hybels built Willow Creek Community Church with a "whatever it takes" attitude. One night his wife begged him to stay home and share a meal with her. He responded, "Kids are dying and going to hell and you want me to stay home and hold your hand?"[18] The only reason anyone knows this story is that Bill and Lynn Hybels courageously shared their mistake in their early ministry so their readers would not repeat them. Hybels is not the only well-known leader who made poor priority choices in the early days of ministry.

Billy Graham has a similar story to tell about when Ruth asked him to stay home with her because she was having labor pains. She asked him to cancel his speaking engagement at a meeting in Alabama. Graham refused. That evening Ruth delivered their daughter Gigi.[19]

In 1949, at the famous Los Angeles crusade, Ruth's sister and brother-in-law came to the meeting. While they were together, Billy admired a child they were holding. "Whose baby is this?" Graham asked.

It was Anne, his daughter.[20] In his later years, Graham, said that if he could do it over again, he would have devoted more of his time to his family.[21]

This is not just an issue with famous ministers. Pastor Dan is not famous at all. In fact, he is a rural pastor who looks after two small rural churches simultaneously. His daughter's third grade teacher insisted that he accompany his wife for the annual parent teacher conference. At the conference, the teacher showed Dan a picture that his daughter drew of his family.

Dan looked at the picture and asked, "Where am I?"

"That's why I called you down here today," the teacher responded. "I asked your daughter the same question. She said you're never home, so she left you out of the picture."

Dan was doing "whatever it takes" to take care of two flocks, and in the process was missing precious years of his daughter's life that he could never replace. Pastors can delegate some things, but not all things.

In an interview with Dennis Rainey and Bob Lepine on "FamilyLife Today," Pastor Ben Freudenburg said, "We have become ministers because we have this great passion to care for and love people to Christ. We'll do whatever it takes, and sometimes we get misguided and put so much energy

18   Hybels and Hybels, *Rediscovering Church*, 44.
19   Graham, *Just as I Am*, 97.
20   Ibid., 156–57.
21   Bumpus, "Billy Graham Answers," 14.

into the work of the church that we don't realize what we are doing to our own families and to our own lives and children."[22]

This attitude does not honor God.[23] Somewhere there is a balance.

The balance is not always easy to find. Pastors are not just working a job, they are fulfilling a calling (chap. 2). During times of acute crisis, a family has to understand when a pastor must sacrifice family time. People die. Adolescents attempt suicide. Families have fatal automobile accidents. And when these things happen, pastors must leave whatever they are doing to go to the aid of those in distress. No one would have sympathy for a doctor refusing to perform an emergency life-saving surgery because the doctor's niece is pitching at a softball game. Neither will a distraught mother understand if her pastor refuses to intervene when her child is threatening suicide. It is not neglectful to miss family time due to an acute situation. It is neglectful, however, when missing family time becomes chronic.

The pastor's family life is not the only casualty of a busy schedule. Busyness can rob pastors of spiritual vitality,[24] their availability to minister to needs,[25] and a full, meaningful life.[26] Just as an engine cannot run full throttle[27] over an extended period, neither can pastors. Excessive work schedules drain time from family, God, and rest. It leaves pastors vulnerable to burnout.[28]

---

22   Rainey, Swindoll, and Zuck, *Ministering*, 2.

23   Stanley and Maxwell, *Choosing to Cheat*, 32: "There is nothing honoring to God about the workaholic who neglects his or her family. But the man or woman who refuses to provide for his family brings no honor to Him either."

24   Goetz, "Pastors Practice the Presence," 33: "Eighty-three percent of the 749 respondents said the top obstacle to their spiritual growth was busyness."

25   Gladwell, *Tipping Point*, 165. In an experiment at Princeton University only 10 percent of students who were placed in a hurried situation stopped to help a person they thought were in need, while 63 percent of those who were not rushed rendered aid.

26   Demarest, *Soul Guide*, 95: "Some relish busyness and speed to avoid facing up to their real selves and the haunting emptiness within."

27   Martin, "Ten Hours," last updated January 31, 2012, http://www .thetruthaboutcars .com/2012/01/ten-hours-800-rpm-full-throttle-how-chrysler-used -to-test-engines. Chrysler could not get an engine to run full throttle for more than 20 hours without doing damage to it.

28   Thoburn, Baker, and Dal Maso, *Clergy Sexual Misconduct*, 10: "The pastors who are more prone to burnout are those who are afraid of intimacy, who overwork out of fears of failure or rejection, or who put their emotional and physical energy into their careers because things are not going well at home.

I Feel your Pain

Just as those who minister with a "whatever it takes" attitude run a risk of experiencing burnout, those who minister out of a "I feel your pain" posture are susceptible to empathy fatigue. Compassion is important. Jesus modeled ministry flowing out of compassion (Matt. 14:14; Mark 6:34) and Paul admonished Christians to do the same (Col. 3:12–13). Compassion is an *inward* emotion that emerges when observing pain in others.[29] It is not an attempt to experience the other person's pain; it moves people to try to alleviate another person's pain. On many occasions, Jesus experienced compassion when viewing other people's pain (Matt. 15:32; 20:34; Mark 1:41; 6:34; 8:2; 9:22; Luke 7:13; 10:33; 15:20).

There is a popular notion in the fields of counseling,[30] cross-cultural ministry,[31] and pastoral care[32] that ministers should minister with empathy, not merely compassion. Some even question pastors' spiritual qualifications if they do not use empathy in their ministries.[33]

This is misguided. If empathy is "concern for others,"[34] then fine, in this usage — empathy is simply a synonym for compassion. However, there is a technical distinction between the two words. Biblical compassion is a motivating, internal feeling that occurs when observing another person in pain. Empathy is an attempt to feel the pain of the other person.[35]

---

29   Bible Hub, "Splagchnizomai," *Greek,* accessed October 25, 2014, http://biblehub.com/greek/4697.htm. Σπλαγχνίζομαι derives from a word literally meaning inward parts, like "the heart, lungs, liver, and kidneys."

30   Stebnicki, *Empathy Fatigue,* 33: "Many in the counseling field suggest that possessing the skills of empathy is a prerequisite for becoming a competent helper."

31   Lingenfelter and Mayers, *Ministering Cross-Culturally,* 110: "His empathy with the people to whom he ministers is so great that he experiences in his own emotional and spiritual life their pain of weakness."

32   Oden, *Becoming a Minister,* 90: "Rigorous behavioral expectations are applied to those who have been, in the mind of the church, set apart for sacred ministry. Consistency, empathy, evenhandedness, and a steady temper are required for soul care."

33   Oates, "The Pastor as Healer," 305: "Yet the pastor who moves at his task as healer without empathy for the hurt of his people has yet to learn of the Holy Spirit."

34   Hoffman, *Empathy and Moral Development*: "Empathy is the spark of human concern for others, the glue that makes social life possible."

35   Valent, "Diagnosis and Treatment," 20: "On the receiving side, empathy is the vehicle whereby helpers make themselves open to absorption of traumatic information."

Empathy is a relatively new concept. It was used for the first time in 1909 by Edward Titchener when he translated into English the German term *Einfühlung*,[36] which means "feeling into."[37] He wrote, "The experimenter must be in full sympathy with his observers; he must think, by empathy, as they think, understand as they understand, speak in their language."[38] However, Titchener does not limit the use of empathy to thinking another's thoughts; he also used the term to relate to experiences[39] and attitudes or feelings.[40] Titchener sought to use "inner imitation"[41] to relate to what is happening inside of another.

Compassion is feeling with someone and then doing something about the pain. Empathy is *feeling into* someone's pain and experiencing it. One problem with experiencing the pain of the other person is it voids pastors of their objectivity, which is necessary to minister and give soul guidance. The transferred suffering[42] can leave pastors unable to help[43] and result in debilitating empathy fatigue.[44] While it is possible to monitor and limit negative effects,[45] empathy works against long-term ministry resiliency.

---

36   Titchener, *Lectures*, 21.

37   Stueber, "Empathy."

38   Titchener, *Lectures*, 91.

39   Ibid., 181.

40   Ibid., 185.

41   Wispe, "History," 20.

42   Kaiser, *Grief and Pain*, 131: "Grief affects more people than the afflicted; it oftentimes enters fully into the lives and feelings of those whom the sufferer loves or knows. Thus empathy with those who suffer produces a new suffering."

43   Lazarus, *Stress and Emotion*, 246: "So we must protect ourselves against unbridled compassion. Too much compassion, paradoxically, can impair our ability to help. To help, we must steel ourselves so as not to fall apart in the face of another's tragic distress."

44   Stebnicki, *Empathy Fatigue*, 68: "However, when deeper levels of compassion and empathy are experienced and communicated by the therapist, there may be a professional cost that results in an empathy fatigue reaction."

45   Lane, *Levels of Emotional Awareness*, 173: "One's ability to empathize cannot exceed one's ability to monitor one's own emotional states."

SOUL HYGIENE

Give God the First Part of Your Energy

When people say "give me the rest," they mean give me what is left-over—what they did not need or use. Sometimes, that is how pastors approach rest. They fill their schedules with activities and give God and their family the "rest." In this case, rest is what is leftover of their time, attention, and energy. However, that was not God's original design. God's Sabbath rest came on the seventh day of creation (Gen. 2:2). After he had finished all of His work, He rested. On the sixth day, He created Adam and Eve (Gen. 1:27). That means that the first full day of their lives, Adam and Eve rested before their work began. God's work resulted in rest (Gen. 2:3). Our work flows out of rest. Rest comes first.

This is consistent with what God requires of finances. Believers do not give out of the leftover money—they give off the top, the firstfruits (Prov. 3:9–10; Ezek. 44:30; 2 Chron. 31:5). This is a matter of faith. When believers give off the top of their resources, they live off the rest. When believers rest before they begin their week's work, they work out of the rest, trusting that they will do what God wants them to do.[46]

Give God the First Part of Your Day

Because pastors spend their week handling the Scripture and praying for others, it is easy to neglect personal time with God in the Word and on their knees. The best way to ensure this does not happen is for pastors to spend the first part of their day with God.[47] Just as the beginning of the day usually includes personal hygiene, it can also include soul hygiene. Make it part of the routine right along with taking a shower and brushing your

---

46　I am not advocating for a certain day of the week for rest here—just that labor flows out of a rested soul. Since Sunday is the busiest day for most pastors, Saturday would be a good day for deep, God-honoring rest. The day of the week is not as important, in my view, as the fact that rest occurs and it isn't what is leftover.

47　I don't mean this in a legalistic way. It may be that it is better to have personal devotionals at another time of the day than morning, especially if a person is not a morning person. (Obviously, some people take their showers at other times of the day also.) However, the time should be intentional, not an afterthought and certainly should not be "leftovers."

teeth. Spend time in the Word, prayer, meditation, confession, and praising God. Do it before, after, or concurrent with your personal hygiene routine, but make sure it is daily. No exceptions. Just as you would not leave the house without showering, do not leave without taking care of your soul.

HEALTHY BOUNDARIES

Understanding that pastors should keep all Ten Commandments, they should schedule one day a week for rest, which leaves up to six days for work. In all of those six days, pastors will need to allocate time for personal devotions, sleeping, eating, family, exercise, and household chores. These things are not optional.

Schedule Boundaries

Each week has seven days, and each day, twenty-four hours. By definition, time has limitations. If it were humanly possible to work twenty-four hours each day, seven days a week, it would still be impossible to work more than that. In other words, pastors are limited in how much they can work. When crisis comes, pastors will have to push past normal limitations; but in an ordinary week, they should be able to find some balance.

Pastors need to develop a reasonable schedule of ministry activities that includes time for all responsibilities, but that does not exceed a fifty-five-hour workweek and no more than a few nights away from home. While it is possible to deviate from the plan when crisis occurs, it is important to honor it the rest of the time. When a request comes to work in a time slot allocated for non-work activities, shuffle the schedule around or simply say, "I'm sorry, my calendar is full at that time, can we meet at another time to talk?"

Pastors reserve time slots for important activities all the time. For instance, they do not schedule counseling meetings during the primary worship service time. Since family, personal devotionals, and the other items in pastors non-work schedule are also important. Pastors should not apologize for offering other times to meet the need.

In the final analysis, pastors will always have to leave some things undone. There is always another book to read, person to visit, lost person to evangelize, verb to conjugate — it never ends. Even if pastors could work twenty-four hours a day, seven days a week, they still could not get everything done. Wise pastors develop reasonable boundaries that help them know what to do — and what not to do.[48] Boundaries are not just about what pastors do with their time; they also involve what pastors do with their relationships and their emotions.

Relational Boundaries

Pastors need normal relationships. Unfortunately, relationships in the church usually tilt in one or two directions. Either church members hold pastors in such high regard that they are usually differential to them, resulting in a sense of entitlement among pastors. Or the members hold them with such low regard that they treat pastors with contempt, contributing to self-loathing. It is unhealthy for church relationships to overshadow other relationships with spouses, children, grandchildren, and friends that do not tilt to either extreme.[49]

Pastors need friends in the church .[50] When I was young and in ministry I heard professors and pastors say, "Don't make friends in the church because they will turn on you and hurt you."[51] Today I teach students to make friends — just know that their friendship does not mean they have to agree with every idea you have.

Pastors also need friends outside of their church life[52] —people to play golf, racquetball, or bowl. While these relationships may lead to opportunities to share the gospel, they are not merely evangelism targets. They are people. They are friends. Pastors need neighbors to exchange favors with, and they need nieces, nephews, aunts, uncles, in-laws, and other family members to share holidays with. Pastors need normal relationships with

---

48   Wickman, *Pastors at Risk*, 11: "Most pastors, studies show, have difficulty saying 'no.' Thus it is easy for him to take on too much and soon feel over his head in work."

49   Wicks, *Handbook of Spirituality*, 253: "Over-involvement with others is unhealthy when one acts upon relationships genitally and/or makes colleagues or parishioners the center of one's life."

50   Thoburn, *Clergy Sexual Misconduct* 10: "The ministry is a lonely calling, with 70 percent of a representative sampling of pastors reporting that they have no close friends."

51   Gula, "Ethics in Pastoral Ministry," 81. Speaking of being friends with members of a pastor's parish, Gula writes, "These dual relationships have not necessarily become a hindrance to effective ministry, but in fact have been healthy for both parties."

52   Smith, *Empowering Ministry*, 176.

people who neither idolize nor marginalize them. They need a life on the other side of the stained glass.

Emotional Boundaries

While pastors must enter into people's pain and demonstrate compassion, they cannot internalize people's pain to the extent that it absorbs them.[53] Pastors cast their cares upon the Lord (Ps. 55:22; 1 Peter 5:10); they do not take them upon their own shoulders. Perhaps one of the most challenging calls of the Scripture is to take up the cross and follow Jesus (Matt. 16:24). Following Jesus means exercising good soul hygiene and having reasonable boundaries as Jesus did.

Jesus practiced good soul hygiene. Jesus spent time reading Scripture, as evidenced by the multiple times he quoted or followed Scripture (Matt. 19:7-8; Luke 5:4; Matt. 5:17-18). Jesus also had a vital prayer life (Luke 5:16; Luke 9:18; Luke 22:39-41; Matt. 6:6; Mark 1:35; Matt. 14:23), fasted (Matt. 4:1-2), and rested (Luke 5:15-16).

Jesus lived His life with the purpose of helping hurting people (Luke 4:18-19). But He also lived live with appropriate boundaries. He spent time in solitude at the beginning of the day (Luke 4:42), walked away from the crowd (Matt. 13:36), asked those He helped not to tell anyone about what He'd done for them (Matt. 8:4) and went into isolation, away from people who wanted Him to heal them (Matt. 15:29).

Pastors who want to follow Jesus will make time for good soul hygiene and will keep appropriate boundaries in their life. And if they do, they will be able to help the hurting and do so without hurting themselves.

---

53 Pembroke, *Renewing Pastoral Practice*, 103: "If we allow ourselves to be overwhelmed by the pain we are encountering we are unable to offer effective pastoral care."

Chapter 6   Celebrate!

A pastor I know shared the ups and downs of his vocation this way:

> I've been threatened, hit, screamed at, and hated. I have been asked to
> minister to parents after their child died and children after their parent
> died. I have sat on the side of the accused and the parents of the victim in
> the courtroom of murder cases. I cannot count the number of times I have
> counseled with those in the midst of a divorce and children caught in the
> middle. I have ministered to rapists, murders, and child molesters as well
> as the victims of such crimes.
>
> Yet, I have also had the opportunities to share in people's most joy filled
> moments: weddings, births, graduations, and baptisms
>
> I have loved and been loved by many. . . . So goes the life of an average
> pastor.[1]

This chapter is about what comes after the word "yet" in the quote
above. Yes, pastoral ministry includes spending time with people on the
most difficult days of their lives, but it also about spending time with them
on the best days of their lives.

Pastors receive invitations to attend football games, Christmas parties, and birthdays. Though they are not always able to accept the invitations, they attend the ones they can because ministry during times of
joy is important. Remember that the occasion of Jesus' first ministry was
a wedding.

WEDDINGS

When Burt called to ask me to perform his wedding, he told me that a
mutual friend, his pastor, referred him to me. We set a date for him and

---

1   Garland, "Ordination of Miles Hanson."

his bride-to-be to stop by my office to talk about their wedding ceremony. That is when I first heard their remarkable story.

When they were very young, they stood barefoot on a beach near the location of the church I served, pledging their undying love to one another. It was the 60s, so it was understandable they exchanged their vows without anyone officiating. In time, they lost touch with one another and went on with their lives.

Both married other people. Both divorced.

Gloria would dial directory assistance after dinner to different locations in the state of California trying to locate Burt. Gloria never gave up, making those after dinner calls for twenty or so years. What she did not know is that Burt had an unlisted number.

One day Burt installed a fax machine in his home office and an hour later, the phone line rang. When the fax machine did not pick up, Burt answered, thinking it was the telephone company testing the line. It was not.

Gloria had found the number. They talked for hours rekindling their friendship, and Burt promised to drive down to see Gloria in a couple of weeks. The next day he called and asked, "What exit did you say I should take?" He could not wait the couple of weeks—he was already on his way.

They were true lovers reunited at the end of their lives.

It was a pleasure for me to stand with them on the beach and officiate their wedding. There was a slight mist in the air that day for which I was grateful, because as you know, real men do not cry. The mist provided an excellent cover story as to why my eyes were so moist.

It is always an honor to perform a wedding ceremony. Each wedding I have been in has a special place in my memory, but some are more personal than others are. It was an honor to perform the wedding ceremony of my oldest son, and to participate in my youngest son's wedding, pronouncing "a father's blessing" over them. Among the most memorable ceremonies I performed came right after losing my voice to cancer.[2] I had been doing premarital counseling with a couple before discovering the cancer, and notified them that one of the other staff pastors could do their ceremony since I could no longer speak louder than a whisper. They refused my offer. I will never forget their kindness in including me in their day of celebration.

Weddings are important, but so are marriages. They are a foundational

---

2   Wilson, *Future Church*, 120–27.

building block of society.[3] From biblical times[4] forward,[5] marriage has had a civil component to it, which includes restrictions on who can and cannot be married (Lev. 18:8, 18; Deut. 7:3) and conditions for dissolution of the marriage (Deut. 22:19; 24:1–4; Matt. 4:31–32; 19:8–9).

Pastors often mention the civil component of the religious wedding ceremony when they say, "Acting in the authority vested in me by the laws of this state," during the final marriage pronouncement. No doubt, performing a wedding ceremony is a ministry function, but it is also a civil function. Pastors have dual responsibilities when they perform weddings, and one of them is to the state.

States regulate who can get married and who can perform those ceremonies. In some states, a pastor must register with the state and gain a "Minister's Credentials" card.[6] Others do not require registration.[7] There are also some variations county by county within a state for filing a certificate of marriage with the county clerk. Before agreeing to perform a ceremony, pastors need to check to see if they are qualified to do so in the jurisdiction of the ceremony.

Civil requirements notwithstanding, pastors, even though qualified to perform a ceremony in a jurisdiction, may choose not to do so. Sometimes pastors turn down requests due to unavailability and life balance issues (chap. 5),[8] but other times they do so because of their church's policies about who can be married on their property or their own personal convictions. Before agreeing to perform a ceremony, pastors should consider each request based on these three questions:

1. Does the state and local jurisdiction allow this couple to marry?
2. Does the church allow this couple to marry in its building?

---

3   Herrnstein and Murray, *Bell Curve*, 168.

4   Trutza, "Marriage," 96.

5   Cott, *Public Vows*, 46.

6   American Marriage Ministries, "Marriage Laws," *Arkansas Code*, accessed October 28, 2014, https://theamm.org/marriage-laws/arkansas/. See specifically, the section tagged "9-11-214: Recordation of Credentials of Clerical Character."

7   American Marriage Ministries, "A Guide to Performing Marriage" *Minister Licensing Requirements in the State of Texas*, accessed October 28, 2014, https://theamm.org/minister-licensing/texas/.

8   McKinley, "Where Does Time Go?," 33: "It's all right to say no. If we're going to get on top of managing our time, we need to say no intentionally, not by default."

3. Can I perform this wedding ceremony and bless this union with integrity?

If a wedding would be legal but not allowed in the church buildings by the congregation, the pastor could decide to perform the wedding offsite since it is the pastor and not the church with the authority to perform weddings. However, a congregation could also permit a ceremony in its building that its pastor chooses not to perform. Pastors' convictions differ on which weddings they will participate in and which they will not. Some have few restrictions, while others have many. They usually revolve around a few key questions.

Should Pastors Join Christians and Non-Christians in Holy Matrimony?

Paul encouraged believers to marry "in the Lord" (1 Cor. 7:39) and not to be "unequally yoked" in their relationships (2 Cor. 6:14). However, since he also encouraged the believing member of a married couple not to divorce their unbelieving spouse (1 Cor. 7:12-14), it would be difficult to say that Paul considered it wrong to be married to an unbeliever. Rather, it would be wrong for a believer to marry an unbeliever. Discovering what Paul meant by "in the Lord" and "unequally yoked" is at the heart of developing solid pastoral practice informed by these passages

Does "in the Lord" mean according to God's will,[9] or does it mean a Christian can only marry another Christian?[10] Does it mean both?[11] Another key question is, Is it possible for two Christians to be "unequally yoked"?[12]

The only place where the term "unequally yoked" appears in the Bible is 2 Corinthians 6:14. Since it includes the word "yoked," it likely is a reference to Deuteronomy 22:10, which prohibits plowing with an ox and a donkey yoked together.[13] Likely, the passage applies to all significant relationships,[14] but should not be taken to the extreme of complete isolationism[15] (1 Cor. 5:10). While this term is not likely referring to marriage

---

9   Utley, *Paul's Letters*, 94.

10 Mare, "1 Corinthians," 237.

11 Wiersbe, *Bible Exposition Commentary*, 593.

12 McDaniel, *Logic of Faith*, 84.

13 Robertson, *Word Pictures*, 2 Corinthians 6:14.

14 Pratt, *1 and 2 Corinthians*, 375.

15 Philip Edgcumbe Hughes, *Paul's Second Epistle to the Corinthians* (Grand Rapids: Eerdmans, 1962), 245.

exclusively, it definitely informs choices about who Christians are to marry.[16] Christians should not ally[17] themselves with people who will influence[18] them not to practice their faith, or if their mere association with them compromises their faith and witness.[19]

Some would say this prohibition was culturally specific,[20] addressing a specific problem in Corinth and has no bearing on people's choices today. However, that view overlooks the striking similarities between the ancient Corinthian and current American cultures. Others stand at the opposite extreme, saying that pastors are never free to perform a wedding ceremony between a Christian and non-Christian.[21] Some take a middle of the road view that a pastor should not conduct a ceremony between a Christian and a hardened, cruel, dangerous unbeliever but can join a "civil" non-Christian to a Christian.[22]

Pastors who take the stand not to marry people because they consider the couple to be "unequally yoked" will likely face unpleasant consequences from the culture who will think they are narrow-minded and have no right to withhold marriage from two people who say they are in love.[23] They might also have conflict with angry church members wondering why their pastor will not perform a wedding ceremony for them or their children.[24] However, violating their conscious also has consequences.

Some pastors will marry couples whether are not both are Christians, because pre-marital counseling session can be effective places for

---

16   Fisher, *1 and 2 Corinthians*, 359: "There is no indication of the exact nature of the 'yoking' which Paul had in mind. It could have been the 'yoke' of marriage or of business partnership. Paul deliberately left it indefinite so that it might apply to all such relationships."

17   Garland, *2 Corinthians*, 331.

18   *The ESV Study Bible*, 2231.

19   Harris, "2 Corinthians," 359.

20   Spicq and Ernest, "ἑτεροζυγέω", vol. 2:80: "To the Corinthians, who were getting used to debasing contact, or rather compromise, with their pagan surroundings (going to temples, entering mixed marriages?), St. Paul gives this charge: 'Do not be unequally yoked with unbelievers.'"

21   Bryant and Brunson, *New Guidebook*, 143.

22   Gerberding, *Lutheran Pastor*, 351: "If the pastor knows the one party to be heartlessly cruel, dangerously intemperate, or affected with disease from lewdness, he should also refuse to become a party to plunging the innocent into a life of suffering."

23   Dobson, "Speaking Truth," 31.

24   Shelley, *Well-Intentioned Dragons*, 129–30.

evangelism.[25] However, they could enter into pre-marital counseling without a promise to do the wedding ceremony. If the non-believer accepts Christ, there is no issue. If not, the pastor could always attend the ceremony as an act of friendship, but not bless the union by officiating.[26]

Should Pastors Marry Those Who Have Been Divorced?

The Bible allows for remarriage after divorce. These allowances are found in cases where the divorced spouse passes away (Rom. 7:2; 1 Cor. 7:39), or if the divorced spouse committed adultery (Matt. 19:8–9). *Porneia*, the Greek word translated for adultery, denotes a wide variety of sexual sins (Mark 7:21; John 8:41; Acts 15:20; 1 Cor. 6:18; 7:2; 2 Cor. 12:21; Gal. 5:19; Eph. 5:3; 1 Thess. 4:3). It is a general term[27] and not a narrowly defined word to mean a married person who has sexual intercourse with a non-spouse while married.[28] Regardless of the status the state grants divorced couples, they may still be married in God's eyes (Mal. 2:14) unless *porneia* was involved,[29] in which case the marriage can be dissolved (Matt. 5:31–32)[30] and remarriage may occur for the innocent party.

Remarriage is also allowed when divorced spouses reconcile (1 Cor.

---

25   Shelley, *Helping*, 78–80.

26   My own practice has been to conduct wedding ceremonies between Christians and non-Christians if I did not feel the non-believer would compromise the believer's witness or dissuade the believer from pursuing his or her faith. I can only think of a handful of people that I married under these circumstances. I did see many non-Christians accept Christ during premarital counseling.

27   Köstenberger and Jones, *God, Marriage, and Family*, 231: "The word *porneia* is a general term for sexual sin."

28   Schaff and Schaff, *History*, 348, footnote 2: "The word πορνεία, without addition, must be taken in its usual sense, and cannot mean illegitimate marriages alone, which were forbidden to the Jews, Exodus 34; Leviticus 18, although it may include them."

29   Mounce, *Matthew*, 181: "The point is that in God's sight the man who divorces his wife for any cause other than her unfaithfulness is still married to her."

30   *Jewish Encyclopedia*, s.v. "divorce." On the necessity of divorce, see Ketub. 3:5, also Israel Abrahams, *Studies in Pharisaism and the Gospels*, 74. Jesus' presentation of divorce in the Sermon on the Mount came against the background of a rabbinical argument between the houses of Hillel and Shammai. The first argued a man might divorce a woman for any cause, provided he provide her a bill of divorce. The latter argued only in the case of adultery is there a legal divorce, because the covenant *has already* been

7:10–11), as long as one divorced spouse had not married someone else after their divorce (Deut. 24:1–4).

As with the previous question of whether a non-Christian and a Christian can marry, some reject the idea of any divorced person remarrying,[31] others allow for it,[32] and still others argue for a case-by-case approach.[33] As it is important to follow biblical teaching, it is also important not to add to its teaching. Clearly, the Scripture allows for some remarriages, so remarrying when the person is the "innocent party" or after the death of a divorced spouse is a legitimate option.

If the divorced spouse is still alive or the marriage did not dissolve due to *porneia*, there is no biblical permission for remarriage, unless the divorced are included in the group of people[34] who would be better off to marry than to "burn with desire" (1 Cor. 7:9).[35] Some pastors, standing on the grounds of grace, will make allowances if the divorce was in the distant past or if it occurred prior to the person accepting Christ, while others will not. Just as refusing to perform an unequally yoked marriage will likely result in conflict, so will opting out of remarrying divorcees,[36]

---

broken. Jesus, then, goes even further, stating not that one *must* divorce, as Shammai would argue based on the broken covenant, but that one *may* divorce in such a case.

31 Leonard, "Barnhouse, Donald Grey," 36: "Barnhouse rejected divorce and remarriage under any circumstances, yet three of his four children were divorced. In the light of their experiences he moderated his view of divorce, claiming that it was 'not the unpardonable sin.'"

32 Bryer, "Burchard," 119: "One noticeable liberal deviation from mainstream Christianity was Burchard's marital teaching, most pointedly his allowance of remarriage by divorced believers."

33 Ferguson, "Murray, John," 464. Murray refused to be dogmatic on the issue of remarriage.

34 *The Lexham Analytical Lexicon to the Greek New Testament*, s.v. "ἄγαμος"; it means "an unmarried one."

35 Since Paul addresses remarriage after divorce in the verses that follow (1 Cor. 7:10–16), and he directs his remarks directly to those who are unmarried and widows (1 Cor. 7:8), it may be that he was excluding divorcees from the better to marry than "burn with desire" caveat. In 1 Corinthians 7:8 and 11, Paul uses ἄγαμος to refer to an unmarried person. The context of verse 11 makes it clear that the usage of the term referred to a separated woman, while in verse 8 it is open-ended. So it is not clear if he is referring to a different class of unmarried person in verse 11, than in verse 8. Regardless, it does beg the question, Is it better for the divorced to "burn with desire" than to marry?

36 Cornes, *Divorce and Remarriage*, 32.

but the probability of conflict should not keep pastors from following their convictions.

Should Pastors Officiate Same-Sex Unions?

Since the Supreme Court's Ruling on *Obergefell v. Hodges*,[37] all pastors in the United States are in jurisdictions that allow for same-sex unions. Because of this, someone may ask them to perform those ceremonies. Actually, this is not new. A same-sex couple asked me to solemnize their union in the early 1990s while I was the pastor of a church in Riverside County, California. What makes this question different from the previous ones is that heterosexual unions are not, by definition, immoral. Some are gloriously affirmed by the Bible (Gen. 2:22–24; Prov. 18:22), while others are strongly condemned (1 Cor. 5:1). Homosexual acts are unbiblical (Lev. 18:22; Rom. 1:24–27; 1 Cor. 6:9–11; 1 Tim. 1:10), and few Bible-believing pastors will likely have to think twice before saying no to the request. That notwithstanding, when pastors speak into this issue, they should do so with truth and grace.[38]

Other Issues to Consider

With large weddings, will the pastor, or will a wedding planner be in charge of the rehearsal? Will the pastor be available to do the pre-marital counseling? Will others do the counseling? Is pre-marital counseling mandatory or optional?[39]

Even if pastors do not require vigorous premarital counseling,[40] they will need to meet with the couple to discuss the biblical view of marriage and to plan the wedding ceremony. Other topics they could broach is temperament compatibility, managing conflict in marriage, intimacy and sex, marriage roles, managing finances, and cultivating their lifelong friendship.

---

37 http://www.scotusblog.com/case-files/cases/obergefell-v-hodges/

38 Wilson, "A Pastoral Model for Engaging Community," 223–36.

39 Huffman, *The Family You Want*, 200–201: "We require at least four premarital counseling sessions at St. Andrew's."

40 Dobson, "Family-Friendly Church," 127: "Mandate a vigorous premarital counseling program. The best ones provide a trained person to do at least six sessions before the wedding and two or more 'check-up' sessions six months afterward."

CHILDBIRTH

Another occasion for the ministry of celebration is the birth of a child. With their education complete, Randy and Lisa began their family. As the weeks became months, Lisa looked tired and ready to have her baby. When they missed church one Sunday morning, someone from the church called the hospital, and sure enough, Lisa was in labor. I smiled when I heard because I knew the next day, I would be able to hold a miracle — I would get to visit their newborn baby in the hospital.

I heard laughter outside the hospital room as I knocked on the open door. "Come in," two female voices blended to invite me into the room. Lisa was smiling from ear to ear, "Hello, Pastor, you've got to see him; he's so cute." There was no time for small talk — she asked Mary, her mother, to walk with me to the nursery for a glimpse of baby Samuel. When the nurse saw us, she brought him to Lisa's room.

Carefully, the nurse handed Samuel over to his mother. She was right — he was cute. I am always amazed at how small babies are. Lisa lifted the cap off his head to show me the full crop of black hair on his head. Finally, she asked the question I was waiting for, "Would you like to hold him?"

After a brief moment of cradling him in my arms, I lead in a prayer of blessing, "Father, thank you for this new life and the joy you brought into this home. I thank you that Samuel was born into a home filled with love and faith. Also, thank you that he will grow up in a church where he will hear the gospel, and I that one day he will have the chance to pray to receive Christ as his Savior."

With great pride, I announced to Susan that evening, "I got to hold baby Samuel today. He's so cute." Susan absolutely loves babies. She was happy for me, but I could tell that she was sad that she had to work and could not go to the hospital with me.

A few weeks after his birth, Randy, Lisa, and Samuel became regular in their attendance at church again. After some time passed, Randy and Lisa left Samuel in the nursery during Sunday school — a big step for new parents. With pride in her eyes and a smile on her face, my wife said to me on the way home from church, "I got to take care of Samuel today during Sunday school."

I replied, "That's great, Honey. That shows they really trust you — new parents don't always leave their babies in the nursery so soon after birth."

However, I was smart enough not to say what I was thinking: *I got to hold him first!*

CHURCH ORDINANCES

Perhaps the most public ministry of celebration pastors lead revolves around the church ordinances. Every baptism is memorable and important, but some of them were especially meaningful to me.

Dave

One church I served had a Saturday homeless ministry where they fed the homeless in a local park and had a Bible study for those that were interested. Dave regularly attended and before long, he helped the workers set up, serve, and tear down after the event. Soon, he was riding his bicycle to the church building on Sunday mornings and attending church on a regular basis.

One of the leaders of the church told me that some of the members were uncomfortable having Dave in the audience. He did not dress, or for that matter, smell like everyone else. "No problem," I said, "we can take care of this."

Then I asked, "You are always well-dressed for church, where do you buy your suits?" He gave me the name of a main street haberdashery. "Great," I said, "why don't you take Dave to your store and buy him a suit. I'm sure he would wear nice clothes if he had them." He was quiet. "Then let's get him some soap and deodorant; I'll unlock the bathroom early for him on Sunday morning and he can clean himself up."

To his credit, the leader did exactly what I asked him to do. On Sunday mornings, Dave rode his bicycle to the church early, entered the unlocked bathroom before others arrived, cleaned himself up, and put on his suit. One morning, I sat down next to him on a bench as we were waiting for the crowd to arrive and asked him to respond to the gospel message. A few weeks later, I stood in the baptistery with Dave. He may not have had a home on earth at the time, but His Savior was preparing a mansion for him in heaven and the whole church celebrated that at his baptism.

It was not long until Dave was not homeless anymore. His sister heard about the transformation and agreed to take him back into her home if he would get back on his medication.

Dave's baptism reminds me that the gospel is for all people. This story is a tribute to the gospel that saved Dave, but also to the gospel that lead a church leader to sacrifice and buy a suit for a homeless man so he would feel comfortable at a church that encouraged formal dress. This story is not about church dress codes — it is about a congregation who would help a homeless man fit in with others so he could sit under the power of the gospel.

Sergio

I rarely rehearsed what I would say at a baptismal service. I had long ago memorized the baptismal blessing and would say the same words before I immersed people in the water: "In obedience to the command of our Lord and Savior Jesus Christ, I baptize you my brother/sister in the name of the Father and the Son and the Holy Spirit." With Sergio, it was different. It would be the first time I would give the blessing in Spanish. "*Por su profesión de fe . . .*" So I rehearsed for days for his baptism.

A few years before, I had enrolled in a Spanish class at the local junior college to learn Spanish so we could launch Iglesia Bautista el Faro in the Spanish-speaking community where the church building resided.[41] With two years of Spanish classes under my belt and the help of a nearby Spanish-speaking church and her pastor, we launched the 3:00 p.m. Spanish-speaking service. The other pastor preached most of the time, but I preached in my broken Spanish once a month. There was pressure from the Spanish-speaking congregation to let the other pastor do the baptism, since he preached more than me. But I insisted on doing it.

It was important to me to make it clear that Iglesia Bautista el Faro was not a separate church. We were two congregations, but only one church. That baptism was a great day of celebration — it was a celebration of the gospel that penetrated both Sergio's heart and the barriers that divide us.

Brian

Hanging in my office is a picture of Brian, a former atheist, standing in an outdoor baptistery, soaking wet with his arms lifted up in victory. His arms obscure my face as the large man towered over me. It was only after his baptism that I heard his full story.

One of the associate pastors of the church agreed to allow Brian do his court-ordered community service with the church. I was serving as their transitional pastor on the weekends while on faculty at a seminary. For his court-ordered service, Brian worked with the set-up crew to unload the

---

41   Wilson, *Future Church*, 230–32.

church-in-a-box and prepare the rented school gymnasium for worship, then went outside until the second service was over when he would help tear down. Of course, I do not know what he would do outside, since I was inside, but I do know he had access to listen to the service because the sound team set up speakers in the courtyard.

Before long, he was not going outside anymore; he stayed inside and participated in the worship service. In time, the staff member in charge of set up and the associate pastor led him to faith in Christ. We scheduled a baptismal service in the courtyard to occur at 10:10 a.m. We chose 10:10 because it was between the two services and because of Romans 10:10. That morning, Brian was one of fifteen people who publically followed the Lord in believer's baptism. His story reminds me that God arranges ways for people who are estranged from Him to find Him (cf. 2 Sam. 14:14).

Baptism is a celebration of the transforming power of the unhindered gospel (Acts 28:31). Economic status, language, or worldviews cannot hinder the gospel. Dave's story reminds me that socio-economic barriers cannot hinder the gospel; Sergio's story reminds me that language barriers cannot hinder the gospel; Brian's story reminds me that the gospel is not hindered by intellectual elitism.

Every baptism is a celebration of the gospel's power, and every baptism can be a *public* celebration of the gospel's power. Non-church people will attend a friend's baptismal service. In addition to encouraging the baptismal candidate to invite their friends, offer to send formal invitations to any mailing list they provide. Before the baptism, ask all friends of the candidate to stand in his or her honor, including them in the celebration.

Yes, baptism is a celebration, but it is more than that — it is a symbol of the Christian faith.

Baptism and the Lord's Supper Are Symbolic in Nature

The water in baptism does not wash away sins and the bread used in the Lord's Supper is not literally the body of Christ. Baptism symbolizes the death, burial, and resurrection of Jesus Christ (Rom. 6:3-4; Col. 2:12.) The new converts are buried with Christ as they go under the water and they rise to newness of life. The fact that baptism symbolizes death, burial, and resurrection is one of the reasons my faith tradition insist on immersion. Another one is the Greek word translated *baptism*[42] literally means "to immerse."

---

42   Bible Hub, "*Baptizó*," Greek, accessed September 20, 2014, http://biblehub.com/greek/907.htm. Βαπτίζω (*baptizó*) means "to dip or submerge."

The bread used in the Lord's Supper symbolizes Jesus' body that is broken for His people. And the fruit of the vine symbolizes the blood He shed for their sins (1 Cor. 10:16). While most believers experience baptism only once, they have the opportunity to partake of the Lord's Supper on a regular basis to celebrate what Jesus did for them on the cross.

Baptism and the Lord's Supper Are for Believers

My faith tradition does not baptize infants because baptism is only for believers. Since the ordinance does not "transmit grace," but symbolizes a new life, it follows that it is for those who have experienced the new life. However, the church does understand the importance of parents expressing their desire to raise their children under the teaching of the church. Therefore, many churches practice baby dedication where parents can stand before the church, declare their intention to raise the child under the teaching of the church, and ask for the Lord's help in raising the child. It is a way that parents can give their children back to God.

Baptism and the Lord's Supper Are Important

When believers are baptized, they follow the example of Jesus (Luke 3:21-22), of New Testament believers (Acts 2:41-42), and are obedient to God's desire for them (Matt. 28:19-20). The Lord's Supper is also important.[43] In the upper room, Jesus took some unleavened bread, held it up, and said, "Take, eat; this is My body" (Matt. 26:17-30). In the Passover meal, the bread had a particular significance. When the Hebrew women made their household bread, they took a piece of fermented dough they saved from a previous day and mixed it into their fresh flour. With time, the yeast would overtake the dough and she could then make her family's daily bread. When God delivered the children of Israel out of Egyptian bondage, there was not time to bake bread or hassle with yeast. They ate their bread unleavened.

Eating unleavened bread became a reminder of the time when God delivered the children of Israel out of bondage (Exod. 13:8-9). At the Lord's Supper, the bread that celebrated the people's deliverance from Egyptian bondage took on a new meaning. Now it commemorates Jesus' broken body and celebrates the Christian's deliverance from eternal bondage. Because

---

43   Henry, *In Remembrance of Me.* This book is full of ideas to communicate the importance of this ordinance to the people.

of Jesus' death on the cross and resurrection from the tomb, eternal life is available for those who believe.

When Jesus handed the cup to the disciples (Matt. 26:27–28), they naturally would have thought of the blood of the lamb smeared on the doorpost of their ancestors' homes in Egypt (Exod. 12:13). In preparation for the tenth plague, God instructed the children of Israel to put the blood of the Passover lamb on the two doorposts and on the lintel of the house. God made a covenant with the people – when the death angel saw the blood on the doorposts, it would pass over that house and not kill the firstborn son. However, if a house did not have the blood on the doorposts and lintel, the death angel would visit their home and kill their firstborn son.

As the disciples drank the wine, they remembered the blood covenant. But Jesus reinterpreted the wine to symbolize a new covenant. In the Lord's Supper, Jesus' blood now symbolizes more than salvation from a single night of terror; instead, it celebrates eternal salvation (1 Peter 1:18–19).

Every time I serve the Lord's Supper, I am mindful that others, whom others served, served those who have handed the elements to me – there is an unbroken chain that goes back the day that Jesus served His disciples in the upper room. The church gathers around the Lord's Table. It is the salvation that He provided with His broken body and spilt blood that the church celebrates.

OTHER OCCASIONS

Ministry during times of joy builds relationships and opens avenues for even more ministry. I have become better acquainted with numerous people watching their children play in sporting events, singing in school recitals, or blowing out candles at birthday parties. By knowing the family better, I build relationships for future ministry.

I have also seen my children's eyes light up more than once because their Sunday school teacher sent them a birthday card or jotted them a kind note. It does not take much time to send a card, email, or text to people on their special days, but it does a lot to communicate a pastor's love.

PART THREE

TEACHING GOD'S PEOPLE

While this part examines the teaching function of pastoral ministry, it cannot be divorced from the preceding (loving) and following sections (leading). One of the ways pastors love the people they serve is to preach well-prepared transformative sermons that meets their congregation's needs and challenges them to grow spiritually. Equally, one of the best leadership tools pastors have is the pulpit, where they cast vision and give commentary on the direction of the church organization.

Pastoral ministry includes many opportunities to teach. Perhaps that is why Paul referred to pastors as *pastor-teachers* (Eph. 4:11). They teach and preach through an intentional public ministry, during informal moments shared while living life in a faith community, and even during volatile conflict situations. This section explores how pastors can better impact others through planned, public teaching and preaching ministry (chap. 7); find teachable moments in everyday life to advance the spiritual growth of those they serve (chap. 8); and capitalize on teaching opportunities during conflict situations (chap. 9).

Chapter 7   High Impact Teaching and Preaching

Paul's admonition to Timothy to "preach the word; be ready in season and out of season; reprove, rebuke, and exhort, with complete patience and teaching" (2 Tim. 4:2 ESV) had a dual orientation: Timothy was to preach a message anchored in the past,[1] but do so to people living in his time. Twenty-first century preachers experience that same challenge.

THEN AND NOW

Sermons are a bridge between *then* and *now*. Preachers must faithfully retrieve a meaning from the text (*then*) and communicate it to people in the contemporary pastoral setting (*now*), which is thousands of years from the original milieu of the Bible. This nimble shifting between then and now is central to the preacher's task.[2]

The then and the now perspective is a helpful way to view the preacher's task of sermon development and communication. Donald Sunukjian writes, "Specifically, the preacher's task is twofold: to present the true and exact meaning of the biblical text ('Look at what God is saying . . .') in a manner that is relevant to the contemporary listener ('. . . to us')."[3]

In Sunukjian's construct, the meaning comes from the *then* domain, the choices of the communication processes and the communication itself comes from the *now* domain, which is formed by what is "relevant to the

---

1   "The Word" in common usage among evangelicals today denotes the Bible; however, it likely did not have that connotation when Paul used it in this text. It is reasonable to think that Paul's intent was to admonish Timothy to preach the message or the gospel, which he learned, from the apostles. That message that he learned from them, we learn from the Bible.

2   Stott, *Between Two Worlds*, 138, Greidanus, *Modern Preacher*, 137.

3   Sunukjian, *Invitation to Preaching*, 9.

contemporary listener." While this approach is reasonable, perhaps even representing the majority view, there is an alternative worth considering. Instead of selecting the communication medium solely from the *now* domain, what if preachers also included information from the *then* domain to help shape their sermon form? Certainly, relevance to the audience (*now* domain) is an important consideration, but is does not have to be the only one.[4] The literary form of the text (*then* domain) should also influence the sermonic form.

As an overall approach, the form of the expository sermon can address both the then and the now if preachers know when to separate and when to blend the two. Extraction of meaning belongs in the *then* domain and communicating the message is in the *now* domain. However, infusing the meaning of the text into sermonic form can combine both domains.

DEFINITION OF EXPOSITORY PREACHING

According to Haddon Robinson, "Expository preaching is the communication of a biblical concept derived from and transmitted through a historical, grammatical, and literary study of a passage in its context, which the Holy Spirit first applies to the personality and experience of the preacher, then through the preacher, applies to the hearer."[5] Robinson's definition clarifies how preachers approach their text and audiences. They approach the text to discover meaning that will flow through them to their congregations in a three-phase communication process: (1) extract meaning from the text, (2) submit to the work of the Holy Spirit as He applies the text to the preacher and then the congregation, and (3) communicate that meaning to the listeners.

Meaning

Extraction of meaning belongs in the *then* domain. The text does not mean one thing to one generation and another thing to another. It does not mean

---

4   Metaxas, *Bonhoeffer*, 261. Bonhoeffer said, "Do not try to make the Bible relevant. Its relevance is axiomatic." It is as important to insure relevant communication does not interfere with the self-evident relevance of the Bible. Preachers must stay out of the way of the text.

5   Robinson, *Biblical Preaching*, 21.

one thing in this cultural setting and another in that one. It can only mean what it meant.[6] Gordon Fee and Douglas Stuart say, "*A text cannot mean what it never meant.* Or to put it in a positive way, the true meaning of the biblical text for us is what God originally intended it to mean when it was first spoken."[7]

Expository preaching begins with the text. Other approaches may begin with a predetermined meaning before approaching the text, but expository preaching does not seek to impose meaning, it demands preachers locate the intent of the author.[8] Sidney Greidanus says, "Respect for the Word of God requires that one do justice to the intent of the text."[9] Brian Chapell states the preacher's task is "to discern what the original writers meant."[10] Alan Jacobs says looking for the authorial intent is "more useful,"[11] and Robert Stein calls it the "basic goal."[12]

Application

The meaning rests with the author from the *then* domain, but the application[13] rests with the interpreter living in the *now* domain. Osborne sees application as a contextualization, whose key "is to seek a fusion of the horizons of both the biblical text and the modern situation."[14] The fusion process takes more than human effort to accomplish. Notice in his defini-

---

6   Carson, *Exegetical Fallacies*, 129. Carson argues that those who promote polysemy (the viewpoint that a text has multiple meanings and must be interpreted subjectively) are inconsistent because they expect readers to understand the meaning of their writings and the meaning they intend to convey.

7   Fee and Stuart, *How to Read the Bible for All Its Worth*, 30.

8   While I use "authorial intent" as the standard, I do understand that there are times that the interpreter must also take into account the speaker's, editor's, compiler's, or redactor's intent.

9   Greidanus, *Sola Scriptura*, 172.

10   Chapell, *Christ-Centered Preaching*, 77.

11   Jacobs, *Theology of Reading*, 16.

12   Stein, *Interpreting the Bible* 9.

13   Ibid., 44. Stein draws this same distinction but uses a different word than application; he speaks of *meaning* and *significance*. While a text can have only one meaning, it can be significant in different ways in different settings to different people. After determining the meaning, preachers are then free to find its significance and to preach it contextually to their people.

14   Osborne, *Hermeneutical Spiral*, 426.

tion of expository preaching, Robinson stresses application is the work of the Holy Spirit through the preacher.[15]

Communication

Robinson does not address what shape the sermon must take, just that the preacher communicates the sermon. He sets perimeters around extracting meaning through "historical, grammatical, and literary study of a passage in its context and that the Holy Spirit first applies to the personality and experience of the preacher, then through the preacher applies to the hearer," but by this definition, he does not seem to restrict preachers' choices in shaping their sermon.

Biblical Form's Relationship to Sermon Form

Robinson's definition includes the need to study the literary form of the passage in developing the expository sermon. The primary reason for paying attention to form is that it "yields essential clues for rightly interpreting the author's intended meaning of a passage."[16] It is difficult, if not impossible, to interpret a text without considering its genre. Form affects meaning; it is not an inert container simply holding a proposition in place.[17] Osborne says, "Meaning is genre-dependent."[18] The genre controls the rules interpreters use to discover meaning in the text. The chosen literary form will nuance meaning at the least and at the most, shape it. Thomas Long writes,

> Texts are not packages containing ideas; they are means of communication. When we ask ourselves what a text means, we are not searching for the idea of the text. We are trying to discover its total impact upon a reader—and everything about a text works together to create that impact. We may casually speak of the form and the content of a text as if they were two

---

15   Wiarda, *Interpreting Gospel Narratives*, 206. Wiarda points out that while human effort is "necessary" to do proper exegetical work, it is not "sufficient"—expositors must depend on the work of the Holy Spirit.

16   Vogel, *Biblical Genres*, 171.

17   Long, *Preaching*, 12.

18   Osborne, *Hermeneutical Spiral*, 26.

separate realities, but if "content" is used as a synonym for "meaning," the form must be seen as a vital part of the content.[19]

Form and meaning are inseparable. Studying the literary form can help preachers know how to communicate the meaning, not just what the meaning is. Jeffrey Arthurs says, "I contend that exegeting the text's literary features helps equip preachers to reproduce the text's rhetorical impact in their sermons. Paying attention to how the text communicates helps us understand how we can recommunicate."[20] Just as the literary form is vital in understanding the meaning, the sermon form is vital in transmitting the meaning with its full rhetorical impact intact. Expository preachers must get out of the way of the text, allowing the text to shape the sermon[21] getting clues from the genre[22] informed by the intent of the author.[23]

What Are the Points?

Some biblical literary forms, such as the epistles, lend themselves to a multi-point, deductive sermonic form. It is often the case that an epistle writer makes a claim and then weaves a logical, multi-point argument to buttress the assertion. In these cases, expository preachers should select the text and do their exegetical work while asking, "What are the points that naturally emerge from this text?" Chapell says, "The main idea of an expository sermon (the topic), the divisions of that idea (the main points), and the development of those divisions (the subpoints) all come from truths the text itself contains."[24] The deductive approach of *read, explain,*[25] *illustrate,*[26] *apply*[27] works well with these type of texts.

---

19   Long, *Preaching*, 12–13.

20   Arthurs, "Old Testament Narratives," 73–74.

21   Stott, *Between Two Worlds*, 229. Stott calls this the "golden rule for sermon outlines." He asserts that "each text must be allowed to supply its own structure."

22   Vogel, *Biblical Genres*, 189.

23   Waltke, *An Old Testament Theology*, 55.

24   Chapell, *Christ-Centered Preaching*, 131.

25   Meyer, *Expository Preaching*, 101. According to Meyer, as preachers explain the text they will show that the teaching is "consistent with reason."

26   Robinson, *Biblical Preaching*, 152. See also Chapell, *Christ-Centered Preaching*, 178.

27   Sunukjian, *Invitation*, 173.

A widespread variation of this approach is verse-by-verse preaching.[28] Origen used a similar approach[29] in the third century,[30] as did John Chrysostom in the fourth century,[31] and many other preachers through the Middle Ages.[32] The strength of this method is that everything is covered and it does not require selecting an expository unit or shaping the sermon by points. However, it difficult to defend this method as the only expository form since there is no correlation between the chapter and verse numbers and authorial intent. The current chapter divisions were not in place until the early thirteenth century, put there by then Archbishop of Canterbury, Stephen Langton.[33] Hugo did not subdivide the chapters until 1248,[34] and Stephanus did not add verses until 1551.[35] Therefore, the form created by verses should not necessarily dictate the final form of a sermon. The weakness of this approach is it tends to become a running commentary or a grammar lesson instead of expressing and applying the point (or points) of a text selection. Chapell calls the type of sermons that emerge from this approach "pre-sermons" because of their lack of relevant application.[36]

A new sermon form emerged after Pope Innocent III gave the Franciscans permission to preach in 1210.[37] Their sermon form mimicked the shape of a tree.[38] The three branches (sermon subpoints) grow out of three boughs

---

28   Blackwood, *Preaching from the Bible*, 39. While acknowledging it is a good form in the hands of a gifted preacher, Blackwood also says, "It would be a pity if verse-by-verse explanation were the only type of expository preaching."

29   I say similar because chapters and verses did not exist yet.

30   Edwards, *History of Preaching*, 40.

31   Stitzinger, "History of Expository Preaching," 44.

32   Edwards, *History of Preaching*, 40.

33   Dahan, "Genres, Forms and Various Methods," 207.

34   Bullinger, *How to Enjoy the Bible*, 34.

35   Carr, *Introduction*, 19. The Masoretes divided the Old Testament into unnumbered verses over three hundred years, beginning in the seventh century, and their work is still seen in the Hebrew Bible. Although similar in many respects, the divisions used in Christianity are traced to Robert Estienne—better known as Stephanus (see McKnight, *Blue Parakeet*, 45). For more information on the ancient divisions of the Hebrew text, see Tov, *Textual Criticism*, 4–8.

36   Chapell, *Christ-Centered Preaching*, 55.

37   Edwards, *History of Preaching*, 216.

38   Larson, *Anatomy of Preaching*, 54. Larson uses the tree metaphor as a model for the modern-day multi-point sermon.

(sermon points) which, emerged from the trunk (the text).[39] This new approach emphasized dividing and subdividing the text into smaller thematic units. The goal was to understand the whole by dividing it into parts. They spiced their exegesis with illustrations to drive home their points.[40]

The Oxford Convention affirmed the division of the text into three parts and that each should have three significant words.[41] Charles Smyth explains the perceived wisdom of their assertion when he writes, "Single things said are soon forgotten. Too many confuse. Arrangement in threes binds them together, and a threefold cord is not swiftly broken."[42] Smyth bolsters his contention with the claims from anthropology, the arts, and personal observation.[43] Anthropologists know of tribal people whom only number things to three, and then say, "a great number." Plays are usually in three acts, and a person can only see three or four things at a time.[44]

The three-point sermon structure that emerged during the Middle Ages survived the Reformation, so that preachers both from the Catholic and Protestant traditions used it as standard fare.[45] However, they were not identical in form to the medieval sermon structures. Influenced by Scholasticism,[46] they included a proposition and a logical flow to the sermon structure, but they maintained the propensity towards subdividing into thirds.[47]

What Is the Point?

Other biblical forms encourage preachers to ask, What is the point? rather than, What are the points? These forms represent genres (or subgenres)

---

39   Edwards, *History of Preaching*, 217.

40   Larson, *Company of the Preachers*, 122.

41   Smyth, *Art of Preaching*, 49.

42   Ibid., 48.

43   Stott, *Between Two Worlds*, 34. Stott comments that Smyth's explanation of the three point sermon is a "rigid structure of the medieval 'sermon scheme."

44   Smyth, *Art of Preaching*, 48.

45   Bayley, *French Pulpit Oratory*, 108–11.

46   Latourette, *A History of Christianity, vol. 1*, 496–98. Scholasticism was not limited to theological studies, but did result in an understanding of the connection to faith and reason. It rekindled an interest in the contribution of the ancients, including Aristotle in matters of faith and rhetoric.

47   Edwards, *History of Preaching*, 223.

that typically have a single primary point. Among them are narrative, parallelism,[48] proverb,[49] and parable.

By itself, the narrative genre comprises almost half of the Bible.[50] When including the other genres, it is safe to say single-point genres comprise the majority of the Bible,[51] which makes the search for a single point appropriate for expository preachers who use literary analysis as part of their sermon preparation process.[52]

Biblical narratives include plot dynamics that propel the story toward a focused theological truth. The plot dynamics are movements, not points. The point is the final resolution,[53] and the movements are the twists and turns of the story that carry the listener to the point. Greidanus explains typical Old Testament narrative as action with a beginning and ending. The action begins with a conflict in a specific setting and context. It climaxes at a point of great intensity, before it begins to unravel and is resolved resulting in a communicated outcome. The action ends, concluding the story.[54] The theological truth emerges at the resolution of the conflict. Again, the resolution is the point, not the plot dynamics that transports the listeners to the resolution.

Synoptic pronouncement stories are a good example of how a narrative passage makes a single point.[55] Usually, Jesus told these stories in response to an observation He made or a question posed to Him. The function of the narrative is to communicate a focused truth to His hearers.[56]

This is not to say that all narrative passages make only a single point,

---

48 Long, *Preaching*, 48. Synonymous parallelism says the same thing in two different ways to add richness to or underscore a single point.

49 Long, *Preaching*, 60. Proverbs typically have two parts (common structures are antithesis, elaboration, or answer) that make one point.

50 Stein, *Basic Guide*, 151.

51 Greidanus, *Modern Preacher and the Ancient Text*, 355. I'm not attempting to draw strict lines here. It is possible to use a one-point narrative approach for a didactic text, a point that Greidanus makes.

52 If preachers take the cue from the literary form to choose their sermon form, there could be more one-point sermons preached then three-point sermons, assuming a normal distribution of text selection.

53 Hunter, *Interpreting the Parables*, 11. Hunter gives four rules of story, the final is the rule of "end stress," that the point of the story is usually at the end.

54 Greidanus, *Modern Preacher*, 204.

55 Tannehill, *Narrative Unity of Luke-Acts*, 1:111.

56 Long, *Preaching*, 77.

only that as a rule, it is wise to look for a single point instead of assuming the complexity of plot dynamics automatically dictate multiple points exist in the narrative.[57]

The prominence of parables in the Bible requires a separate category, even though they are a type of narrative. Many contemporary Bible interpreters agree that parables have a single point,[58] but that has not always been so and does not enjoy universal acceptance. In 1899, as a reaction to the practice of allegorical interpretation of parables,[59] Adolf Jülicher contended that parables should have only one point.[60] Today, Craig Blomberg offers a differing view of the interpretation of parables. He writes the interpreter should look for one point per main character, not one point per parable,[61] and allow those points to shape the sermon. In about two-thirds of the parables, according to Blomberg, that would be three points.[62] However, his sermon "Pray and Persevere," based upon Luke 18:1–8,[63] is a three-point sermon, even though he sees the text as having a single point with two lessons.[64] He says that he wrote it with three points to make it a fuller, richer, and clearer sermon and because he has a "predilection for three points!"[65]

Klyne Snodgrass writes, "In short, some parables make one point, and some make several points. A formulaic approach to parable interpretation, as for all biblical studies, just does not work. One must discern from context the intent of the analogy."[66] So it is true that not all parables have one point, but many do, making it very important for pastors to pay attention to the text when choosing the sermon form.

If biblical genre is not an inert vessel, what about a sermon form? If

---

57   Osborne, *Hermeneutical Spiral*, 221. Osborne states a preference using multiple points in a didactic sermon, but treating the shifts in action in a narrative passage as movements, rather than points.

58   Stein, *Basic Guide* 141.

59   Long, *Preaching*, 95.

60   Blomberg, *Preaching the Parables*, 14.

61   Ibid., 15.

62   Ibid., 83–84.

63   Ibid., 169–77.

64   I do not mean to imply that Blomberg's sermon distorted the meaning of this text. I cite this as an illustration of a decision that preachers face as they sculpt the form of their sermons.

65   Blomberg, *Preaching the Parables*, 177.

66   Snodgrass, *Stories with Intent*, 29.

a text has only one point, as Blomberg affirms in the case of Luke 18:1–8, should not the sermon have just one point to maintain its meaning and impact? As previously stated, choosing the medium of communication is a then-and-now task. Certainly, elements from the now,[67] such as a preacher's predilections and congregational norms, are germane in selecting sermonic form, but so are the elements[68] from the then domain. It may be possible to preach a multi-point sermon based upon a text with a single point without altering the meaning, but it may also result in distorting the conveyed meaning and its impact.[69]

Preachers who are looking for three points are likely to find them. It would be easy to see Matthew 7:7 in thirds: (1) "*ask*, and it will be given to you," (2) "*seek*, and you will find," (3) "*knock*, and it will be opened to you." The genre of this verse is parallelism; therefore, *ask, seek, and knock* function as synonyms, not three modes of praying.[70] However, the tripartite sermon structure can imply that there are separate actions involved in praying.

Taken as a separate point, seeking or knocking could lead the hearer to the conclusion that the petitioner should actively attempt to bring about the desired resolution through human activity. In this case, prayer becomes a secondary solution to the problem, human activity being the primary — God just helps the petitioner who is seeking for a solution. While this idea is consistent with Benjamin Franklin's philosophy that "God helps them that helps themselves,"[71] it counters the context of Matthew 7:7, which encourages those who pray to do so with "an expectant attitude"[72] because God is dependable and loving. He cares for His people and will answer their prayers. The emphasis is on a God who provides, not on the mental and kinesthetic energy the petitioner puts into the act of praying.

In this case, ignoring the context and the organic unity of the synonymous parallelism used in Matthew 7:7 and instead imposing a three-point structure shifts the emphasis away from *expecting that God will answer* to

---

67   I have refrained from making a case for the one-point sermon structure from the *now* domain, so as not to detract from my argument that the literary form of the text should influence the form of the sermon.

68   Specifically I mean the genre and context.

69   Greidanus, *Modern Preacher*, 19–20.

70   France, *Gospel of Matthew*, 280.

71   Benjamin Franklin, *Poor Richard's Almanac*, 82. Although popularized by Franklin, Algernon Sidney originated the phrase in 1698 in his *Discourses Concerning Government*, Section 23. It was also the moral of Aesops's story, *Hercules and the Wagoner*.

72   Blomberg, *Matthew*, 129.

an entirely different message: *pray and do your part in answering the prayer.* This example, no doubt takes the meaning from the *then*,[73] but it untethers the message from the textual form. While being a coworker with God is a biblical concept (1 Cor. 3:9), it does not emerge from this text. An expository sermon must extract meaning from its text.

Preachers who gravitate toward the common three-point propositional sermon without regard to understanding of structure derived from the literary genre limit themselves.[74] Stott uses stronger language; he says they confine themselves in a "strait-jacket."[75] Craddock goes even further by asking, "Why the gospel should always be impaled upon on the frame of Aristotelian logic."[76]

The notion that a preacher can proclaim the meaning of an immutable text with an interchangeable sermon chassis has the feel of homiletical Gnosticism — one being sacred, the other not. There is an organic unity between form and meaning; they affect one another[77] and should stay unified throughout the sermon writing and preaching event. Craddock calls the separation of the two "fatal for preaching."[78] Stott says, "Each text must be allowed to supply its own structure."[79] The inspiration of the Holy Spirit, and the intent of the author,[80] forever link the form and meaning together. Long refers to this linking as "form of the content."[81]

---

73   If the meaning does not arise from the selected text itself, it might come from somewhere in else in the Bible. Even though a sermon does not accurately reflect the intent of the author of a certain text, does not mean it is not theologically sound or unbiblical — just that it is not an expository sermon.

74   Equally, an argument that those who lean toward a one-point structure also limit themselves if they do not look for sermon points in genres that typically have multiple points.

75   Stott, *Between Two Worlds*, 230.

76   Craddock, *As One Without Authority*, 38.

77   Larson, *Anatomy of Preaching*, 63. Even though Larson argues for a multi-point sermon form, which does not align with my assertions, he does affirm "substance and form affect one another."

78   Craddock, *As One Without Authority*, 5.

79   Stott, *Between Two Worlds*, 229.

80   Long, *The Witness of Preaching*, 24. Long argues that the biblical writers are not just concerned with what they said, but how they were saying it. Genre therefore is part of authorial intent. I link it with the message and affirm it is inspired by the Holy Spirit.

81   Long, *Preaching*, 13.

If the biblical author, under the inspiration of the Holy Spirit, used a genre that makes a single point,[82] the meaning extracted from the text the preacher conveys through the sermon cannot be independent from that textual form. The application can and the significance can, but the meaning cannot.[83] Sunukjian writes, "The sermon outline may indent or symbolize a bit differently than the passage or truth outline. It may slightly change the author's structure (but never his meaning!)."[84] Then, can changing the structure (as dictated by the literary genre and context) change the meaning?

The Medium Is the Message

Communication theorist, Marshall McLuhan coined the phrase "the medium is the message" to describe the effects communication media have on a message. He contended the way communicators say something is as important as what they are saying. Actually, he argued the medium was more important. "The content or message of any particular medium has about as much importance as the stenciling on the casing of an atomic bomb."[85] In a macro sense, as in the introduction of the Roman alphabet, Gutenberg press, or electronic media into culture, he argued media itself shaped the cultural environment to such an extent that the medium is more important than the words the alphabet formed, the printing press printed, or the electronic media broadcasted.

Each technological innovation rewired how people processed information and what they did with their time. The Roman alphabet,[86] not the words it formed, reshaped thinking from pictures to words, from spatial to linear. It made changes as far as the east is from the west. Philosophers might point to Aristotle and Confucius to highlight the differences between the cultures, McLuhan would indicate that the difference began with the western adoption of the Roman letters,[87] instead of something like the logographic Chinese characters.[88]

---

82   Edwards, *Deep Preaching*, 65.
83   Ibid., 169.
84   Sunukjian, *Invitation*, 39.
85   McLuhan and Zingrone, *Essential McLuhan*, 238.
86   While Egyptian hieroglyphics and Phoenician cuneiform made this shift centuries before the Roman alphabet, McLuhan's argument focused on the Roman alphabet.
87   McLuhan, *Understanding Media*, 121.
88   McLuhan and Zingrone, *Essential McLuhan*, 122.

The printing press made orality antiquated and flattened time. After the mid-fifteenth century, readers could easily spend their leisure time in isolation interacting with thinkers from another time and place, instead of exchanging their heritage stories in their community, resulting in a less tribalism and more individualism.[89] McLuhan would argue that it was not the words that the press printed that made post mid-fifteenth century generations more individualistic, but that the introduction of the printing press itself caused the transformation.

The electronic media formed a global village that blurs the lines between here and there. The world came into the living room in McLuhan's day and into the palm of user's hands today. While it shrinks the world into a tiny screen, it also expands the users' world. It creates a cultural fusion where the East and West constantly churn and blend resulting in fewer distinctions, less privacy, and more awareness.[90] McLuhan argued that it was not the words that producers broadcasted that ushered in these changes, but the electronic media itself.

Most of the time, when McLuhan used the phrase "the medium is the message" he was referring to this macro sense of how media shapes its environment and does more to influence people than the words spoken, read, or heard. However, he does make an important distinction between *hot* and *cold* mediums.[91] Some communication mediums, such the narrative form, invoke a higher level of participation from the audience. It is a cool medium requiring the use of multiple senses and mental capacities. Other communication mediums are hot, requiring only a single sense. A photo projected on a screen is a hot medium (requiring only the visual sense) or a lecture is a hot medium, requiring only the single sense of hearing.

Imposing a three-point, deductive sermon structure upon a one-point, inductive biblical narrative shifts the communication medium from cold to hot, invoking lower audience involvement. This movement, taking a literary cold medium and shifting it to an oratory hot medium, has the possibility of altering the impact of its meaning, if not the meaning itself. The author of an inductive narrative intended the listeners to immerse themselves in the story and discover the truth as the tension

89   McLuhan, *Understanding Media*, 122.
90   Ibid., 53–55.
91   McLuhan, *Understanding Media*, 39. "Hot media are, therefore, low in participation, and cool media are high in participation or completion by the audience."

in the story resolves. Instead, with the three-point, deductive sermon structure, the storyline no longer requires their involvement, just their attention to the expert who will explain its significance and make an application for them.

Remember, the biblical authors wrote their words for listeners not readers.[92] Prior to Gutenberg, the text was not widely available and the people would gather to listen to it. They did so after rebuilding the walls of Jerusalem (Neh. 8:5-6) and during Domitian's reign[93] (Rev. 1:3).[94]

On a micro sense, shifting the temperature of the communication medium from cool to hot may affect the impact of the message and obscure the intended meaning, but on a macro sense, it can change the way the listeners come to regard the Bible. In the same way the introduction of the Roman alphabet, printing press, and electronic media affected western culture, altering the literary genre from a single point focus to a multi-point sermonic form can shift the way listeners view the Bible. The medium is the message.

Sermons based on narrative passages that tilt away from the story to propositions-for-living communicate something besides their content. They shape the congregations' view of the Bible. Long says, "Idea-centered sermons are prone to communicate, over time, that the Christian faith itself can be boiled down to a set of concepts to which people are supposed to give assent. The gospel thus gets presented as a list of propositions, and sermons become didactic devices tor explaining these truths and how each of them logically connects to the others."[95] A steady diet of propositional preaching of narrative passages can result in people viewing the Bible as an answer book for life's problems, or an owner's manual for the Christian life, or a textbook for a Christian education. While the Bible may be useful in those pursuits, its purpose is greater. The Bible is not a collection of propositions for Christians to understand and apply. It is God's story to be experienced. The Bible does not just contain narratives. It is narrative. Even the epistles have a "narrative bedrock," [96]

---

92   Long, *Witness of Preaching*, 24.

93   Mounce, *Revelation*, 32.

94   Ἀναγινώσκων (*anaginoskon*) is a word that denotes reading aloud. In Revelation 1:3, John blessed the one that would read his words aloud to God's people.

95   Long, *Witness of Preaching*, 101–102.

96   Goldingay, *Old Testament Theology*, 31. In an explanatory footnote to the sentence, he says that "the biblical gospel is not a collection of timeless statements such

Greidanus writes, "A vibrant story lies just beneath the surface of many an epistle text."[97]

Long says, "The first-order work of the biblical writers was to 'reveal the enactment of God's purposes in history.'"[98] More times than not, expository sermons will reveal something about God and the way He works in redemptive history. If preachers align their sermons with authorial intent, the majority—if not all—of their sermons will be Theo-centric[99] and will encourage the listeners to respond in faith to God as revealed in the sermon. The literary form will provide clues to how many points the sermon will have, and in some cases, the structure of the sermon can come from the movements within the text.[100]

ONE-POINT SERMON FORMS

According to Chapell, "As preachers mature, they will discover that rhetorical 'moves,' homiletical 'plots,' concept-rich 'images,' thoughtful transitions, implied ideas, and other measures can often substitute for the formal statement of points in their outlines."[101] Typically, one-point sermons are inductive in nature and use movements instead of points to progress their listeners through the sermon. Just as movements in plot presented above, these movements are not the same as points. Multiple points subdivide a concept into equal or progressive concepts. They either show the smaller components of the whole or a cascading list (ascending or descending) of interrelated ideas. Movements are oratory devices that propel the message forward, usually using the conflict or tension inherent in the structure of a story. Buttrick says, "In speaking of 'moves,' we are deliberately changing terminology. For years, preachers have talked of making points

---

as God is love. It is a narrative about things God has done." Goldingay elaborates, "The narrative form of the Gospels makes this point evident, but a 'narrative bedrock' also underlies the non-narrative form of Paul's writings."

97   Greidanus, *Modern Preacher*, 335.

98   Long, *Preaching*, 70.

99   As the title suggests, in *Christ-Centered Preaching: Redeeming the Expository Sermon*, Chapell encourages Christ-centered preaching. Since our God is triune, I encourage Theo-centric preaching to encompass all three persons of the Trinity.

100   Taylor, "Shaping Sermons, 140.

101   Chapell, *Christ-Centered Preaching*, 134.

in sermons. . . . Instead, we are going to speak of moves, of making moves in a movement of language."[102]

In the case of preaching through a biblical narrative, movements often come from plot dynamics of the text itself.[103] In other cases, the preacher provides the movements for the sermon structure. Long argues, "Even though the possibility of matching sermonic movement to text movement is clearest when the biblical text is a narrative, non-narrative texts possess their own inner movements that can also serve as the patterns for sermons."[104] (For three samples of one-point sermons, see the appendix.)

Whatever form sermons take, the sermon must make a difference. The strength of a multi-point sermon is it provides several options for information and inspiration; if one point does not apply, there is a chance the next one will. Not so for the one-point sermon, it delivers a single point, and if it is not strong and well delivered, the hearers leave with little benefit. The one-point sermon must have atomic impact upon the congregation. It must be powerful and it must be clear. The strength of a one-point sermon is that it does not force any point to compete with another for the audience's attention. Instead of the pressure to develop a point in a third of the time allotted for the sermon, preachers can devote all their time to develop the single point to make that clear, atomic-sized impact.

TRANSFORMATION

Teaching should be transformative.[105] The purpose of the sermon is not to teach the Bible or the audience,[106] but to transform people's lives.[107] Transformation is impossible outside of the empowering work of God. Paul writes in Romans 12:1-2: "I appeal to you therefore, brothers, by the mercies of God, to present your bodies as a living sacrifice, holy and acceptable to God, which is your spiritual worship. Do not be conformed to this world,

---

102   Buttrick, *Homiletic*, 23.

103   Wilson, *Write Narrative Sermons*, 11–33.

104   Long, *Literary Forms*, 131.

105   Edwards, *Elements of Homiletic*, 63.

106   Dave Earley, *Pastoral Leadership Is . . .* , 147: "Effective preaching evokes *change* in the hearer. It is more than giving information. It is a means of *transformation*."

107   Chapell, *Christ-Centered Preaching*, 57.

but be transformed by the renewal of your mind, that by testing you may discern what is the will of God, what is good and acceptable and perfect."

Paul uses the word translated "transformed" twice in his writings (2 Cor. 3:18 in addition to Rom. 12:2). Each time it denotes a work that happens inside the believer brought about by an outside force.[108] The verb is in the passive voice, meaning that an outside force, in this case, God, is doing the transformative work. Mark uses the divine passive with this same verb to describe Jesus' transfiguration (Mark 9:2).[109]

Even though God is doing the transformation, there is a human response involved. God's people need to do something.[110] They must submit themselves to Him and not allow the world to shape them. To that end, teaching and preaching can be one of the tools that God uses to transform His people through the renewing of their minds (Rom. 10:17). The transformation happens at the intersection of trusting and obeying. God's people must trust Him and put their faith into practice (Matt. 7:23-27).

The present tense of the verb indicates that transformation is a continual pursuit, not solitary event.[111] Transformation is a process. It does not occur instantly, but it can happen over time. With a steady diet of listening to God's story, as revealed through the text and unaltered by an imposed structure, God's people can experience His transformative power.

DEVELOPING THE TRANSFORMATIVE POINT

The sermon climaxes with the transformative point—a call for the people to respond in faith to God as revealed in the text and proclaimed in the sermon. Writing the transformative point is a two-step process. First, through exegesis of the text, preachers discover what the biblical author is revealing about God, His nature, His attributes, or His glory. Second, by way of applying the truth, preachers then suggest an appropriate way for their audiences to respond to God as revealed in the text (see samples of transformative points in the sermons in the appendix). A transformative point is different from a sermon thesis, which encapsulates the sermon's meaning. Rather, a transformative point is a concrete, memorable

---

108   Behm, "Μορφόω," 758.
109   Selby, *Comical Doctrine*, 224-25.
110   Melick and Melick, *Teaching That Transforms*, 5.
111   Mounce, *Romans*, 232.

statement of the preferred response a listener should make to God's nature, attributes, or glory as revealed in the text.

Transformation is the point of teaching and preaching. The primary thing pastors can do to aid in the transformation of their people is to stay out of the way of the text and let it do its transformative work. They can stay out of the way by knowing how to bring a transformative message, anchored in the biblical text to a contemporary audience.

This method is different from moralistic preaching that looks for signs of virtue in the Bible characters, then calls on the listeners to emulate them. Bible characters have no virtue (Rom. 3:10) apart from their faith response to God (Rom. 1:17). It is also different from how-to preaching that turns the Bible into a self-help book.[112] The transformative point follows the sermonic explanation of how the story's main character — the triune God — is working to call the listener to resist conforming to the world and submitting to Him in faith.

---

112   Chappel, *Christ-Centered Preaching*, 221.

Chapter 8   Teaching While Walking Around

In one church I served, I met with three retired pastors on a regular basis so I could benefit from their wisdom. At one of the "brain trust" meetings, I asked two questions: "What were your greatest accomplishments in ministry?" and "What are your biggest regrets?"

When the two older ministers spoke, I could tell they had made peace with both sides of their ledgers long ago. Not so with Fenton, the third pastor, who was freshly retired. When he spoke, he had a distant look in his eye. I could tell his thoughts were from current analysis.

In the late 1970s, Fenton left the business world to plant a church in Southern California with a core group of five people. He thought he could grow the church to three or four hundred people within a couple of years, and then the new church would become a base of church planting throughout the Los Angeles Basin. His ambitious plans never materialized.

After pouring five years of his life into the effort, the church constituted with 135 members. It never grew any larger, nor did it become a center of church planting as he hoped. Fenton said he always thought if a pastor could not grow a church, he was either incompetent or carnal. He did not want to consider himself either. With a doctorate in Church Growth from Fuller Seminary, he knew church growth principles, which he diligently applied. Still, the church did not grow.

The work was tough. As a rule, the church had to reach three new members to net an increase of one. Part of it was the transient nature of the community. In one year, fifty-one out of 110 members moved away. In that same year, Fenton crashed. "It was almost like a death," Fenton said. And the church was never the same again. As hard as that year was, he did not hit bottom, but he would.

Some of the losses felt more personal than the rest. Fenton poured hours into John, who lived out of his van when they first met. In time, Fenton brought John to faith in Christ and helped him live a more stable life. About the time Fenton was seeing real fruit in John's life, John left to go to a larger church with a drama program and a theater. The cycle repeated itself with others like John. Fenton would do the hard work of cultivating, witnessing, and baptizing the converts only to lose them to the great choirs, fantastic youth programs, and magnificent drama programs of larger churches.

It was frustrating.

John was not the only devastating loss Fenton suffered. Fenton watched God transform Judy, a nurse with addiction issues. Fenton baptized her and helped her grow spiritually. Then *it* happened and when it did, it was three times worse than before. Judy's lapse haunted him. *I should have spotted this,* he thought. *I should have been more cautious and warned her. I should have paid more attention to her.*

Fenton lost track of her; he does not know whether she is dead or alive. His honest, gut-wrenching evaluation as he entered retirement was that he had not been as effective of a leader because he was not able to grow his church into a large, influential church that planted other churches, nor had he been effective in caring for the hurting people that God sent him — as evidenced by Judy's relapse.

However, that was not a new evaluation. After ten years of serving the church, Fenton came to believe this congregation was not going where it should go. He went to the Lord in prayer, pleading for answers. All he heard back was, "For the church to grow it needs a new vision." Since he did not have a new vision, he resigned. He spent most of the rest of his ministry as a writer[1] and a missionary to the Jewish people, largely providing for his own financial support. At our brain trust meeting, Fenton stopped short of saying he regretted going into the ministry, but he left the impression that he had mixed emotions about whether he had fulfilled his calling. We did not talk about it again for months — not until we were returning home from a conference.

Fenton was driving. Chaplain Scott, one of Fenton's converts, rode shotgun, and I relaxed in the back seat, eavesdropping. For thirty minutes or so, they discussed the good old days at their church and some of the people that surrendered to the ministry from that church plant — about a dozen.

I could not believe it.

I interrupted their conversation, "Fenton, do you remember the conversation we had in the brain trust meeting a couple of months ago where you talked about your regrets in ministry?"

"Sure," Fenton said, "what about it?"

---

1 Ward, *What to Say.*

"Let me get this right," I answered. "You served a church for ten years that produced a dozen ministers like Scott and you question your effectiveness as a pastor?"

Whether or not Fenton was effective at leading (part 4) or loving (part 2) God's people, I will leave for others to decide. From my point of view, the fact that the church he planted did not meet his expectations might have more to do with unrealistic expectations than poor leadership execution. The true test of effectiveness in loving God's people is the willingness to get involved in their lives. He did that with John and he did it with Judy.[2] The fact that John went to a different church or Judy returned to previous addictions does not necessarily reflect on Fenton. If that were true, the same would be true of Jesus, who had one disciple deny Him (John 18:15-27) and another betray Him (Luke 22:48).

Fenton was effective at teaching God's people. The evidence is clear. A dozen people serving the Lord in ministry leadership positions, three of whom he led to faith in Christ provide ample evidence that Fenton knew how to "teach while walking around."[3] From the pulpit, he preached that the gospel was true, and because it was true, all other concerns of life are trivial. He did not stop with mere words; he lived the message among the people. Fenton and the church members poured their lives out in ministry to those God sent them. There was no artificial distinction between the laity and clergy (chap. 2), and he encouraged all the people to live out their calling. For about a dozen of them, that meant becoming pastors, chaplains or some other form of vocational minister, but for everyone it meant recklessly pursuing God's kingdom (Matt. 6:19-34).

Teaching includes what pastors do in formal settings, what they say in everyday conversations, and how they model their values in the faith communities where they serve.

---

2   These stories were representative of dozens of similar stories Fenton experienced in his ministry.

3   Peters and Waterman, Jr., *In Search of Excellence*, 137. I borrow the phrase "while walking around" from Tom Peters, who popularized the concept of managing while walking around when reporting on a practice of managers at Hewlett-Packard who did not cocoon themselves in corporate offices, but walked among their employees to stay in touch with their most valuable resource – the people who worked for them.

JESUS' TEACHING MINISTRY

In the Gospel of Matthew, Jesus taught in formal settings like the synagogue (Matt. 4:23; 9:35) and public venues when crowds gathered around
him (Matt. 5–7; 13:3–33; 15:10–20; 22:1–14; 23:2–39). Jesus also taught as life
happened. He taught at His baptism (Matt. 3:15), during His wilderness
temptation (Matt. 4:1–11), after healings (Matt. 8:10–13; 9:2–6; 17:17–21),
during His betrayal (Matt. 26:47–56), in conversations with His disciples
(Matt. 10:5–42; 13:37–52; 14:27–31; 16:5–11; 16:23–28; 17:9–12; 17:22–23; 18:20;
18:21–35; 19:11–12; 19:23–20:16; 20:18–19; 21:21–22; 24:2; 24:4–25:46; 26:2–13,
17–30, 31–35; 28:18–20), and with non-disciples who asked Him questions
or engaged Him in conversation (Matt. 8:20; 9:12–23; 11:4–30; 12:3–8, 11–13,
25–37, 39–45, 48–50; 13:57; 15:3–9; 16:2–4; 17:25–27; 19:4–9, 16–22; 20:22–28;
21:16, 24–44; 22:18–22, 29–32, 37–40, 41–45).

No doubt, Jesus preached in public, but that was a small percentage of
His teaching ministry. Much of this teaching was while walking around
with His disciples ministering to people.[4] Teaching while walking around
was a common method of teaching in His day.[5] It was later used by Paul
in the latter half of the first century (Acts 20:20),[6] and before that, by Aristotle and his disciples in the fourth century BC.[7]

Actually, teaching while walking around has ancient roots. In the
greater context of the *Shema* (Deut. 6:4–9),[8] Moses included instructions
for parents to conduct religious training with children in the course of

---

4   Polhill, *Acts*, 384. I do not mean to imply that peripatetic teaching must replace
other types of teaching by virtue that Jesus did it. Cynic philosophers also used the
methodology and did not have a great reputation among the people. "Cynic philosophers were peripatetic, traveling from town to town, often preaching to crowds on
street corners and in marketplaces." "Some seem to have fallen somewhat short of the
ideal and had a reputation for fleecing the gullible crowds."

5   Blomberg, *Matthew*, 90: "As Jesus is walking about the vicinity of his new home
in Capernaum, perhaps in conscious imitation of the peripatetic ministries of many
rabbis and philosophers of the day, he finds two brothers who are fishermen and
commands them to become his disciples."

6   Tidwell, *Educational Ministry*, 30: "Paul taught wherever and whomever he
could."

7   De Villiers, "Philosophical Trends."

8   Merrill, *Deuteronomy*, 162: "It is the expression of the essence of all of God's
person and purposes in sixteen words of Hebrew text. Known to Jewish tradition as
the *Shema* (after the first word of v. 4, the imperative of the verb *shama*, 'to hear'), this

everyday life, including "when you walk along the road" (Deut. 6:8). The message of the unity of God and the obligation to love Him was so important that it required both formal and informal instruction.[9] Pastors in the twenty-first century do teach while walking around as well. They cannot keep from teaching through word, example, and deed.

PASTORS TEACH WHEN THEY LIVE WHAT THEY SAY THEY BELIEVE, AND WHEN THEY DON'T

In general, people tend to trust others who live what they say they believe, but are less likely to believe the veracity of those who say one thing and do another. When there is an inconsistency between the two, they tend to believe actions more than words.

If you saw a sign in a repair shop window that says WE CAN FIX ANYTHING next to a sign that says PLEASE KNOCK ON THE DOOR — THE BELL DOESN'T WORK,[10] would you believe they really can fix anything? If you heard that an outspoken wildlife advocate, who had been critical of the mining industries practice of generating pollution that kills sheep and cattle, pled guilty to a poaching charge,[11] would you really believe he really cares about laws and animals? If you read a book by a famous football coach that describes discipline as "what you do when no one else is looking,"[12] but later learned the he had to resign after looking the other way at his players misconduct and then lying about their deeds in an attempt to cover up their violations. Would you trust his integrity?

What about a pastor who preaches on a Sunday morning from Ephesians 4:32 to be kind to others, and then later in the week yells at a clerk at the grocery store who makes an error? Or a pastor that encourages the

---

statement, like the Decalogue, is prefaced by its description as 'commands, decrees, and laws' (or the like) and by injunctions to obey them (6:1-3; cf. 4:44-5:5)."

9   Smart, *The Teaching Ministry*, 14: "It is noteworthy that, in this sixth chapter of Deuteronomy, emphasis is laid upon the importance of persistence in teaching and upon the utilization of informal opportunities."

10   Mehta, 143.

11   Associated Press, "Idaho Wildlife Advocate Pleads Guilty to Poaching Two Elk, Casper Star Tribune, December 19, 2013, http://trib.com/news/state-and-regional/idaho-wildlife-advocate-pleads-guilty-to-poaching-two-elk/article_563fd3b1-1e37-59c8-acce-04c8b2b16ffa.html.

12   Sean Gregory, "Jim Tressell," *Time*, June 13, 2011, 19.

church members to give sacrificially, but doesn't tithe? What happens when pastors do not live what they say they believe? Preachers cannot expect people to apply a sermon when the preachers do not practice what they preach themselves.[13] What we do matters more than what we say.[14] There is an inseparable connection between the message and the messenger. People will not believe the words of leaders that they do not trust.[15] People have a right to demand that their leaders live up to their beliefs.

There is a riveting moment in the motion picture *The Patriot,* which is set during the days of the American Revolution. Gabriel Martin (played by Heath Ledger) interrupts a worship service already in progress to enlist soldiers for the militia. As Rev. Oliver (played by Rene Auberjonois) resisted allowing the disruptive announcement, Anne Howard (played by Lisa Brenner) took the floor to support Gabriel's request.

> Dan Scott, barely a week ago I heard you railed for two hours about independence. Mr. Hardwick, how many times have I heard you speak of freedom at my father's table? Half the men in this church, including you, Father, and you, Reverend, are as ardent patriots as I. Will you now, when you are needed most, stop at only words? Is that the sort of men you are? I ask only that you act upon the beliefs of which you have so strongly spoken and in which you so strongly believe.[16]

After her stirring speech, Gabriel asks, "Who's with us?" and one by one, men stand. The key to her speech was the question, "Will you now, when you are needed most, stop at only words? Is that the sort of men you are? I ask only that you act upon the beliefs of which you have so strongly

---

13 Waggoner, *The Shape of Faith,* 188: "Preaching that fills the head with a lot of biblical facts is vastly different from preaching that focuses on putting truth into practice. We must call the people of God to action, and they must see that we are practicing what we preach."

14 Melrose, *Making the Grass,* 13: "No matter what our talk may be, it is our walk, our behavior that reveals our true beliefs."

15 Kouzes and Posner, *Encouraging the Heart,* 131: "Above all, people want to believe in their leaders. They want to believe that the leaders' word can be trusted, that they do what they say. Our findings are so consistent over such a long period of time that we've come to refer to this as the first law of leadership: if you don't believe in the messenger, you won't believe the message."

16 Emmerich, *The Patriot* (DVD, 57:58–60:55).

spoken and in which you so strongly believe." In short, she said to live what you say you believe.

There is never a time when a pastor is not a pastor. Pastors can never drop their guard in the name of authenticity or relaxation and act in a way that is unbecoming to the office. Just as President Reagan never took off his suit coat in the oval office,[17] pastors should never act in a way that lessens their office.[18] The size or location of a church does not diminish the importance of the office of pastor. It is the same office Charles Spurgeon, W. A. Criswell, Adrian Rogers, and Jim Henry held. The office is a good thing something worth aspiring to (1 Tim. 3:1).

People are watching, perhaps even more than they are listening. Pastors teach when they hold the door open for a disabled person, when they yell at an umpire who makes a bad call, or when they stop to talk to a homeless person outside a fast food restaurant. They teach by example — an example their people are commanded to follow (Heb. 13:7).

However, there are times that pastors, like everyone else, fail to live what they believe (cf. Rom. 7:14-25). What then? What happens when there is a discrepancy between pastors' realized beliefs (what they actually do) and their aspirational beliefs (what they believe in) and want to do? They should learn from their hypocrisy,[19] determine to grow spiritually, be transparent about their failings, and desire to be more like Christ. There is a difference between saying, "I'm human,[20] cut me some slack," and saying, "I'm a sinner in need of the grace of God." Paul affirmed his need for God's grace (1 Tim. 1:15), yet was able to ask others to live like he lived (1 Cor. 11:1).

Fenton was effective in communicating his belief in word and deed. He did not just preach that the gospel was true, and because it was true all other concerns of life are trivial. He lived the message among the people. His teaching while walking around corresponded to his teaching while standing behind the pulpit.

---

17   D'Souza, *Ronald Reagan*, 201.

18   My point here is not about dressing formally, but is about aligning conduct with the importance of the office of pastor.

19   Dufrensne and Chair, "Mind the Gap," 108: "Embracing hypocrisy and *moving in the direction of integrity* is indeed more important for leadership effectiveness and ethical leadership."

20   To see what it means to be fully human, look at Jesus. He was fully human (Gal. 4:4; Mark 6:3), yet never sinned (Heb. 4:15).

Pastors Equip People for Ministry

In the Great Commission, Jesus gave the command to make disciples of all nations. The imperative verb in the command is "make disciples." While the participles "going," "baptizing," and "teaching" all carry the imperative force of the verb, the verb itself, "make disciples," is at the heart of the commission,[21] which begs the question, What is a disciple? In its most basic sense, a disciple is a follower.[22] Jesus commanded His disciples, who followed Him to make other disciples by going, baptizing, and teaching people from all nations to observe His commands. This further refines the definition of a disciple as a baptized, obedient believer.[23]

After studying the commands of Jesus, one church I served adopted the following as a definition of disciples: "Devoted followers of Jesus Christ are transformed people who, under the leadership of the Holy Spirit, seek God, deny self, love, serve, and teach others to follow Jesus Christ."[24] Some converts, while they may be involved in church activities, fall short of observing Jesus' commands and are not experiencing the required spiritual growth to classify them as true disciples. Sometimes that is evident in their relationships[25] or the way they demonstrate their love God and others.[26]

Just as preachers need to practice what they preach,[27] their hearers need to do what they hear. Disciples are not foolish people who hear

---

21   Blomberg, *Matthew*, 431.

22   *Greek-English Lexicon of the New Testament*, s.v. "μαθητεύω." This word is defined as "(1) follow and (2) make followers."

23   Wilder, "Establishing and Training,"16. Disciple was a primary name for Christians in the book of Acts. Its use only declined due to consistently having to tighten the definition due to general use of the term in the Greco-Roman world.

24   Valencia Hills Community Church, "Core Beliefs," accessed November 17, 2014, http://www.valenciahills.com/core-beliefs.

25   Mulholland, *Invitation to a Journey*, 42: "If you want a good litmus test of your spiritual growth simply examine the nature and quality of your relationships with others."

26   Hawkins and Parkinson, *Reveal*, 4: "Among the findings, nearly one out of every four people at Willow Creek were stalled in their spiritual growth or dissatisfied with the church — and many of them were considering leaving."

27   Waggoner, *Shape of Faith*, 49: "We need sermons that are will prepared, biblically substantive, and delivered by sincere, humble preachers who model what they teach."

but do not do what they are commanded (Matt. 7:26–27); instead, they are wise people who hear and do (Matt. 7:24–25). Hearing is not enough. Disciples must hear (Rom. 10:17), but they also must do what they hear (Luke 11:28).

The capacity for disciples' spiritual growth is the discrepancy between the life Jesus commanded His followers to live and the life they are currently living. While they may never completely close that gap this side of heaven, there should be positive movement in that direction.[28] One key to closing the gap between the real and the ideal is hearing transformative sermons (chap. 7), but hearing is not enough. Real growth occurs when the disciples love God and others,[29] which is the distillation of His commands (Matt. 22:36–40). One way pastors can help the people live those commands is to release and equip them to be ministers (see Be-the-Minister model in chap. 2), which is a primary responsibility for pastors (Eph. 4:12).

There is no best way to teach or learn. People are individuals with different learning intelligences,[30] preferences, temperaments, and learning styles.[31] As such, they benefit from a multi-modal approach.[32] Just as there is no one-size-fits-all approach to classroom instruction, there is not a single learning venue that will always achieve optimal results. When pastors work to equip the people for ministry, they do so in formal teaching venues like a worship service or a retreat setting, but it can also be done while doing ministry. The combination of hearing and doing is a powerful learning duo.[33] For some people, the truth they have heard does not become real to

---

28   Rainer and Geiger, *Simple Church*, 136: "According to the Scripture, a believer's life is to be transformed more and more. People are not supposed to be the same. There is to be progression, movement."

29   Ortberg, *Life You've Always Wanted*, 45: "The true indicator of spiritual well-being is growth in the ability to love God and people."

30   Howard Gardner, *Disciplined Mind*, 186–213.

31   Knowles, *Adult Learner*, 150–54.

32   Snowman and McCown, *Psychology Applied to Teaching*, 216: "[In ADHD students] multimodal programs were most effective in reducing classmates dislike and fostering more effective prosocial skills and positive peer interactions."

33   Hopson, *Managing for Development*, 70: "Some theory can help learning (we can read books or watch videos on how to drive a car or play golf, and so on), but most learning comes from doing rather than hearing, and in most cases learning involves both theory and practice."

them until they begin applying it.[34] While doing cannot replace hearing, neither is hearing alone enough.[35]

The combination of *hearing, observing,* and *doing* is an effective way to learn how to do something.[36] However, when it comes to ministry, it also helps people grow spiritually. Getting involved in church activities may not catalyze spiritual growth,[37] but serving others in a sacrificial way can.[38] People grow spiritually when they minister.[39] When pastors equip the peo-

---

34   Eyler and Giles, *Where's the Learning*, 69: "When we asked our reflection inter-view subjects what they learned from service, they agreed that it was easier for them to make sense of material because 'hands-on experience is definitely a lot better than hearing it, because it doesn't click in your mind until you experience it or relate to it.' They found that the understanding attained through service-learning enhanced what they learned from books and lectures. 'We learn these theories and ideas in school, but until we really apply them or see them in action, they're not real. And we come out of school – if we haven't done something like this – come out of school not understand-ing.' Students recognize that understanding is more than acquisition of information or memorization of theories."

35   Mertens, "Incorporating Service-Learning," 111: "Participating in service as part of a course has a positive effect over and above the effect of generic community service."

36   Nelson-Jones, *Life Coaching Skills*, 112: "The Chinese proverb says I hear, I forget. I *see,* I remember. I do, I understand. Learning by doing is essential to successful coach-ing. Knowledge gained by exploring oneself, hearing and observing gets clarified and consolidated when clients learn by doing. You do not learn to drive a car without driv-ing. Likewise clients acquiring and strengthening particular lifeskills need relevant ac-tivities that help them to improve the skills and to integrate them into their daily lives."

37   Hawkins and Parkinson, *Reveal*, 35-36: "We discovered that higher levels of church activities did not predict increasing love for God or increasing love for other people. Now don't misread this! This does not mean that people highly involved in church activities don't love God. It simply means they did not express a greater love for God than people who were less involved in church activities. In other words, an increasing level of activities did not *predict* an increasing love for God."

38   Greenleaf, *Servant Leadership*, 159: "There is now seeking on an unprecedented scale, and the land abounds with gurus who are feeding the hunger of the seekers. The change that I anticipate is a new awareness among seekers in which those whose needs with be met *only* as they serve others will separate themselves from those who are satisfied to remain committed almost wholly to meeting their own needs – which, in the nature of things, will probably never be met because one is rarely satisfied with what one only seeks for oneself."

39   Waggoner, *Shape of Faith to Come*, 140: "Serving God and others is a mark of spiritual maturity. In fact, without service, spiritual transformation is impossible."

ple to minister, they are helping them to do the works God prepared for them to do (Eph. 2:10), but also, they are helping them become the disciples God called them to be (Matt. 28:19-20).

PASTORS TEACH WHEN PEOPLE ASK QUESTIONS OR ENGAGE THEM IN CONVERSATIONS

Teaching while walking around includes being a good example in word and deed, mentoring others in ministry, but it also includes living life in community and responding to questions people ask in informal settings. While it is impossible to prepare for every question (cf. Luke 12:11-12), you can be sure that people will have questions about their faith when it is being tested with various trials.

Data collected by LifeWay Research in a yearlong longitudinal study of twenty-five hundred Protestant churchgoers indicated that 3.5 percent of the respondents grew, while 3 percent declined spiritually.[40] That number represents a negligible overall increase. However, when the researchers went past the statistical data and read the narratives of those who experienced growth, they found the most frequently mentioned contributor to spiritual growth was a life event, like cancer, death of a loved one, abandonment, or a near-death experience.[41] This research hints that life transitions are ripe for growth.

In "Caring for the Hurting" (chap. 3), I made the case for listening to people when they have questions instead of stifling them with clichés. Active listening in a non-judgmental way is a way that pastors love God's people when they are hurting. However, it is also appropriate, after the initial numbness dissipates to teach the hurting people how to trust in God when their souls are throbbing.

In those times, the key decision believers have to make is will they blame God for their pain, or will they invite God into their sorrow and trust in Him. In Romans, Paul writes of one possible outcome of trials: "And not only this, but we also exult in our tribulations, knowing that tribulation brings about perseverance; and perseverance, proven character; and proven character, hope; and hope does not disappoint, because the love of God has been poured out within our hearts through the Holy

---

40   Ibid., 266.
41   Ibid., 281-83.

Spirit who was given to us" (5:3-5 NASB). Notice the chain reaction of how tribulation becomes hope.

Figure 1. Development from Tribulation to Hope

One thing builds upon the other — the person who trusts in God during the tribulations develops perseverance.[42] That perseverance builds character, and character leads to hope. There is a connection between trusting in God and surviving tribulations. However, what happens when those suffering do not trust in God and instead blame Him? Could it be the opposite happens?

If, instead of trusting God in trials, believers choose to blame Him — or taking it to an extreme, choose to curse God (Job 2:9)—they begin a downward spiral from giving up to experiencing a deep empty void, ending in despair. [43] The difference between a life of despair and a life of hope is the choice to trust in God and not blame Him for circumstances of life. Trust defeats fear (Ps. 56:3), gives direction (Prov. 3:5-6), and strength (Isa. 26:4).

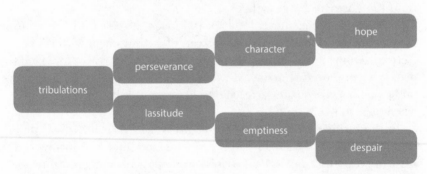

Figure 2. Development from Tribulation to Despair

---

42   Jesus connects faith with the ability to perseverance (Luke 22:32). And Paul and Barnabas encouraged the believers to continue in the faith through their troubles (Acts 14:22).

43   Luke 18:1 (AMP): "They ought always to pray and not to turn coward (faint, lose heart, and give up)."

Trust is not possible to those in denial about their tribulations. They must name the pain. The great verse of hope in Lamentations, "[Because of] the Lord's faithful love we do not perish, for His mercies never end. They are new every morning; great is Your faithfulness! I say: The Lord is my portion, therefore I will put my hope in Him" (Lam. 3:22-24). These verses are preceded by an honest lament, where Jeremiah names his pain—a sense of abandonment and ill-treatment at the hand of God (3:1-23). Yet, in the midst of his pain and depression, he found hope by remembering God's faithfulness, his unending mercies, and faithful love. From the pain sprung hope (Lam. 3:24).

Faithfulness is not a feeling—it is a matter of trust. Often, Christians view the world through the eyes of an actor on center stage and think of God is playing a supporting role, and feel He is not being faithful when He does not cater to their every desire. God does not play a supporting role to anyone.

The confusion does not stop with who is playing the leading role; there is often a misunderstanding about the location of the stage. The stage is not on earth, it is in eternity. This life is not the main event; it is a dress rehearsal for what is to come.

Job learned this lesson when God answered him out of the whirlwind. The trials he endured, in the end, brought glory to God as he proved a point God was making to Satan.[44] The stage was heaven, the main actor was God, the antagonist was Satan. Job simply played a supporting role as the person whose life proved God's point.

After naming the pain, God's people need to invite God into their sorrows.[45] They can do so with confidence because He promised never to leave or forsake His people (Deut. 31:8) and has promised to be with His people until the very end (Matt. 28:18-20). The Psalmist never promised that God's people would not have to walk through the valley of the shadow of death, just that they would not have to walk through it alone (Ps. 23:4). Like many pastors, I've been in the valley of the shadow—sometimes that shadow belonged to someone I loved (a few times, it was my shadow), but I've never walked in the valley alone. In the midst of the pain, doubts, and suffering, I have felt the unseen hand of God.

After inviting God into their sorrow, God's people need to choose to trust in God's faithfulness. God's faithfulness is higher than the heavens

---

44   Tabb, *Out of the Whirlwind*, 46.
45   Wilson, *Soul Shaping*, 102-107.

(Ps. 36:5), is declared by angels (Ps. 89:5), is unmatched by any other (Ps. 89:8), and will never end (Ps. 100:5). While trials may come, they will never destroy God's people (Rom. 8:38-39) because He shelters (Ps. 91:4) and protects (2 Thess. 3:3) His people. God can be trusted.

PASTORS TEACH IN TIMES OF CONFLICT

In the midst of the conflict, pastors love the hurtful (chap. 4). But that is not all they do—they also teach. Paul wrote, "A servant of the Lord must not quarrel but must be kind to everyone, be able to teach, and be patient with difficult people. Gently instruct those who oppose the truth. Perhaps God will change those people's hearts, and they will learn the truth."[46] In this passage, there are several words or phrases that indicate that Paul is referring to a conflict environment: "quarrel," "difficult people," and "oppose the truth." There are also several phrases that indicate the role of God's servant in these situations is to teach: "able to teach, gently instruct, and learn the truth."

Pastors should not run from conflict fearing personal pain; rather, they should lean into it, knowing it is one way they teach while walking around. It is not personal. The difficult person is not opposing the Lord's servant (2 Tim. 2:24-25). It is the truth they oppose. Conflict is an opportunity to teach (chap. 9).

---

46   2 Timothy 2:24-25 (NLT).

Chapter 9 *Teaching in Conflict Situations*

N ot all conflict is destructive, painful, or negative. Rather, it is a vital part of every pastor's experiences – just another context for ministry. Just as in literature, conflict surfaces inner tensions in the main characters, thickens the plot, and moves the story towards its climax,[1] conflict is the context for everyday life.

Conflict is an environment for ministry (chap. 4), leading (chaps. 10 and 11), and teaching. In the Gospel of Mark, Jesus' primary response in conflict situations was to teach. There are only six exceptions in Mark's Gospel. One exception is a low-intensity conflict where Mark is narrating the story and does not report a response from Jesus (Mark 3:20–21). Other exceptions are four of the five conflict episodes in which the intensity of the conflict was high.[2] In two of them Mark was narrating the story and Jesus had no opportunity to respond (Mark 12:12; 14:1–2). In the other two, Jesus disengaged with the antagonists (Mark 3:6–7; 15:1–16:14).

Jesus Had High-Intensity Conflict with Supporters and Those Who Opposed Him, His Teachings, or His Purposes

However, in one of the five high-intensity conflict episodes, Jesus used it as an opportunity to teach. The conflict began with Jesus explaining to His disciples that the betrayal was about to happen, followed by the betrayal it-self that turned violent (Mark 14:42–50). Jesus taught them in this instance by saying what was happening was a fulfillment of prophecy (Isa. 53:7).

---

1 Thomas, *Script Analysis for Actors*, 145.

2 Bullard, *Every Congregation*. As mentioned in chapter 3, Bullard gives seven intensities of conflict. For this chapter, I am not attempting to assign a numerical level to the conflict since the tool is specific to congregational conflict. Instead, I will differentiate between low-intensity conflict (corresponds to levels 1–3) and high-intensity conflict (corresponds to levels 5–7).

In all the low-intensity conflict episodes, except Mark 3:20–21 (as noted above), Jesus' consistent response was to teach (Mark 2:5–12, 16–17, 18–22, 23–28; 3:1–5, 22–30; 4:36–41; 5:25–34; 6:2–6; 7:1–13, 26–30; 8:11–13, 31–33; 10:2–12; 11:27–12:11; 12:13–17, 18–27; 14:3–9, 10–25, 27–31). He taught supporters, and He taught those who were not sympathetic to Him, His teachings, or His purposes.

JESUS TAUGHT DURING
LOW-INTENSITY CONFLICTS WITH SUPPORTERS

Ten of the twenty-six conflict episodes Jesus experienced in Mark's Gospel were with supporters — those who were friendly to Him, His teachings, and His purposes (Mark 3:20–21; 4:36–41; 5:25–34; 6:2–6; 7:26–30; 8:31–33; 14:3–9, 10–25, 27–31, 42–50). Two of those occurred with people He ministered to (Mark 6:2–6; 7:26–30), and the remainder were with those in His inner circle.

Conflict with Recipients of His Ministry

In Mark 6:2–6, Jesus taught in the synagogue and the people were astonished at His teaching. At first, there is no hint they would take offense at what He was saying or doing — the reader could think their astonishment was hometown pride. But it becomes evident the astonishment was negative — they were offended by His wisdom because He was not trained by a rabbi. He was missing an important credential that was keeping them from taking Him seriously.[3] They referred to Him as a carpenter, a tradesman, a common man, and as Mary's son, perhaps drawing attention to the fact that He was conceived out of wedlock.[4] In other words, it got personal. Since Jesus was not, in their view, a trained rabbi,[5] what business did He

---

3   Brooks, *Mark*, 98.

4   Hurtado, *Mark*, 92: "It has been suggested many times that this expression may have been a slur upon the legitimacy of his birth used by people of his hometown. It is possible that this slur might have resulted if, as Matthew 1:18–25 indicates, it became known that Mary had become pregnant before her marriage to Joseph. Though Christian tradition attributes this to a miraculous act of God, in ancient Jewish tradition Jesus is referred to as an illegitimate child."

5   Lange, Schaff, and Shedd, *Mark*, 53: "According to the custom of the Jewish

have teaching them in their synagogue? This rejection ended Jesus' public teaching ministry in the synagogue. After this event, those who wanted to hear Jesus preach would have to go to less formal arenas.

In response to this personal conflict, Jesus inserts the word "prophet" into familiar proverbs that were similar to our saying "familiarity breeds contempt."[6] In doing so, He was not arguing for His legitimacy based upon formal training, but on His prophetic role (Matt. 21:11). Unencumbered by errant traditions recycled through rabbinical schools, Jesus taught from a fresh source of authority that promoted genuine faith (Mark 1:22).

Mark provides an interesting parallel thought in Mark 6:6 between the people's lack of belief, which amazed[7] Jesus, and Jesus' lack of traditional training, which astonished[8] the people. Because of their lack of faith, Jesus only did a few miracles among the people, foreshadowing a teaching that emerges later in Mark about the direct connection between God's work and people's faith (Mark 9:23).

A second conflict episode with a recipient of His ministry emerges out of Jesus' faith and practice, but is not as personal in nature. He has a conversation with a Syrophoenician woman who asks for Jesus' assistance with her demon-possessed daughter (Mark 7:26–30). In this conversation, Jesus teaches an important lesson about His mission. He responded to her request for assistance with a proverb that could have caused her to take offense: that children must eat before feeding the dogs. In doing so, He was implying the Jews (children) were a priority for ministry (Rom. 1:16), but not the Gentiles (dogs).[9]

Her response—that puppies under the table at least ate the children's scraps—demonstrated her faith (she referred to Jesus as Lord) and Jesus healed her daughter. In doing so, He taught the observers a single lesson in two ways: one in tone and the other in action. When Jesus referred to Gentiles as dogs, He did not use the typical word that Jews used to

---

people, even the rabbis learned some handicraft." There is a difference between a rabbi having a trade and someone being a tradesman. In this instance, they were dismissing Jesus as a teacher because he was a carpenter.

6   Wessel, "Mark," 665.

7   Ἐθαύμαζεν.

8   Ἐκπλήσσω.

9   Brooks, *Mark*, 121: "Jews often used the word 'dogs' to refer to Gentiles. Even though it seems out of character for him to have done so, Jesus almost certainly used it in the same way."

describe Gentiles as wild dogs or street scavengers;[10] instead, He used a word meaning a household pet. His tone communicated something about His mission in general and His intent in this specific instance. His actions were congruent with His words. He did not stop at mere words; He acted on truth and healed the daughter.

Conflict with His Inner Circle

Jesus also had a significant number of conflict episodes in the Gospel of Mark with people in His inner circle, which included His family, friends, and disciples. Some of those conflicts were issue-centered concerning His faith and practice (Mark 8:31–33; 14:3–9, 27–31), but the majority of those were personal in nature (Mark 3:20–21; 4:36–41; 5:25–34; 14:10–25, 42).

Issue-Centered Conflicts

In Mark 8:31–33, Jesus gives the first of three predictions to His disciples about His impending death and resurrection (Mark 9:30–37 and 10:32–34 for the other two times). Peter took Jesus aside to rebuke Him over this new teaching. When Jesus saw the disciples listening, He turned the tables on Peter and rebuked him in very harsh terms, calling him Satan because Peter was not seeking God's interest. With this rebuke, Jesus taught the importance of seeking after kingdom purposes, not human comfort.

Mark records an instance of Jesus teaching while walking around (chap. 8), or more accurately, teaching while reclining at the table (Mark 14:3–9). An unidentified woman anoints Jesus with an expensive perfume. Some in the home criticized her for wasting the perfume on Jesus, noting that its value was equivalent to a full year's wages for an average worker. In their view, she should have sold the item and given it to the poor instead of lavishing it upon Jesus in this intentional act of worship.

In this instance, Jesus comes to her aid, rebuking them for their criticism of her good deed. And He teaches them that, while ministering to the poor is important, it is never-ending. However, the ministry of anointing His body for burial had a deadline. He elevated her action to say

---

10   Hurtado, *Mark*, 119: "It is true that Jewish tradition sometimes referred to Gentiles derogatorily as 'dogs,' but this may not be relevant here. The Greek term Mark uses seems to refer to household dogs, while 'dog' as a slur used a Greek term applied to wild dogs or to scavenger dogs of the street."

that preachers should mention her deeds whenever they preach the gospel throughout the entire world.

Mark includes one more issue-centered conflict episode in his Gospel. It is between Jesus and His inner circle (Mark 14:27-31). Peter resists Jesus' prediction that the disciples will fall away after His death, even though Jesus clearly stated that He would return to them in Galilee after the resurrection. Peter says, "They may deny you, but I will not." Jesus teaches Peter something about his human frailty when He points out that Peter would deny Him and it would happen that very evening. Peter continued to resist and the others joined him in rejecting Jesus' teaching. In this text, Jesus teaches, but the disciples do not learn—at least not yet.

Personal Conflicts

While there were only two personal low-intensity conflicts with those who were not sympathetic to Jesus, His teaching, or purposes (Mark 3:22-30; 11:27-12:11), there were five with those in His inner circle. The most common conflict Jesus had with those in His inner circle surrounded issues of His identity and was personal in nature.

In two of the instances, Jesus does not respond or attempt to teach (Mark 3:20-21; 14:42). In the first occurrence, Mark, serving as a narrator, explains that Jesus' inner circle rescued Him from the multitude because He was not eating as He should. What makes this one personal is their comment that He had lost His senses. The second instance finds Jesus telling His disciples they needed to leave the place of solitude in the Garden of Gethsemane to meet the betrayer. This account is personal because of the nature of the conflict. Judas did not merely reject Jesus' ideas; he betrayed Jesus.

In the other three instances (Mark 4:36-41; 5:25-34; 14:10-25), Jesus responded to the personal conflict by teaching. After leaving the multitudes, Jesus lay down and went to sleep on the boat. However, a storm came up that threatened the safety of those on the boats, so the disciples awoke Jesus and accused Him of not caring about them and their safety. Jesus ignored the insult and rebuked the weather. The sea calmed down and Jesus chided them. He did not rebuke them for the unfounded allegation that He did not care, but He did rebuke them for not having sufficient faith.

Another time Jesus suffered their sarcastic wit after He asked members of a crowd that pressed around Him, "Who touched Me?" (Mark 5:25-34). Pointing out the obvious, but missing the import of Jesus question, the disciples say, "You're asking who touched you when you have many people touching you—the crowd is pressing all around you." As before, Jesus ignored the personal jab and began a search for the person He healed with His touch so He could heal her spiritually with His words. With His actions, Jesus taught the importance of healing people spiritually.

The third personal conflict with a member of His inner circle (perhaps the most personal of all) happened while reclining at the Passover table (Mark 14:10-25).[11] Before the meal, Judas met with the chief priests to work out the details of the betrayal and two of Jesus' disciples arranged, at Jesus' instruction, for the Passover meal. As they were eating, Jesus initiated the conflict. He changed the dinner conversation to the subject of betrayal and a direct accusation that one of those at the table would betray Him that evening. As they did with Jesus' prediction about denying Him (Mark 14:27-31), all of the disciples said it was not them, but Jesus identified who it was—the one who dips with Him in the bowl. As they ate the Passover meal, Jesus reinterpreted the meaning of the elements and He taught them about the significance of what He was doing.

Because of His teaching, the Passover bread that celebrated the people's deliverance from Egyptian bondage took on a new meaning. Before, it was a reminder of the time when God delivered the children of Israel (Exod. 13:8-9); now it commemorates Jesus' broken body and celebrates the Christian's deliverance from eternal bondage (1 Cor. 11:24).

When Jesus handed the cup to the disciples, they naturally would have thought of the blood of the lamb smeared on the doorpost of their ancestors' homes in Egypt. In preparation for the tenth plague, God instructed the children of Israel to put the blood of the Passover lamb on the two doorposts and on the lintel of the house. God made a covenant with the people: when the death angel saw the blood on the doorposts, it would pass over that house and not kill the firstborn son. However, if a house did not have the blood on the doorposts and lintel, the death angel would visit their home and kill their firstborn son (Exod. 11:1-13:16).

As the disciples drank the fruit of the vine, they remembered the blood

---

11   I classified Judas' intended betrayal as a low-intensity conflict in this instance for two reasons. First, Judas was a pawn in the destructive plot lead by the religious leaders, not the driving force. Judas, in my view, was an opportunist who capitalized at every turn for a profit. Personal enrichment (John 12:6) was his motive, not destruction. Second, because the impending betrayal was the background of this conflict, not the conflict itself. This conflict was a confrontation about what was going to happen.

covenant (Exod. 12:13). However, Jesus reinterpreted the wine to symbolize a new covenant. It was not a salvation from a single night of terror (Matt. 26:27-28); instead, it celebrates eternal salvation (1 Peter 1:18-19).

JESUS TAUGHT DURING LOW-INTENSITY CONFLICTS WITH THOSE WHO OPPOSED HIM, HIS TEACHINGS, OR HIS PURPOSES

As might be expected, most of the conflict episodes in the Gospel of Mark that involved Jesus were with those who were not sympathetic to Him, His teachings, or His purposes. Mark records Jesus teaching on twelve different occasions under these circumstances (Mark 2:5-12, 16-17, 18-22, 23-28; 3:1-5, 22-30; 7:1-13; 8:11-13; 10:2-12; 11:27-12:11; 12:13-17, 18-27). Mostly Jesus taught the Pharisees, but on a few occasions, He taught the chief priests, scribes, elders, Herodians, or Sadducees.

Personal Conflicts

Only two of these low-intensity conflicts were personal in nature (Mark 3:22-30; 11:27-12:11). In the first one, right after Jesus' disciples called Him out of His mind (Mark 3:21), the scribes ratcheted up the intensity by calling Jesus demon-possessed. Jesus refuted their claim by showing them the error of their logic. Since Jesus cast out demons (Mark 1:23), He could not be demon-possessed. Jesus then teaches the importance of a united house and warns against the blasphemy of the Holy Spirit.

In the other instance of a personal, low-intensity conflict episode, the chief priests, scribes, and elders (the group that would ultimately influence His crucifixion) challenged Jesus about His authority. Of course, they were the local religious authorities, and they were ready to end Jesus' rogue teachings and actions by reminding Him that He needed to submit to their authority. Jesus did not take the bait. Instead, He offered to answer their question if they would answer one from Him. He asked them about the authenticity of John's baptism—Did John's authority come from heaven, or from men? In essence, Jesus answered their question—just as John's authority was from heaven, so was Jesus' authority. Fearing the people, the religious leaders declined to answer Jesus' question. Jesus responded by teaching the crowd with a parable that clarified His role in the kingdom of God, that is, He is the chief cornerstone, rejected by men but established by God (Mark 12:1-11).

Their response, one of the high-intensity conflicts mentioned at the beginning of this chapter, was to plot His destruction. They wanted to destroy Him, but they did not make their move. At least not yet, because they feared the people (Mark 12:12).

Issue-Centered Conflicts

Ten of the twelve low-intensity conflicts episodes in the Gospel of Mark, in which Jesus taught those who were not sympathetic to Him, His teachings, or His purposes were not personal, but centered on His faith and practice.

After Jesus forgives the sins of a paralytic man, the scribes assumed Jesus was being presumptuous since God is the one who forgives sins (Isa. 43:25), and Levitical priests were the ones that announced that God had forgiven sin (Lev. 4:20). Jesus, according to the scribes, was neither.

Jesus perceived what they were thinking and challenged them by asserting that He did have the authority to forgive sins. As a sign of that authority, He healed the man and the man walked out of the place, carrying the bed he was lying on (Mark 2:5-12). He did not correct their assertion that only God can forgive sins. By using ascribing the title "Son of man" to Himself, and by doing the miracle, He did clarify that He had that authority.[12] In other words, He taught them that He was (and is) God.[13]

The scribes and the Pharisees noticed that Jesus was fellowshiping with some unsavory people and asked Jesus' disciples why He did such a thing. Jesus overheard the conversation and answered their question by teaching them that, since sinners need to repent, He was spending time with them just as a doctor would spend time with sick people (Mark 2:16-17).

Later, the Pharisees and John's disciples noticed that Jesus' disciples were not fasting as they did (Mark 2:18-22), and they wanted to know why Jesus and His followers did not conform to their traditional approach to religious practice.[14] Jesus not only answered their question, but also taught

---

12   Wiersbe, *Bible Exposition Commentary*, 116: "Jesus affirmed His deity not only by forgiving the man's sins and healing his body, but also by applying to Himself the title 'Son of man.'"

13   Ultimately, this is the charge, which the religious leaders used to persuade Rome to condemn Jesus to death (Mark 14:61-64).

14   Brooks, *Mark*, 64: "So important was fasting for ancient Jews that an entire tractate of the *Mishna, Taanith*, was devoted to it."

them something about His purpose. In answer to their question, He indicated that the current season was not one for fasting, but for celebration. Implicit was that there is a season for everything (Eccl. 3:1), and that the time for fasting would come later, but not while He was with them. At the conclusion of this conflict, Jesus corrected their assumption that He was coming to fit in with the old ways. He was not. He taught them that their old wineskins could not contain His new wine.

The next conflict episode, Mark 2:23-28, is one in a series of conflicts that revolved around the Sabbath day (see also Mark 3:1-5; 3:6-7; 6:2-6). Jesus and His disciples plucked some grain from a field, which was allowed under Deuteronomistic law (Deut. 23:25). However, the Pharisees called the action "unlawful" because the disciples plucked the grain on the Sabbath day (Exod. 20:8-11). Jesus explained that David ate showbread when he was hungry (1 Sam. 21:4-5), even though it was set apart for the Lord (Lev. 24:5-9), therefore it was permissible for Jesus' disciples to eat grain plucked on the Sabbath day when they were hungry. He taught them that Sabbath rest is a gift from God to His people – God instituted it for them, He did not create people for it.

Jesus' teaching did not end the discussion. In Mark 3:1-5, He healed a man on the Sabbath. Jesus was in the synagogue and performed the miracle in full view of the Pharisees, who were watching Him to gather evidence against Him. Jesus did not disappoint them. Before the healing, Jesus asked if it were permissible, in their view, to do good things and serve life on the Sabbath, or only do evil (a commentary on the trap they were attempting to set for Him). Following the question, Jesus healed the man immediately. Therefore, the Pharisees and the Herodians began to plot Jesus' destruction, which is a high-intensity conflict mentioned at the beginning of this chapter (Mark 3:6-7).

Just as the Pharisees did not appreciate Jesus' views on fasting and the Sabbath day, they objected to His non-compliance with ceremonial washing laws (Exod. 30:19), which they applied to everyone, not just the priests (Mark 7:1-13).[15] Quoting Isaiah 29:13, Jesus called them hypocrites for elevating their traditions above God's commandments. After pointing out some commandments they were ignoring while holding to their traditions, Jesus taught them that their actions were destructive.

---

15 Witherington, *Gospel of Mark*, 224: "In order to understand the Pharisees, one must recognize that they attempted to apply the Levitical laws for the cleanness of priests to everyone."

After Jesus' feeding miracle (Mark 8:1-10), the Pharisees began arguing with Jesus, (Mark 8:11-13), asking Him to give them a heavenly sign that would validate Him and His teaching. Jesus refused, and in doing so hinted that genuine faith is the evidence people need (Heb. 11:1) and that a sign will not convince people to believe if they did not already have faith (Luke 16:31).

In Mark 10:2-12 the Pharisees take a different approach in their attempt to trap Jesus; they stop asking Him about His practice and begin to question what He believes by asking about divorce. Jesus answered with His own question, asking them to explain what Moses taught on divorce. They gave a partial answer, but omitted the indecency clause. They said that Moses allowed divorce as long as the husband certified the divorce in writing (Deut. 24:1-4). Jesus agreed that Moses allowed divorce, but noted that it was because of the hardness of people's heart that he did so. Then Jesus taught the purpose of marriage in God's design. In private, the disciples asked Him to clarify and Jesus explained the long-term damage divorce does in people's lives.

Collaborating with the Herodians, the Pharisees continued attempting to trap Jesus (Mark 12:13-17). This time, they ask about the lawfulness of paying taxes to the state, which was an issue the Herodians would value. Jesus asked to see a coin, then asked whose image it bore. When they said Caesar's, He replied, "Give Caesar what belongs to him, but reserve for God what belongs to God." Since people have God's image on them (Gen. 1:26-27), Jesus was teaching them the importance of giving their lives to God.

In Mark 12:18-27, the Sadducees get a turn at Jesus.[16] They questioned Jesus about the resurrection, a doctrine they rejected but affirmed by the Pharisees. They mentioned Moses' teaching on levirate marriage (Lev. 25:25-28) and gave a hypothetical situation of a woman that married seven brothers, one at a time, as each one died off. Then they asked whom she would be married to after the resurrection. Jesus clarified that marriage was for earth, not heaven, and that the resurrection is true since the living God identifies Himself as the God of the patriarchs. Since He is the God of the living, not the dead, even those patriarchs who have died are now alive.

---

16   Wessel, "Mark," 735: "In the NT the Sadducees are mentioned only fourteen times whereas the Pharisees are mentioned about one hundred times."

Table 3. Summary of Jesus' Conflicts in the Gospel of Mark

Mark	Intensity level	Faith & practice (F&P) or Personal	Friendly to Jesus, His teachings and His purpose	Did Jesus respond or disengage?	Did Jesus teach in word or deed?
2:5–12	Low	F&P	No	Respond	Yes
2:16–17	Low	F&P	No	Respond	Yes
2:18–22	Low	F&P	No	Respond	Yes
2:23–28	Low	F&P	No	Respond	Yes
3:1–5	Low	F&P	No	Respond	Yes
3:6–7	High	Personal	No	Disengage	NA
3:20–21	Low	Personal	Yes	NA	NA
3:22–30	Low	Personal	No	Respond	Yes
4:36–41	Low	Personal	Yes	Respond	Yes
5:25–34	Low	Personal	Yes	Respond	Yes
6:2–6	Low	Personal	Yes	Respond	Yes
7:1–13	Low	F&P	Not	Respond	Yes
7:26–30	Low	F&P	Yes	Respond	Yes
8:11–13	Low	F&P	Not	Respond	Yes
8:31–33	Low	F&P	Yes	Respond	Yes
10:2–12	Low	F&P	Not	Respond	Yes
11:27–12:11	Low	Personal	Not	Respond	Yes
12:12	High	F&P	Not	NA	NA
12:13–17	Low	F&P	Not	Respond	Yes
12:18–27	Low	F&P	Not	Respond	Yes
14:1–2	High	Personal	Not	NA	NA
14:3–9	Low	F&P	Yes	Respond	Yes
14:10–25	Low	Personal	Yes	Respond	Yes
14:27–31	Low	F&P	Yes	Respond	Yes
14:42–50	High	Personal	Yes	Respond	Yes
15:1–16:14	High	Personal	Not	Disengage	NA

JESUS TAUGHT IN CONFLICT SITUATIONS

Jesus used conflict situations as an opportunity to teach. Teaching is not reserved for formal settings (chap. 7), but is done while walking around (chap. 8), which include seasons of conflict. While different readers of the Gospel of Mark could divide the conflict episodes differently (and rendering a different total), the twenty-six occurrences I have identified in the sixteen chapters of Mark demonstrate that conflict was a big part of Jesus' teaching ministry. It is especially significant in light of the observation that He taught in word or deed in twenty-one of those conflicts. His default response was to teach when the conflict was low in intensity and disengage when it was high.

Jesus Had Conflicts with Supporters and Non-supporters

The conflicts that Jesus had with supporters tended to be more personal than those He had with the religious leaders. More times than not, Jesus ignored the personal insults and dealt with the issues at the core of the conflict.

Most of the conflicts that Jesus had with religious leaders revolved around their desire for Him to conform to their practices and beliefs. Jesus instead insisted on promoting genuine, heart-felt faith, which made conformity impossible. Throughout His teaching during these conflict episodes, He unveiled His identity and kingdom purposes. To a large degree, Mark used conflict episodes to unveil Jesus' teachings.[17]

God Accomplished His Will through These Conflicts

While many of the antagonists in these conflicts are villainous and act in despicable ways, their aggression provided Jesus an opportunity to teach that benefited His hearers and Mark's readers. Ultimately, the greatest thing that emerged from these conflict episodes was not a teaching, but redemption. Without the final conflict in the Gospel of Mark (Mark 15:1–16:14), salvation would not have been possible.

No one took Jesus' life from Him (John 10:18); He gave it freely for the

---

17   Donahue, *Gospel of Mark*, vol. 2, 22: "Plot dynamics emerge either from conflict or from the resolution of an initial tension. Plot elements in Mark include the early conflict between Jesus and authorities (3:6), the mounting misunderstanding between Jesus and disciples (1:36), the frequent question about Jesus' identity: 'Who is this?' (1:27; 2:7; 4:41; 6:2, 14; 8:27; 11:27; 14:61–62; 15:2, 31–32), and the suspense that arises from the early enthusiastic reception of Jesus by the crowds along with intimation of lethal opposition."

sins of the world (John 3:16). He died for the chief priests, scribes, and elders that conspired to take His life. He died for Judas, His friend who betrayed Him. Jesus died for the Pharisees and Sadducees who pestered Him along the way. He died for you and me. His death was necessary.

Jesus' Example of Teaching in Conflict Situations and Pastoral Practice

Even though Jesus did not hold the office of pastor in a local church, pastors can apply Jesus' example of teaching during conflict situations to their pastoral practice. Remember, Jesus is the Good Shepherd (John 10:11) and pastors who imitate Him are following Paul's example (1 Cor. 11:1).

LIFE AND MINISTRY IS BETTER WITH FRIENDS, EVEN THOUGH PASTORS WILL HAVE CONFLICT WITH THEM

Having friends in the church can create problems such as giving the appearance of favoritism[18] or creating the possibility for betrayal;[19] yet friends are essential to health,[20] longevity,[21] and spiritual vitality.[22] Life is better with friends. While it is possible to have friends in the community and with pastoral colleagues and neighbors, the church is one of the most likely places where pastors can make friends.[23]

The need to maintain confidentiality, keep professional and personal boundaries, and remain friendly with everyone in the church are some of the unique challenges pastors face if they have close friends in the church.

---

18   Miller, *Secrets of Staying Power*, 161.

19   Cedar, "Leading or Responding?" 61–62.

20   Mackereth, "Friendfluence." Research found that being with a good friend lowers blood pressure and helps sick people get better quicker.

21   Hamilton, "Friends." In 2010 researchers at Brigham Young University published a summary of over one hundred other studies involving over 300,000 individuals. The results agreed that people with strong social ties were likely to live 7.5 years longer than people without those kinds of friendships.

22   Waggoner, *Shape of Faith to Come*, 74: "Biblical spirituality is not consistent with Lone Ranger attitude. We need one another for support and encouragement."

23   Smith, *Empowering Ministry*, 177: "Pastors who shun friendships within the congregation are likely to be lonely because they have little opportunity to make friends elsewhere."

Pastors should be careful in entering into such friendships,[24] insisting their friends respect boundaries and not attempt to use the friendship as a fulcrum point of power. On the other hand, pastors must exercise care not to take advantage of their friends to advance their personal and leadership agendas. Pastors must understand that friends can disagree with them in congregational meetings and still be friends. Friends can oppose the pastor's ideas and still be friends.

However, even assuming that all concerned are spiritually mature people who handle boundaries well, there will still be conflict. That reality should not dissuade pastors from making friends in the church any more than the inevitability of conflict with family should dissuade pastors from marrying or having children. Life is better with friends.

Opportunities to Teach Will Be
Squandered if Pastors React to Personal Insults

Sometimes conflict gets personal, and if the conflict episodes Mark recorded in his Gospel are typical, they tend to be more personal when they are with friends. Pastors must hold their temper and be self-controlled in all situations (Titus 1:5-9), even when friends engage in personal attacks against them. Jesus ignored the personal attacks and focused on people's potential to learn. He taught them.

SINCE PASTORS ARE SINFUL, THEY CAN EXPECT
TO HAVE CONFLICTS CAUSED BY THEIR FAILURES

Jesus never sinned (2 Cor. 5:21). Everyone else has (Rom. 3:23). This fact is one place where applying Jesus' conflict episodes in the Gospel of Mark to pastoral ministry gets tricky. People accused Jesus of wrongdoing, but He never did anything wrong. If there were twenty-six episodes of conflict in Mark's Gospel for the perfect Savior, how many more episodes will sinful pastors have in their ministries? Pastors create their own conflict with their bad decisions and sinful choices.[25]

---

24   Wilson and Hoffman, *Preventing Ministry Failure*, 161: "While we don't have the luxury of deciding who we minister to, we have every right to decide who we let in as friends."

25   Iorg, *The Painful Side of Leadership*, 53-54: "Leaders cause painful situations

Admit Mistakes

When pastors make mistakes, they should admit and take responsibility for them. When they do, it helps build healthy relationships between pastors and the people they serve. It can build loyalty,[26] breed confidence,[27] and reassure the people.[28] Besides, it is the right thing to do (Prov. 28:13).

Ask for Forgiveness

Especially in the case of sinful choices, pastors, like all Christians, should first confess the sin in the circle it is committed,[29] then ask the offended parties to forgive them (James 5:16), and finally be willing to accept the consequences for their actions. Sometimes the consequences involve stepping down from the leadership position,[30] other times the consequences are less drastic, but in every case, pastors should accept forgiveness and the lingering consequences for their sins.

CONFLICTS ARE OPPORTUNITIES TO LEARN AS WELL AS TEACH

After noticing that Jesus' default response in His conflict episodes recorded in the Gospel of Mark was to teach, it is wise for pastors to follow His pattern and look for opportunities to teach in conflict situations. But when

---

by bad decisions or sinful choices. Sometimes a decision is one or the other—oftentimes a little bit of both. Both bad decisions and sinful choices, depending on the scope of the decision, can have wide-ranging consequences. On lesser issues, leaders can often recover quickly by admitting their mistakes, changing course, and moving in new directions. But other times, our bad decisions and sinful choices can have devastating results."

26 Mittelstaedt, *Your Next Mistake*, xix: "Don't they know that customers are often more loyal if you admit a mistake and fix it?

27 Kepcher and Fenichell, *Carolyn 101*, 102: "Contrary to popular wisdom, and this is something I wish more politicians understood, saying you're sorry doesn't make you seem weak, it makes you seem strong."

28 Maxwell, *Leadership Gold*, 107: "When you admit your mistakes, it is not a surprise to them; it is a reassurance. They'll be able to look at each other and say, 'Whew! He knows. Now we don't have to keep pretending!'"

29 Orr, *My All, His All*, 23.

30 MacArthur, *Called to Lead*, 162.

taking into account that sometimes conflicts result from bad decisions or sinful choices they make, pastors should also be willing to learn from their mistakes.[31]

Conflict situations provide opportunities for loving God's people, when they are hurtful, teaching God's people, and leading God's people to accomplish the church's mission. While it is possible to resolve a specific conflict situation, there will never be a time when ministry is void of conflict. Pastors will miss opportunities to love, teach, and lead God's people if they let the conflict consume them instead of determining to fulfill their calling in it.

---

31   Maxwell, *Failing Forward*, 18: "People who fail forward are able to see errors or negative experiences as a regular part of life, learn from them, and then move on."

PART FOUR

LEADING GOD'S PEOPLE

Whenever conflict spreads past the boundaries of a few people, it requires pastors to shift from caregiver or teacher to leader. The first two chapters in this part provide tools to look at the conflict systemically so that the pastor can remain calm and lead the church through the difficult days. The chapters that follow show how to lead a congregation to change and how to lead with or without power.

Chapter 10 Leading During Seasons of High Conflict

"Please state your full name for the record." Neighbour panned his surroundings, sensing this was just another workday for everyone else in the boardroom. They pushed camera buttons, they typed on the stenograph machine, they served coffee, they represented their clients—just another workday, except, that is, for him.

He cleared his throat and said, "Ralph Webster Neighbour III."

"I am sure your attorney has explained the deposition process to you, but let me explain it again for the record."

Neighbour could not believe what was happening to him—a seventh generation pastor. Yet there was no arguing the facts. Here he was, giving a deposition in a sexual misconduct lawsuit.

This is not what I signed up for! Neighbour thought.

THE DREAM

With the help of the Church on Brady (now Mosaic), Ralph and Pam Neighbour planted Inland Community Church in Chino, California, in 1984. Within five years, they averaged around two hundred on the typical Sunday. That was before they went into overdrive. At a conference, Neighbour heard John Maxwell say, "I'm praying for a thousand churches to reach a thousand in attendance." Immediately he knew that was his goal. Neighbour says, "I wanted to lead one of those churches reaching a thousand people for Christ. I started doing the necessary things to grow the church."

The first step was to "staff for growth," so he hired a high-octane organizational genius who had a knack for identifying a trend, programming to it, and then rolling out events for the target group. The man was amazing.

Soon the children's ministry was reaching more than two hundred kids, the youth group was almost that size, and the church attracted thousands of seekers with special events like the drama *Heaven's Gates and Hell's Flames.*

They also brought in Oliver North who spoke to a packed house and helped create a positive buzz about the church in the community.

Within fifteen years, they reached a peak attendance of one thousand. Because of the growth, they added more staff and planned for a new building. "The sky was the limit. I was living every church planter's dream," Neighbour says.

THE NIGHTMARE

A few years later, one of the church's staff members was having problems at home. He and Neighbour mutually agreed that he should do something other than church ministry. What Neighbour did not know then was that within the next seven months, he would have to dismiss two other staff members, and one of them was the executive pastor who had done so much to help them grow.

"Looking back now, I realize I had ignored the warning signs," Neighbour says. "But his productivity was so high that I overlooked them. Yes, he got a lot done, but he did it, in a large measure, by running over people."

Neighbour's son noticed. "Dad," he said, "I can't keep coming to church here if you continue to let that man hurt people the way he is." Neighbour soon discovered that much of the staff was ready to leave because of this man's approach. Neighbour knew that the confrontation could not wait any longer. He let him go. The dark cloud lifted and for the next few weeks, they experienced a sense of freedom. Unfortunately, the dark cloud was not the only thing missing.

The church's financial administrator went through the executive pastor's expense account for the previous year and found large inconsistencies. "Pastor, we can't account for a lot of these expenditures, and some of them are major!" she said. When she finished her investigation, she detailed more than thirty thousand dollars she suspected the executive pastor had embezzled from the church. Though they tried, they were unable to resolve the issue with him. Neighbour turned the information over to the police and let them investigate.

These were difficult days. The church was short-staffed, yet they were spending valuable time cooperating with the police department investigation alongside trying to minister to the people they had reached and administering a new building program. The days were bad, but the nights were worse. "I dreaded the evenings," Neighbour said. "I found it impossible to unwind and I didn't sleep well at all." However, one night in February was not just bad—it was horrible.

Good grief, Neighbour thought, *it's after midnight. Who could that be?* He fumbled around on the nightstand to find the phone. "Yes, this is Ralph . . . no, that's okay. What's wrong? Please . . . calm down and just tell me what happened . . . Say that again—the girls are accusing your husband of what?"

The charges against the youth pastor proved serious. The following Sunday, Neighbour told the church that he'd dismissed the youth pastor because of "inappropriate sexual behavior" and asked that people let him know if the dismissed staff member had acted inappropriately with anyone else. Sadly, there were more.

"I hated that he harmed young people. I hated what this would do to our church. I hated that it happened on my watch. I hated how alone I felt," Neighbour says. Leadership under such circumstances gets very lonely.

He prayed and hoped they could overcome the setbacks, and even felt they had made the right decisions on the personnel matters. They did not downplay anything. Instead, they notified the child protection agency, procured legal counsel, talked to their insurance company, and notified the congregation. They had responded promptly and decisively and Neighbour knew that his and the elder's motives were pure.

At Neighbour's prompting, the elder board decided to push forward with the plans to construct a new building and to do their best to weather the storm. "We trusted God to turn things around for us," Neighbour said. "We knew He could."

Two years later, the church was beginning to regain some momentum, but it was not the same. Then a sequel to the nightmare occurred—another allegation of sexual misconduct. This time a sixteen-year-old girl accused one of the church's elders, a key leader in the building project, of molestation. Once again, they notified the congregation and the authorities. Soon, disenfranchised people were talking and rumors spread all over town. A foul stench lingered in the air.

A few weeks later, Neighbour and his leadership team headed out to a retreat center to get away for a few days. While they were there, one of the elders got a call from his wife. "I just picked up the paper," she said. "It isn't good—the church is on the front page." As it turned out, the sixteen-year-old victim was a sister of one of the victims of the youth minister two years before. Their stepmother was a paralegal and organized the others to join them in a lawsuit against the church.

Neighbour had suspected it might happen, but could not believe the irony of announcing the lawsuit while they were on retreat, trying to escape the madness. Neighbour was hoping the pressure would let up. It did not. It increased.

THE PERFECT STORM

Meteorologists say it takes three convergent weather patterns to make the perfect storm, and Neighbour had his three storms raging: the lawsuit, the rapid decline of the church, and a mysterious illness now plaguing his daughter, Ruth, who was rapidly losing weight. He was overwhelmed.

Negative publicity took its toll on church attendance and giving. It is amazing how fast a lifetime of work can unravel. The negative momentum sucked the life out of their gatherings. Inland Community was no longer a fun place to be. Just surviving Sunday morning became Neighbour's weekly goal.

"Normally I am a people person. I'm energized being around them," Neighbour says. "Even when I'm preparing my sermons, I don't want to be holed up in an office. I take my laptop to Starbucks and write my sermons surrounded by people. For most of my ministry, I arrived for the gatherings early and stayed late. Then I'd want to go out for coffee with friends. Not anymore. Most Sundays I wouldn't arrive at the service until it was time to take the platform, and then I'd leave during the closing prayer. I hadn't stopped loving people, but I dreaded Sundays."

By the look of the dwindling crowd, Neighbour was not the only one. Inland Community began an attendance death spiral. The decline began before the lawsuit and accelerated afterward. As the numbers plummeted, so did their hopes to complete the building project.

"We'd already put so much money into it, I felt we'd already crossed the point of no return, but frankly," Neighbour said, "I wasn't sure how we could go forward with it either."

Six months before Neighbour gave his deposition, he got an email from Bob, a special friend and long-time member. In the early days of the church plant, he had prayed with Bob to receive Christ and baptized him. Later he walked with Bob's family through the death of a child and had the privilege of bringing him into leadership.

"Bob knew I was going to the doctor with my daughter today," Neighbour said. "I expected an encouraging word from him when I opened the email – like I'd always provided to him when his child was ill."

"You're a total failure," Bob wrote. "You've disgraced yourself and the ministry. I can't believe I ever trusted you!"

How dare he! Neighbour thought. *How could he say these things to me? How dare he say them now!*

When he was most vulnerable, a trusted friend kicked him.

In the final scene of the movie *The Perfect Storm*, the captain handcuffed himself to the helm. He went down with the ship and Neighbour resonated with what the captain did. "I was determined to do the same thing," Neighbour said, "to go down with the ship. I told myself that it didn't matter what Bob said, I wasn't going to resign."

With time, Neighbour became willing to move on. One evening, Neighbour and his wife drove to a park in Diamond Bar that overlooks the valley to talk. "Pam, I am wondering if perhaps it's time for us to find someone younger to take the church, someone without history here." To his surprise, she agreed.

"I hate to admit it, but I think you're right," she said. They hashed everything out and decided that for the good of the church, he needed to relinquish control of the helm. *Maybe I shouldn't go down with the ship*, he thought. *Maybe I'm sinking it. And it can't survive with me at the helm. Perhaps Bob was right.* Neighbour began to think, *I'm not fit for ministry.*

A good shepherd would never abandon his people and Neighbour would never do that. So he needed to begin planning for a smooth exit. Not knowing where else to turn, Neighbour approached Mosaic, their mother church, to see if they might want to do a new church plant in Chino with their assets and people. What he did not expect was the response he got from Pastor Erwin McManus.

"We will come on one condition," McManus said, "and that's if you stay. You have too much invested here. We'll only do it if it is with you."

"I honestly couldn't believe what he was saying." Neighbour said, "This man was putting everything on the line for me, and I didn't have a clue why. At best, I expected that he'd send a younger pastor over to rebuild the church, and maybe I'd help with the transition. In my wildest dreams, I never thought he'd want me to stay."

Hope sprouted.

Their attorney reported that things were going well with the lawsuit, but church attendance and finances were still struggling and Ruth was still sick. The elders had a huge decision to make and they did not have unity over whether or not to merge with Mosaic. Some of the elders felt they could orchestrate resurgence. The elder board decided not to rush the decision. It was important to Neighbour to have everyone onboard. He wanted unanimity. The elders prayed about it and discussed it but could not come to consensus. The decision process dragged on while the church continued hemorrhaging.

McManus preached at the church a few times to communicate the Mosaic vision to the people, even before they decided what their relationship to Mosaic would be. One of those days, McManus joined Neighbour's family for dinner. He was sitting across from Ruth and they began to talk.

At the dinner, Ruth told McManus about her health problems. For a brief time, everyone else at the table seemed to disappear as Neighbour listened to Ruth share her soul with McManus. In a very prophetic way, McManus looked her in the eye and told her, "It's going to be okay. Ruth, you're going to be okay." Within a short time, the disease began to reverse and Ruth started her journey back toward health.

Then the tide turned with the elders. The church's insurance company sent the church a letter informing them that they were going to drop their sexual liability coverage. "At our next elder meeting, I played hardball," Neighbour says, "Do you want to continue on as an elder where you will personally be financially liable for whatever happens here?" In that moment, the board realized they were out of options. Inland Community could not continue as they were. They needed help—they needed their mother church. The elder board unanimously decided to become the Chino campus of Mosaic.

Neighbour's story is larger than life. Most pastors have not faced a lawsuit because a staff member's sexual misconduct,[1] but what pastor does not know the sting of betrayal. That sting is the dirty little secret of ministry. Most pastors are going through some sort of conflict most of the time,[2] but think other pastors are not. Pastors mingle in the halls at a conference and talk about how well things are going. They downplay the negative

---

1   In an article for *America: The National Catholic Weekly*, Patrick J. Schiltz, associate dean at the University of St. Thomas School of Law, states there will be an increased number of sexual abuse cases against the church. He has provided counsel for over five hundred clergy sexual abuse cases. See Patrick J. Schiltz, "Future of Sexual Abuse."

2   Faith Communities Today's (FACT) study of 14,301 American congregations (in 2000) found 75 percent experienced "some level of any kind of conflict" and 25 percent experienced "serious level of any kind of conflict" in the previous five years. Dudley et al., "Congregational Conflict," 1.

in their ministry and intensify the positive when they talk to colleagues. Because other pastors do the same thing, they think Pastor Appreciation Days, church growth, and miraculous offerings are the norm while their ministry has contentious board meetings, petty criticisms, and self-doubts. The truth is, conflict in ministry is not new. It is part of every leader's story.

CONFLICT IS CONSTANT

They said Jesus was a drunk (Matt. 11:19), Paul was not really an apostle (1 Cor. 9:2), and anyone could do Moses' job (Num. 12:2). You are in good company if people are criticizing you. Fish swim in water, alligators live in swamps, and pastors minister in an environment of conflict. It is not necessarily a sign of bad leadership or ministerial deficiency. After all, Jesus had twenty-six conflicts in the sixteen chapters of the Gospel of Mark (chap. 9), including conflicts with friends, enemies, family members, and colleagues. People criticized him for what he did and what he did not do. Conflict was as much the environment of His ministry as it is ours. It is a constant, but there is more than one way to view it. You can view it in black and white, or in high-definition, full-spectrum color.

Viewing Conflict in Black and White

One of the great movie genres is the old Westerns. In them, the protagonist always wore white hats and the antagonists always wore black hats. No doubt, that is one way to view conflict. Most people race to grab a white hat for themselves and quickly assign black hats to those on the other side. These actions polarize conflict, which creates a more volatile environment and increases the intensity.[3] A sign of unhealthy conflict is taking sides,[4] which is, in effect, crowing themselves with white hats while assigning black hats to the other side.

Evil does exist. Satan is active and wants to destroy churches. No doubt, sometimes there is a personal source: a demon-possessed person may wreak havoc in a church or a hard-core antagonistic person might go out of his

---

3   Gerzon, *Leading Through Conflict*, 94: "Think twice before you call someone an *enemy*. Like the word *foreigner*, the word *enemy* alerts us to the possibility that our capacity to think systemically has reached its limit."

4   Bullard, *Every Congregation*, 53.

or her way to attack a leader without provocation or cause. In the latter case, typically an antagonist makes unreasonable demands that cannot be satisfied. They are self-absorbed and want to destroy, not build up.[5] Hard-core antagonists are "seriously disturbed individuals. They are psychotic—out of touch with reality."[6] In those cases, the black-and-white hats are appropriate and helpful. Leaders who are dealing with evil need to call it evil. Most leaders have encountered an antagonist. King David certainly did. He knew what it was like to have an antagonist during his ascendancy to the throne.

Antagonists in Need of God's Discipline

The day David and Israel defeated the threat against their national security should have been a day of great celebration. Goliath was dead and his army was defeated. Saul's army was victorious in battle and the women came to cheer the soldiers as they returned home, but their song did not please the king. "Saul has killed his thousands," they said, "and David his ten thousands!" Instead of rejoicing with the crowd at David's success, Saul became jealous and paranoid (1 Sam. 18:1-9).

When Goliath defied the army of the living God, Saul had his armor with him and he was quick to loan it to David, but he was not willing to wear it himself to protect his kingdom. When David came up with a plan and volunteered to help, Saul was eager to criticize his plan and belittle David for offering to help. But never did he say to the shepherd boy, "No, I'll do this. It is my place, not yours." As soon as the fighting was over, Saul wanted to ride at the front of the parade and take credit for the victory. Actually, the women were gracious to Saul, they could have said, "Saul has really nice armor that he is willing to loan to men of courage, while David has courage that needs no armor." Instead of being angry that David was included in the song, he should have been grateful that the gracious women even mentioned his name.

Before the women welcomed them from the battlefield, Saul appeared to be pleased with David and promoted him through the ranks. In effect, he gave him a battlefield commission, making him a commander. The more seasoned soldiers and officers took no offense in the promotion. They did not become jealous of David's success; instead, they were pleased with

---

5   Haugk, *Antagonists in the Church*, 25-27.
6   Ibid., 27.

it. After all, David had conquered the giant. I'm sure they were proud to serve under a man of such distinction, even if it meant they had to follow a younger, less experienced person. Saul's men were able to do what he could not. They were happy for David's success. Unfortunately, Saul could not comprehend that when a man under his command distinguishes himself, it reflects well on his country, his fellow soldiers, and on his king. Instead, Saul became jealous.

The next day, while David played the harp to soothe Saul, Saul grabbed a spear and threw it at him, intending on pinning him against the wall. David leapt out of the way and ran for his life. Why would Saul try to kill his son's best friend? Why would he try to kill his armor bearer—his bodyguard—and a commander in his military? He had morbid jealousy,[7] the kind of jealousy that kills.

Saul had an inflamed and fragile ego. His insecurity formed the petri dish for Saul's jealousy to grow. David's success threatened Saul. Saul's view of David contrasts starkly with those of the people. The people loved David but Saul became afraid of him. His fragile ego could not take someone else being successful, even if it meant David's success made him successful.

Saul's jealousy pushed him down a morbid path, plotting to kill David. First, he offered David his oldest daughter in marriage if David proved himself a real warrior. Saul did not want David to prove anything; he wanted the Philistines to kill him (1 Sam. 18:17). David refused, not because he was afraid to prove himself "a real warrior" (he had already done that) but because he did not consider himself worthy to be the king's son-in-law, and Saul gave his daughter to another man.

Then when another of his daughters, Michal, wanted to marry David, Saul asked him again to become his son-in-law. David confessed he could not afford a dowry, so Saul instructed him to kill a hundred Philistines, which would suffice as the dowry. Saul said all he wanted was vengeance on his enemies, but that was not true. Saul wanted David's death (1 Sam.

---

7   Writing for "The Spectator," the oldest continuously published magazine in the English language, Theodore Dalrymple coined the helpful term "morbid jealousy," writing in reference to sexual jealousy. I am not intimating by using the term here that Saul had any sort of sexual attraction toward David. Regardless, the term appears to fit the type of jealousy Saul had. It was a morbid jealousy—one that leads to death. Dalrymple writes, "But the morbidly jealous person does not love his lover; he loves himself, unfortunately, with a tender, extremely inflamed and fragile ego." http://www.spectator.co.uk/features/11321/blackeyed-monster/ (accessed June 22, 2015)

18:25). David succeeds and brings back proof he killed twice as many men than Saul asked, so Saul gave his daughter to David in marriage.

Saul's jealousy increased (1 Sam. 18:28-30) because his daughter loved David, but also, because God was with him. This last point led to Saul growing even more afraid, Saul continued making attempts on David's life, even trying to involve his children as accomplices. He was relentless—he wanted David dead no matter what it cost his kingdom or his children. In short, Saul's jealousy was ruining him, while in the midst of the turmoil, David was becoming a great man because of God's blessing

David did not deserve this mistreatment. He had not done anything except serve his king. When he offered to fight Goliath, it was not because he sought fame or wanted to upstage Saul; it was because the Spirit of the Lord was upon him and he could not stand listening to anyone—let alone an uncircumcised Philistine—mock the armies of the living God. When he refused to wear Saul's armor, it was not because David was ungracious—he knew he could not wear it while fighting his battle, his way.

Whenever Saul needed David, he jumped. An evil spirit would torment Saul, causing terrible mood swings, and David would come and play a harp to soothe his soul. Beyond his musical duties, David worked hard to protect Saul and was willing to lay down his life for him if necessary. He was always humble in Saul's presence, such as when Saul offered his oldest daughter in marriage and David refused, since he believed his family was not worthy of such an honor. David also showed his humbleness by refusing to raise his hand against God's anointed (1 Sam. 24:6). In time, it was God who removed Saul, allowing David to ascend to the throne.

Saul was an antagonist. However, David did not attack him. God protected David and eventually gave him the kingdom.[8] In this story, David's hat is definitely white and Saul's black. When an antagonist is attacking an innocent leader or a wolf stalks among the flock, assigning the black-and-white hats are helpful. Church discipline is also necessary for unmanageable people who will not follow the group's code of conduct (Matt. 7:15; Acts 20:29-31).

The imagery used in Matthew 7:15 and Acts 20:29-31 is of a wolf that invades the church and tears it apart. A similar analogy is cancer. A cancer

---

8   I am not implying that a leader cannot defend himself from an antagonist. David was by no means a pacifist and there are instances in the Scriptures where he encouraged others to avenge him (1 Kings 2:5-9). But in this particular case, David would not fight him because Saul was God's anointed leader.

cell lacks the ability to self-regulate and overtakes the surrounding cells. Without intervention, it will continue to invade healthy cells until the cancer has spread through the entire body. Cancer is deadly if left to spread. On both occasions when I received a cancer diagnosis, I scheduled surgery to remove the cancerous tissue and took the prescribed follow-up treatment immediately. I took aggressive action to stop it.

If the maladjusted person behaves like cancer, cannot self-regulate, and does not respect appropriate boundaries, or if he or she becomes invasive, then removal is appropriate. Matthew writes in 18:15-17:

> If your brother sins against you, go and rebuke him in private. If he listens to you, you have won your brother. But if he won't listen, take one or two more with you, so that by the testimony of two or three witnesses every fact may be established. If he pays no attention to them, tell the church. But if he doesn't pay attention even to the church, let him be like an unbeliever and a tax collector to you.

While I wanted the doctor to remove the cancerous cells, I also wanted him to leave the healthy ones alone. Unfortunately, when people view conflict in black and white, lines between the two can blur, especially since people instinctively reach for a white hat for those who agree with them and a black hat for those who do not. It is possible to misdiagnose a situation and hurt innocent people.

Some sick people in the world want to harm others. Sometimes the harm they intend is physical; but more often than not, it is emotional. I am not minimizing this reality, but I also want to underscore it is not always the case. Mislabeling people and then assigning them a black hat can block the ability to solve the problem at hand, which can lead to conflict escalation and contribute to an unhealthy, volatile environment. If people are antagonists, put the black hat on them and discipline them. If they are not antagonists, however, and if they are simply sinners in need of God's grace, then treat them gracefully.

Sinners in Need of God's Grace

In *Firestorm* Ron Susek writes, "It's all too easy to assume that someone who intensely disagrees with you is either dead wrong at best, or demon-possessed at worst. Be sure that the person is clearly sinning before God and not merely engaging in valid disagreement. What is the difference?

Valid disagreement is negotiable. People resolve issues, even at personal loss, for the sake of Christ."[9] In valid disagreements, both sides should attack the problem, not one another. Unfortunately, when under attack, the natural thing to do is to revert to fight-or-flight survival tactics.[10]

The good- and bad-guy labeling also ignores a basic theological reality—a fallen nature exists in all Christians. At our best, we are sinners saved by grace. Putting a black hat on one group of Christians and white hats on another ignores our shared status as saved sinners who continue to have the capacity to sin. Instead of accepting some blame for the misunderstanding or miscommunication, those Christians assigned white hats ignore their own sinfulness and the ongoing process of grace in the lives of those assigned black hats. Rarely is there a situation where one group is right and another group is wrong. However, the unhealthy, volatile environment breeds dichotomous thinking. There are no shades of gray—only black and white, good and evil, right and wrong. After a while, dichotomous states become unchangeable states, leading to negative sentiment override (chap. 4). When these states become unchangeable, the chances of reconciliation diminish. Unfortunately, both leaders and others, no matter the color of hat, can enter into negative sentiment override.

There is a better way to view conflict: switch to seeing it in high-definition with a full-color spectrum.

---

9   Susek, *Firestorm*, 158.

10   For a discussion on fight or flight survival tactics, see Changing Minds, "Fight-Or-Flight Reaction" *Brain*, Explanations, accessed September 9, 2011, http://changingminds.org/explanations/brain/fight_flight.htm.

Chapter 11 Leading Using a Systems Approach

There is a high-definition, full-color spectrum alternative to viewing conflict in black and white. Picture yourself on vacation, sitting at a bistro table enjoying a cup of coffee on sunny afternoon. A man walking towards you is struggling to maintain his equilibrium. Then he bumps a nearby table and falls to the ground. Is he drunk? Does he have vertigo? Unless there is a medical condition that you do not know about, you are sure you can get out the black hat, right?

These assumptions are reasonable, but I failed to mention the bistro table sits the deck of a ship experiencing rough waters. Certainly, the man might have been drunk, he could have had vertigo and tripped over something, but chances are he lost his balance because the ship was tossing in the waves. In other words, there is a systemic causation. Systems theory is a look at what is happening around a person to understand behavior. It aids in understanding and explaining the dynamics of people's reactions to one another and their behaviors.

George Parsons and Speed Leas write, "A systems approach to organizational problems does not deny that difficulties can be caused by individuals and/or by problems the organization needs to address, but it also observes the reactive patterns or non-conscious agreements or understandings that people have about how they are supposed to act or how to get along."[1]

Leaders can never afford to view conflict in exclusive black and white and ignore what is happening in the emotional system of their organization. Steinke[2]

---

1   Parsons and Leas, *Understanding Your Congregation*, 5.

2   Steinke, "Addressing Anxiety in Congregations." Steinke is a family therapist and a Lutheran minister who served in the parish for fifteen years and served as a therapist for Lutheran clergy for fourteen years. For nine years, he led a program that promoted healthy congregations. Currently he works with congregations in conflict. Steinke studied with Friedman for nine years. He has authored nine books, three of them, including *How Your Church Family Works: Understanding Congregations as Emotional Systems*, which deals with emotional processes in the local church.

says, "The church is more than its emotional processes, but it is never less than these processes."[3]

Systems theory shifts the focus away from a person back to the problem. It is a perspective that helps leaders understand what is happening in their organization so they can limit their reactivity and distraction to keep their organization working the mission.

The systems approach began in the field of psychiatry, later becoming interdisciplinary. Murray Bowen (1913–1990) pioneered the systems theory approach that bears his name to understand human behavior. Instead of exclusively searching the patient's past to understand his or her behavior (psychoanalysis), Bowen suggested therapists could find clues by examining the family system.[4] It is a unique way to approach family counseling. For instance, instead of focusing on the "rebellious teenager," Bowen Theory practitioners look at the behavior of those in the entire system against whom the rebellious teenager might be reacting. Bowen Theory is not an attempt to excuse behavior, nor condemn it. Rather, it tries to explain it and empower others in the system not to make matters worse by reacting to it.

Edwin Friedman (1931–1996) introduced systems theory into congregational life. He was a licensed family therapist who studied twenty years with Bowen and used his theory to promote health in his clients. He was also a rabbi and used it to lead his congregation. His book *Generation to Generation: Family Process in Church and Synagogue* is a watershed work that equips a minister to use a systems approach to counseling. It also includes a section on leadership, which he later expanded in *A Failure of Nerve: Leadership in the Age of the Quick Fix.*

Key Concepts

It would be easy to interpret Inland community's story by labeling Bob a bad person, Neighbour a victim, and McManus a hero. At some level, there is justification for those labels. After all, Bob did betray Neighbour's friendship and said some horrible things to him; Neighbour certainly did not deserve the abuse he took and the suffering he experienced; and

---

3   Steinke, *How Your Church Family Works*, x.

4   "History of the Center," The Bowen Center, accessed May, 10, 2011, http://www .thebowencenter.org/about/history-of-the-center.

McManus did lead Mosaic to do some extraordinary things for Neighbour, his family, and his church. However, that simplistic analysis fails to identify what happened systemically. Before putting a black hat on Bob and allowing Neighbour to ride into the sunset wearing a white one, it is helpful to consider some key concepts in systems theory and to reflect on his story systemically.

Bowen Theory has several key survival strategies people use when an event introduces stress, trauma, or anxiety to an emotional system. The overarching survival goal is both to keep the group together and to fight it from changing into something else.

Emotional Triangles

"If I Can Shift Some of Our Tension to Someone Else, We Can Be Closer"

Stools come in two versions, three legged, and four legged. There are no two-legged stools because they would not have enough stability to handle people shifting their weight. For one-on-one relationships to be stable, they need a third leg so tension can shift without being overwhelming. For instance, whenever you have a conflict at work, you likely will talk to a friend about it. Getting the problem "off your chest" not only feels better, but it is also a mechanism to get feedback about your own culpability. If you have a healthy friendship, your friend will not only listen, but also offer some perspective and advice.

When we triangulate, we often seek out people who will take some of our stress from us, or who will go and fight the battle on our behalf. Friedman writes, "The basic law of emotional triangles is that when any two parts of a system become uncomfortable with one another, they will 'triangle in' or focus upon a third person, or issue, as a way of stabilizing their own relationship with one another."[5] There are several common triangulating strategies.

"Let's You and Him Fight"

In the classic sense, "Let's you and him fight" is an invitation for two suitors to duel for the affection of a woman.[6] However, a variation of this

---

5   Friedman, *Generation to Generation*, 35.
6   Berne, *Games People Play*, 124.

form of triangulation takes place anytime one person (instigation position) influences a friend (squeezed position) to fight on his or her behalf with a mutual friend (target position).

Authority figures can easily find themselves in the squeezed position in this emotional triangle. Police officers, for example, have to come between couples in domestic disputes. In these situations, the violent actions often shift from the victim to the officer.[7] In the squeezed position, a leader may be flattered when asked to arbitrate a dispute between two friends in an emotional triangle; however, it can be unpredictable. Instead of fighting other people's fights, it might be wise to encourage them to work it out themselves when possible, or at least, become a true arbitrator and meet with both people in the room.

Triangulation can also cause the person in the squeezed position to be an anxiety receptor. Steinke says, "Triangulation is a natural way of handling anxiety. If anxiety in one relationship is not resolved, it will be played out in another relationship. A person feels relief from tension when anxiety is shifted to a third party, yet the anxiety in the original relationship is unchanged. It has been merely relocated."[8] It is easy for a pastor to become an anxiety sponge, soaking in other people's stress.

"People Are Saying . . ."

Some leaders find themselves in the target position of an emotional triangle when a person in the squeezed position comes representing the views of a number of anonymous people. One way to handle that situation is to only deal with the views that the person in the squeezed position can personally validate. On one occasion, I was speaking to a person who was representing a group of others who had a complaint against me. I asked her specifically for the name of the person who instigated the complaint, and to my surprise, she told me the name. I picked up the phone and called the person with the complaint, closed the triangle, and was able to satisfy the person in the instigation position. It also stopped the instigator from sending anyone else to my office with her complaints.

---

7   An editorial for *The Daily Courier* begins, "Ask the question and many, if not all, law enforcement officers will tell you they fear 'domestic violence in progress' calls far more than rushing off to thwart, say, a robber holding up a bank." Editorial, *The Daily Courier*, March, 18, 2011.

8   Steinke, *Healthy Congregations*, 66.

"Can You Pass This Along for Me?"

Do you remember sitting in a high school class and a classmate asks you to pass a note to someone else? Your friend needed your help because his or her arms could not reach the target of the note. The practice continues in adulthood even though physical distance is not an impediment. An instigator will put you in the squeezed position to pass information along to a target to imply tacit support on your part, or to filter or soften the reaction of the target. For instance, I often ask my wife to communicate something to our children. Because she has a softer approach, she can deliver the same information but do it in a less threatening way. We have also discovered over the years that our boys will open up to her more than they do me probably because I served as the primary disciplinarian and she was the primary caregiver in our family system. The reverberation of past roles colors current communications, so Susan is often a go-between in our family dynamics.

Unfortunately, I sometimes ask Susan to be a go-between in our other relationships. I ask her to call my mom or one of our friends to communicate something. Sometimes, she boldly tells me to call them myself; she grows tired of being in the squeezed position, especially when I place her there out of my own laziness.

"Whose Side Are You On?"

Children of divorced parents know the pressure from mom and dad to take sides in the divorce. So do church leaders. Whenever there is a high-intensity conflict going on, people often expect pastors to assign the black-and-white hats and throw in with one side or the other. It is difficult to maintain a neutral position when two friends or colleagues are fighting, but unless leaders do, they automatically alienate one side and make it difficult to lead. It may be the conflict intensity has reached such a fevered pitch it is impossible to maintain a neutral position,[9] but at healthy intensities of conflict, it is not only possible but also necessary.

---

9   Bullard, *Every Congregation Needs a Little Conflict*, 68–82. This is the fifth of seven intensities in Bullard's model. It is unhealthy, destructive conflict.

Groupthink: "We Must Agree to Remain Together"

In Hans Christian Andersen's fairy tale *The Emperor's New Clothes,* the townspeople praised the emperor's new clothes made from cloth that the designers said stupid people could not see. Of course, the emperor and the townspeople would not admit that they could not see the garment because that would insinuate their stupidity. Instead, the group praised the beautiful garment that did not exist and the emperor paraded around town in his birthday suit. Then a little boy spoke the truth: the emperor had no clothes. Before long, everyone agreed. Everyone, that is, except for the emperor who would not admit his mistake.[10] The townspeople and the emperor were involved in groupthink (aka herding). The little boy who spoke up was not.

Groupthink is common. Decades of psychological research have revealed that people tend to go along with the majority view even if that view is objectively incorrect. A study published in the journal *Neuron* uses brain imaging to support those beliefs. The research involving 222 participants found that when people hold an opinion differing from others in a group, their brains produce the equivalent of an error message that makes them think they are too different. When participants learned their rating in an objective test differed from a group average, individuals tended to move their thinking to be more in line with the average.

Commenting on the research, Gregory Berna, professor of psychiatry and behavioral sciences at Emory University of Medicine in Atlanta, said that "the two leading theories of conformity state that people tend to look to the group when they are not sure what to do, or when they are afraid of being different." The research found mechanisms associated with fear and anxiety play a role when a person feels their opinion goes against the grain. Berna says, "Brain images indicate participants were not just being deceptive to fit in; instead, they suggest group opinion actually changed participants' perceptions. Further, conformity is good in terms of survival, because there is an advantage to being in a community." He adds, "Our brains are exquisitely tuned to what other people think about us, aligning our judgments to fit in with the group."[11]

Groupthink happens in nature as a survival mechanism. A buffalo hears

---

10   Andersen, *The Emperor's New Clothes.*

11   Elizabeth Landau, "Why So Many Think Alike," CNN, last updated January 15, 2009, http://www.cnn.com/2009/HEALTH/01/15/social.conformity.brain.

a rattlesnake and flees; others in the herd follow at a run. The herd is not running from the rattlesnake, they did not hear it. Rather, they ran because other buffalos were running. When there is legitimate danger, herding protects the group. The problem comes when there is no danger; rather, it is a maladjusted person who is upsetting the group's equilibrium. Now do not reach for the black hat too quickly. Just because people are maladjusted does not mean that they are evil or sinful. The emperor was neither of those things in the fable. He was just wrong.

The herding instinct can work against church health. Leaders can give in to the need to fit in and fail to make a stand contrary to what a maladjusted person is taking and the group is affirming. When this happens, the leader is relinquishing leadership control to an unstable person.

One striking example of groupthink at Inland Community was when Neighbour missed the warning signs his executive pastor was running over people, focusing instead on his productivity. It took a wake-up call from his son to alert him to the problem. In an emotional system, group-think is one way to insure togetherness, but in this case it actually was separating people.

Later in Inland Community's story, the elder board was stuck. They could not give up on the building dream. They could not support the merger with Mosaic even when it was the last and best hope. Unfortu-nately, the need for togetherness blocked seeing creative solutions even when Neighbour, by this time a self-differentiated leader, was finding them. The problem with groupthink is that it abolishes creativity. In an atmosphere where everyone is going along with the group, no one can find a creative solution to the problems of the group and they become stuck.

It is easy to interpret silence as betrayal or cowardice when someone in the group will not come to your aid in the midst of a disagreement. It might not be either of those things; it could just groupthink in action. Neighbour demonstrated wisdom in giving the elders time to decide and superior leadership by asking, "Do you want to continue on as an elder where you will personally be financially liable for whatever happens here?" He called it playing hardball. I just see it as healthy, self-differentiated leadership. He worked past his need to fit into the group and assisted them in seeing reality as it was and as it could be.

The group does not always listen to those who pull out of groupthink and declare the emperor has no clothes. Sometimes the group maligns them and that is where the rub lies. Instinctively, people want to be part of the group and fear others' view them as part of the problem when they make a contrary stand, rather than just pointing out the problem. In a black-and-white world, it does not matter what color hat you think you wear — it is the black or white color the group assigns you that counts.

Scapegoating: "If We Blame One of Us, the Rest of Us Can Stay Together"

A polar opposite reaction to herding is scapegoating (aka cut off), yet it has the same goal, which is homeostasis, that is, to keep the group functioning the same. This strategy avoids group bifurcation by sacrificing a member of the group. They blame him or her for the problem, and then cut him or her off from the organization in order to maintain togetherness. On this surface, this sounds reasonable — run off the troublemaker and the problem will go away.

Scapegoating is why Bob sent Neighbour that horrible email. He needed someone to blame for the turmoil in the group. Moreover, the blame usually flows to the most vulnerable or powerful person in the organization. Steinke writes,

> When anxiety ushers in its relatives — anger, anguish, and grief — the temptation to scapegoat is strong. Scapegoating is an attempt to pinpoint a culprit or to find fault with someone. The blame throwers at first will hurl charges indiscriminately at any target. Most likely, however, anxiety will be projected onto people in the most responsible or the most vulnerable positions in the congregation.[12]

In this case, Neighbour was both powerful and vulnerable. His power is self-evident — he was the founding pastor of the church. His vulnerability came from the church's decline and his daughter's illness. No doubt, he was down and Bob kicked him square in his vulnerability.

However, just as not every rattle is a rattlesnake, not every person who alerts an organization to trouble is a troublemaker. It could be that troublemakers are just an early warning system, so to speak. They may not be the problem; they may just be alerting the system to the problem. Those who view life through black-and-white lenses fall prey to this behavior — the act

---

12   Steinke, *Congregational Leadership*, 13.

of assigning black hats is a precursor to scapegoating. Neighbour was not the problem. The church needed his steady hand at the helm.

Scapegoating is different from church discipline. As mentioned in chapter 10, if a person is unregulated and invasive, or not respecting appropriate boundaries, they must come under church discipline. The church did not scapegoat the executive pastor, who embezzled funds; they disciplined him. The same is true of the youth pastor and elder, who acted inappropriately with minors. Since their actions were invasive (not to mention illegal), the church had no choice but to discipline them.

Underfunctioning: "If I Don't Manage Myself or My Responsibilities Well, Someone Else Will, Insuring Our Closeness"

Long before people resign from a position of leadership, people will usually pull back. Their attendance gets shaky, their giving decreases, and they are just generally less reliable. A leader cannot ignore these warning signals. When stress is piling up in an emotional system, some people need to back away (distancing) to regain equilibrium. Underfunctioning is never less than this, but it usually is more. It is a shifting of responsibilities without negotiation.

Underfunctioners are not trying to distance themselves from the group. It is a dance of sorts—a play for attention. Unfortunately, it changes the whole leadership dynamic of the organization. It puts the underfunctioner in the lead and the leader reacting to the problems he or she creates, enabling the underfunctioning and hurting the organization. Before long, the leader stops working the mission and casting a vision and is constantly occupied with the counter move to the underfunctioner's behavior.

A healthy leader will not give in to the temptation to rescue the organization from the consequences of irresponsible behavior. To do so would result in a combustible reactive environment, not stability. Steinke says,

> Certainly, we are to turn the other cheek, to walk the second mile, and to forgive our offenders seven times seventy. But we are encouraged to do "the Christian thing" to advance mutuality, not to abolish it. Our goal is to restore relationships, not to reinforce sulking, irritable, stubborn, even brutish behaviors. There is a world of difference between extending the hand of generosity and enabling reactive processes.[13]

---

13   Steinke, *How Your Church Family Works*, 59.

There is a difference between practicing the Golden Rule (Matt. 7:12), helping people in need (chap. 4), and perpetuating neediness. Colleen Barrett, president emeritus of Southwest Airlines says, "I demonstrate love as patience when helping people who are down on their luck by showing them that I care about their problems. I want to help them rebuild their self-confidence so that they can, in turn, do the same for someone else who needs help in the future."[14]

One of Barrett's hallmarks is her insistence on Golden Rule behavior at her company. She does more than assist people down on their luck — she also attempts "to help them rebuild their self-confidence." Instead of merely meeting the presenting need, she bolsters confidence. She does this, not just to meet the need, but so that the person she is helping can help others. Not only does she not perpetuate neediness, she empowers others to meet needs she has yet to encounter.

Overfunctioning: "If I Rescue the Group from the Consequences of an Underfunctioner's Failure, We Can Stay Together"

One of the easiest traps for a leader to fall into is to begin overfunctioning to compensate for the underfunctioning of others. A pop psychology term for this is "co-dependency"—the attempt of a responsible person to fix the problems created by an irresponsible person's behavior.

Sometimes a leader overfunctions to compensate for another person's underfunctioning, other times the leader overfunctions because of an intrinsic need to rescue others.

Because Christian leaders are often compassionate, it is easy for them to fall into this trap. They attempt to help, but there can be unintended consequences — they may create an environment for the irresponsible behavior to continue, or worse yet, they can end up hurting others in an attempt to rescue the person underfunctioning.

In 1988 King Rama IX of Thailand performed an exceptional act of grace on his sixtieth birthday that had unintended consequences. He granted amnesty to over thirty thousand prisoners, releasing them from jail. His intent was to be gracious, but removing discipline from these criminals did not turn out very well for his country. Up until then, AIDS was not a problem among the public but was rampant in the prison system.

---

14   Blanchard and Barrett, *Lead with LUV*, 107.

Thailand is infamous for its sex trade and it did not take long for the prisoners to find the prostitutes, who became HIV-positive and spread the disease to straying men who gave it to their wives who spread it to their newborn children. Within five years, an estimated one million people living in Thailand were HIV-positive. All because a king overfunctioned on his sixtieth birthday.[15]

Henry Cloud and John Townsend say, "Rescuing a person from the natural consequences of his behavior enables him to continue in irresponsible behavior. God did not repeal the law of sowing and reaping. It is still operating. But the doer is not suffering the consequences; someone else is."[16] That is exactly what happened to the prisoners. King Rama IX removed the consequences for their behavior, which resulted to innocent children contracting AIDS. Overfunctioning does more than just enable irresponsibility; it leaves the underfunctioner powerless to change.[17]

The overfunctioner also suffers. This pattern robs the overfunctioner of spiritual vitality. Friedman says, "One of the subtlest yet most fundamental effects of overfunctioning is spiritual. It destroys the spiritual quality of the overfunctioner. Several ministers and rabbis have reported after switching professions: 'Now I can go back to being a good Christian/Jew: now I can enjoy prayers and the Holy Days again.'"[18]

Distancing: "When I'm Overwhelmed, I Back Away
Emotionally So I Can Stay Connected with the Group"

Once you have allocated the black-and-white hats, it is difficult to want to maintain an emotional closeness to those wearing black. The natural tendency is to keep a safe distance. This, however, can intensify the negative behavior. Friedman says, "Criticism is a form of pursuit."[19] He states that "the most intensely negative members of a congregational family were as invested personally in their spiritual leaders as those who were most

15   Patterson, et al., *Influencer*, 26.
16   Cloud and Townsend, *Boundaries*, 87.
17   Ibid., 43: "To rescue people from the natural consequences of their behavior is to render them powerless."
18   Friedman, *Generation to Generation*, 212.
19   Ibid., 264.

positive to him."[20] In other words, just as children can misbehave to get their parent's attention, members of churches may be critical of you because they want you to take notice.[21]

At one point during the conflict at Inland Community, Neighbour began to distance himself from others in the church. Like a turtle's head retracting into its shell, Neighbour protected himself from the pain by taking a step back. He arrived late and left early from the worship services, which was atypical behavior for him. Neighbour is a warm, caring person who thrives in a crowd of people. He gains energy from a crowd; it does not tax him at all. You cannot explain his behavior as a character flaw or a change in his personality; it was a survival mechanism in reaction to the anxiety in the church's emotional system.

Fusion: "To Experience Closeness, I Immerse Myself in the Group"

There is a danger that loving, empathetic pastors lose themselves in the emotional systems they lead. They become "fused" with the people or the organization itself. Some pastor's families have felt an emotional triangle between the pastor, the organization, and the family, and they sense that the pastor's first love is the organization. This happens when the leader fuses with the organization. Fusion occurs when leaders are absorbed into the organizations they lead and the lines between me and we are blurred.[22] In effect, there becomes so much "we" that there is no longer a "me."

In a state of fusion with an organization, leaders lose the capacity to lead. They lose objectivity and lack the capacity to take a stand apart from groupthink. Beyond that, they lose the ability to remain calm and take on the anxiety of the group. Steinke says, "But how can anyone function effectively as a leader if his or her anxiety is at the same level of those being lead?"[23]

This situation is not either-or since there is a scale of differentiation. In other words, people are rarely completely fused or completely

---

20 Ibid.

21 I am not insinuating that your critics are children; rather, those under authority often pursue those in authority with criticism.

22 Steinke, *Congregational Leadership*, 144.

23 Steinke, *Church Family Works*, 110.

differentiated.[24] The goal is to be differentiated enough to have the capacity to lead in an objective, calm manner.

Neighbour showed signs of fusion with the church's emotional system. He lost the ability to view himself apart from the church itself. When things were not going well at the church, nothing else in his life was either. He could not sleep at night because of the church. He had strained relationships at home because of the church. He felt like a failure because of the church. How things were going at church became a filter for his entire life. He related to the captain in the movie *The Perfect Storm*, who chained himself to the helm of the ship. He was willing to go down with the ship.

Self-Differentiation: "Remaining Me and Still Be in a Relationship with the Group"

The opposite of fusion is self-differentiation, which is the ability to stay connected while remaining independent from the emotional system. Friedman says,

> Differentiation means the capacity of a family member to define his or her own life's goals and values apart from surrounding togetherness pressures, to say 'I' when others are demanding 'you' and 'we.' It includes the capacity to maintain a (relatively) non-anxious presence in the midst of anxious systems, to take maximum responsibility for one's own destiny and emotional being. . . . Differentiation means the capacity to be an 'I' while remaining connected.[25]

Differentiation is about proper balance between autonomy and connectedness. In fusion, a leader loses self in the group. In differentiation, a leader maintains self so he or she can properly lead the group. Scazzero writes, "Differentiation involves the ability to hold on to who you are and who you are not. The degree to which you are able to affirm your distinct values and goals apart from the pressures around you (separateness) while remaining close to people important to you (togetherness) helps determine your level of differentiation."[26]

A turning point in Neighbour's story is the drive he took with his wife

---

24   Gilbert, *Eight Concepts*, 31.
25   Friedman, *Generation to Generation*, 27.
26   Scazzero, *Emotionally Healthy Spirituality*, 82.

to Diamond Bar to overlook the valley he served. Physically, he got perspective — he could see everywhere — but he also got emotional perspective and with it. He recognized his existence as a unique person apart from the church. The moment he was willing to give it up, he became qualified to lead it again.

Health Returns

"For me, church is fun again. This is an exciting place to come — people want to bring their friends. There is a much different ethos in our gatherings." Neighbour says, "We are seeing people coming to Christ, and we are seeing leaders birthing new ministries."

"I don't want to give the impression that it's been easy." Neighbour says, "It hasn't. Not for either side. Mosaic paid off a $650,000 second mortgage on our building program that we completed within a year of the transition. This mortgage on the inherited property continues to be a tremendous burden during the economic downturn."

Many of the people they reached over the years decided that Mosaic Inland is not their idea of church and have moved on. In other words, the transition did not make the church conflict free (remember: conflict is the ministry environment for pastors). The church may still have conflict and problems, but they have reduced their reactivity and are ministering to one another in grace — something that is much easier to do when people are not insisting on everyone either wearing a black or white hat.

LEADING IN SEASONS OF CONFLICT

If there were no conflict, leaders would be less necessary. History judges Abraham Lincoln among the most respected presidents of the United States due in large part to his extraordinary leadership during a time of great conflict. Without the context of the Civil War, history may never have known the full measure of his leadership. We know of Lincoln's character and leadership abilities, due in large part to conflict.

Seasons of conflict reveal a leaders' true character. Since conflict is inevitably a part of every ministry, churches then need leaders with "above reproach" characteristics (chap. 1). Those pastors can lead during seasons of conflict if they stay connected, remain calm, avoiding reactive behavior, and prepare for sabotage.[27]

Stay Connected

Staying connected is essential in caring for hurtful people (chap. 4) and teaching in conflict situations (chap. 9), but it is also necessary for leading in seasons of conflict, anxiety, or transition. A natural gravitational pull separates leaders from people who are energy leaks, difficult to be around, pessimistic, unbalanced, or unsupportive, which results in a tendency for leaders to engage in distancing (see prior section of this chapter). However, it is essential to stay connected with everyone, during seasons of conflict, anxiety, or transition.

Public Communication

One way to stay in touch is to communicate in public meetings. In the absence of information, people will usually think the worse. While the people may not be entitled to confidential information about leadership discussions, they to have the right to know the criteria and processes leaders are using to make decisions. Most people are willing to wait for information if they have confidence that leadership will communicate decisions when leaders make them.

Neighbor did this well with the staff dismissals. While he was not free to publish the personnel files on each staff member, he did notify the congregation about the severances as soon as they happened. The operational principle is this: *while discussions are confidential, decisions are not.* And leaders should make them public as soon as possible.

Public Forums

Communication is never one directional. While it is important to keep the congregation informed about decisions, it is equally important to solicit their feedback. In one church I served, we closed the monthly business meetings sessions with a public comments time. During this agenda item, any member of the church could give a public commendation or

---

27   Friedman, *Generation to Generation*, 220–49.

air a complaint. I suspect some readers are asking right now, "You did what?" Yes, we gave a time for any appropriate public comments. It never turned ugly.

A few years ago, I served Valencia Hills Community Church, a church going through a difficult time, as their transitional pastor. Their average attendance had plummeted from over a thousand to fewer than four hundred in a period of two years, including many of their staff members and founding pastor. I came in on a six-month contract to help them navigate through this season of high anxiety and uncertainty.[28] One of the things we did in the opening months was open up feedback lines. We hosted several town-hall meetings where I listened to the concerns, hopes, and dreams of the people. Staff members took notes and I circulated a "Did I hear you right?" questionnaire during the weekend services where participants could provide a 1-5 scale on the questionnaire statements to enhance the feedback loop.

At first, some on the leadership team asked me not to have the meetings, thinking they could become volatile. However, I felt transparency was especially important because of the anxious environment. Please note: I did not listen and ignore what I heard. I listened, made sure I was hearing them correctly, and then considered their feedback as I led the church through the anxiety back to focusing on their mission.

Disagreement was okay. People did not have to agree with me and I did not have to agree with them.[29] What was important was that we communicated in a respectful way and worked out a strategy for the future.

Personal Touch

At the request of the staff member who led the First Impressions Team at this church, I stood at the back during the beginning of the service as people entered the gymnasium.[30] I had never done that any other place I had served—I always sat at the front through the entire worship service. It was important to mix with the people as they arrived. In true Southern

---

28   After the six-month period, the administration of the church extended the contract for me to serve until a new pastor was called.

29   Scazzero, *Emotionally Healthy Spirituality*, 82. "I may not agree with you or you with me. Yet I can remain in relationship with you. I don't have to detach from you, reject you, avoid you, or criticize you to validate myself. I can be myself apart from you."

30   This church rented a school gym.

California fashion, many people arrived as the service was underway. So I was at the back to greet them when they did. I hugged them, welcomed them, had private conversations with some, and prayed with others. It was important way to stay connected.

I also came into town a day early and stayed in a hotel so I could be available to visit with the people on Saturdays. It would have been more cost-efficient and less physically draining to preach on Sundays, hold staff meetings on Mondays, and then return to my duties at the seminary during the week. But because of the circumstances, I knew it was important to stay connected with the people in informal settings.

Remain Calm

If leaders feel threatened by the anxiety and reactivity of others, they may fall into a reactivity trap, responding from the lower-brain functions. While these functions are necessary in situations requiring fight-or-flight reactions, they are not useful in situations requiring a thoughtful response (see discussion of de-escalation and maintaining self-control in chap. 4). Cool heads need to prevail, especially when everything around a leader is falling apart.

In *Decision Points* George W. Bush writes, "The first step of any successful crisis response is to project calm."[31] It is impossible to lead anxious people if caught up in the anxiety.[32]

There is a temptation to fuse with the anxiety in the emotional system, empathize with the most unregulated and anxious people, and add fuel to the combustible environment. If pastors make a commitment to care for the hurtful (chap. 4), teach in conflict situations (chap. 9), and stay connected, they will find themselves in regular contact with anxious people. If pastors succumb to the empathy temptation and become anxious themselves, the congregation has no one to keep the organization on mission. But if they show compassion, instead of empathy, they will be able to resist becoming an anxiety receptor and spreading anxiety throughout the entire organization.

In her book *The Eight Concepts of Bowen Theory*, Roberta Gilbert writes,

---

31   Bush, *Decision Points*, 129.

32   Steinke, *How your Church Family Works*, 110: "But how can anyone function effectively as a leader if his or her anxiety is at the same level of those being led?"

As we have examined the various concepts of Bowen Theory, it is rather apparent that the way out of many of the dilemmas people face in their systems is for one person to calm his or her emotional reactiveness, start to think systems, and step out of the patterned positions (and thus the togetherness), taking a position based on principle. This is a step up for self, and as it turns out, for the whole system, for when one can go to a better level of functioning, significant others will follow.[33]

Calm leaders can cast a vision, reactive ones cannot. Once leaders lose self-control, or relinquish control to group think, they cannot lead the organization they serve. The presence of a calm leader gives people hope for the future. Calm can spread as fast as anxiety.[34]

The Scripture provides guidance for dealing with anxiety. We are to cast our cares on God, who cares for us (Ps. 55:22; 1 Peter 5:6–7) and avoid worrying (Luke 21:34; Phil. 4:6–7; Matt. 6:25–31). It is a matter of trust. Pastors can trust that God will take care of them, even in the midst of anxious times. If they cast their problems on the Lord, they are in a better position to lead the church to accomplish its mission.

A few months into the Valencia Hills pastorate, at the prompting of a church member, I led the church in an aggressive evangelism strategy. At first, I resisted. While I had always been an evangelistic pastor, I saw my role in this church as being a stabilizer with a responsibility of preparing the church for the future, not an evangelist. However, this concerned church member reminded me that God had not removed the requirement for the church to fulfill the Great Commission just because of its problems.

I did something I had never done before. I went public with an evangelistic goal. One Sunday I announced to the church, "Between now and the time our new pastor comes, we will baptize forty people."[35] The church returned to working its mission, refusing to let the anxiety keep them

---

33 Gilbert, *Eight Concepts*, 111.

34 Steinke, *Congregational Leadership*, 134: "Self-management is critical, even more so in the boat-rocking times. Your calm, reflective, and principle-based action can be as infectious as anxiety. While anxiety spreads fast, the effects of a thoughtful approach are slower but eventually more effective and beneficial."

35 Forty was not a random number. Before setting it, I called Dr. Randy McWhorter, the leader of the Healthy Church Group of California Southern Baptists to get a definition of an evangelistic church. He told me that he considered a church evangelistic if they baptized 10 percent of their average attendance.

from being who they are at the core, that is, a church who cares about people's souls and a church founded to reach people that other churches were not reaching.

Two things happened over the next nine months that are noteworthy. First, much of the anxiety abated and the emotional system of the church calmed down. Second, the very Sunday Pastor Dennis preached in view of a call, we baptized the fortieth person. Remain calm and work the mission. There is never a time a church can afford to ignore the Great Commission and the Great Commandment. They must work their mission, even during difficult trying times. The first-century church did not let difficult days derail their mission. Nothing can hinder the gospel.[36]

Lead during Sabotage

Staying connecting and remaining calm are both important, but there is a third key to leading during anxious times: prepare for and be ready to deal with sabotage.[37] Expect it. It is not personal. People do not sabotage you because they do not like you; it is because they don't like change. Even if they want the change, they prefer things to remain as they are.

Friedman writes, "People choose leaders because they promise to lead them to a happier or more fruitful state, but after the election, the followers invariably function, either individually or in concert, to frustrate their leaders' efforts."[38] Sabotage was at the core of most of the conflicts Jesus had with those who supported him (Mark 3:20–21; 8:31–33; 14:3–9, 10–25, 42–50). Whether they were saying He was "losing His mind" because of His mission focus, rebuking Him for His insistence that He would die, or the betrayal, those close to Jesus attempted to sabotage Him.

When people are attempting to sabotage the mission, leaders should not capitulate or compromise.[39] The pastor cannot tolerate mission creep, a gradual shift in emphasis or objectives, not even in an attempt to exercise

---

36   Stagg, *The Book of Acts.*

37   Friedman, *Generation to Generation*, 230.

38   Ibid., 224.

39   Ibid., 204: "Whenever I saw one of the members who had been most critical of my functioning at a congregational gathering, I went out of my way to express precisely those positions in which I believed most strongly and with which he or she most disagreed. I did not do it in pointed ways but always as a self-expression of my own views on life."

kindness.[40] There is a time to care for hurtful people (chap. 4) and teach in the midst of conflict (chap. 9), but there is also a time to provide steady leadership when the mission is in jeopardy.

Expect it. Sabotage comes in response to wanting togetherness and things to stay the same. It is possible for pastors to lead their congregations to change, even though people naturally resist it and will attempt to frustrate their leaders who attempt change. It requires the ability to define reality, discover a preferred future, and develop a change strategy to move the current reality into the preferred future.

---

40   Steinke, *Congregational Leadership*, 121: "Resistance, leaders must remember, is part of the leadership process. Too many leaders retreat or capitulate when resistance becomes loud, rude, and messy, because the unspoken rule is 'so as not to upset anyone.' Leaders become pleasers. In return for the pleasing they escape hostilities."

Chapter 12 Leading the Church to Change

Yes, it is hard to change. Yet at the same time, it is impossible not to change. Positive change is hard. There is a constant gravitational pull towards homeostasis—a desire for things to stay the same. This is true in relationships[1] and in congregations.[2] Homeostasis is a stabilizing force; it would be as difficult to navigate life without homeostasis, as it would be to walk around without gravity.

Negative change is easy. It occurs without any effort. For instance, without maintenance, the most manicured lawn on the block will deteriorate into a weed patch. Negative change also occurs when people resist positive change. The attempt to resist change can cause them to change to become an angry, tense, perhaps even a more fearful person.[3] The leadership challenge is to manage the change process to achieve positive outcomes.

THE CHANGE PROCESS

Personal Change

In many ways, Liz Murray raised herself. Though she lived with her drug-addicted parents in New York, she and her sister were on their own from

---

1   Flanagan and Hall, *Christianity and Developmental Psychopathology*, 357: "Homeostasis refers to a process of self-regulation within a system with a goal of maintaining stability in that system. When applied to family systems, *family homeostasis* helps to explain the tendency of families to resist change and maintain a certain balance of functioning."

2   Friedman, *Generation to Generation*, 28.

3   Sweet and McClaren, *"A" Is for Abductive*, 175: "If you resist change you will change. Your act of resistance to change will change you—into an increasingly resistant person, a tenser person, an angrier or sadder or more combative person. The change you were resisting may have been bad. But the change in you may be worse."

a very young age. Her father was a gifted and intelligent man, but lived a diminished life because of drugs. Her mother, suffering from both addiction and mental illness, was content to live from one high to the next. She paid for her drugs with her government checks and prostitution.

What makes Murray's story remarkable is not her dire upbringing. Unfortunately, these stories are all too common. Her story is remarkable because she graduated from Harvard and authored *Breaking Night*, and she is the subject of a Lifetime movie *From Homeless to Harvard*.

As a child, Liz was bright and intelligent but rarely went to school. She opted to stay home with her mom, seeking love, acceptance, and approval. The only real education she had was from educational TV, game shows, and reading an old set of encyclopedias. At the end of each school year, she would begin attending, take the finals (and pass them), then be promoted to the next grade. That got her an eighth-grade education.

During her teenage years, she was either homeless, couch surfing at friend's houses, or living in low-rent hotels with Carlos, her boyfriend. Carlos turned out not to be her knight in shining armor. He was everything Liz hoped to get away from—he was a drug dealer with a short fuse. After reading a headline in the *New York Times* about a woman killed in her neighborhood, Murray realized the murder was the reason the police and ambulance were outside her building the night before. She writes, "Rosa Morilla, age thirty-nine, mother of five, had bled out on the floor of her room in the Holiday Motel, just three doors down from my room."[4] She knew it was time to get out. Murray borrowed a couple of quarters from the maid, called a friend to see if she could crash at her house, and left for good.

Murray defined reality, and she was not content for things to remain as they were. She had put her fate in the hands of a drug-dealing boyfriend to escape her drug-infested home life, and knew she had no future with Carlos. As a temporary measure, she bounced from one friend's house to another, but she knew she wanted more. She did not just want to survive; she wanted a life of her own and took responsibility for the change she wanted. In other words, she discovered her preferred future and took responsibility for it. She writes, "My friends weren't going to pay my rent."[5]

One night she stayed up and wrote two things of significance in her

---

4   Murray, *Breaking Night*, 238.
5   Ibid., 264.

journal. One was an assessment of her current academic situation (furthering her defined reality). Her academic standing looked bleak. She had no idea how many credits she would need to graduate, but she knew that at seventeen years old, she only had one academic credit and did not have a permanent address to use to enroll in school. Her reality was bleak, but the future was bright.

The other thing she wrote in her journal was a list of things to look forward to when she got her own place to live (she discovered a "preferred future"). She was looking forward to the day when she had privacy, could be warm, have plenty of food to eat, have her own bed, being able to sleep through the night, and take warm baths.[6]

Discovering the preferred future empowered Murray. She was not stuck. "If life could change for the worst . . . then maybe life could change for the better,"[7] she wrote. She had been discontent with the way things were, and she had excitement about how they could be. Murray had hope, but she needed a strategy.

Murray developed a strategic change plan to transform her current reality into her preferred future. She found a summer job that paid enough to support her needs and she located an alternative school where she could do four years' worth of schoolwork in two years. As she progressed through high school, it morphed into finding a way to get a college education. She had many obstacles along the way, but she was determined not to let them stop her.

Liz saw obstacles as signs that she was on the right track. Just as in the track and field event, hurdles are on the track, not in the grandstand.

> I pictured a runner running on a racetrack. The image was set in the summertime and the racetrack was a reddish orange, divided in white racing stripes to flag the runners' columns. Only, the runner in my mental image did not run alongside others; she ran solo, with no one watching her. And she did not run a free and clear track, she ran one that required her to jump numerous hurdles, which made her break into a heavy sweat under the sun. I used this image every time I thought of things that frustrated me: the heavy books, my crazy sleep schedule, the question of where I would sleep and what I would eat. To overcome these issues I pictured my runner bolting down the track, jumping hurdles toward

---

6   Ibid., 245.
7   Ibid., 251.

the finish line. Hunger, hurdle. Finding sleep, hurdle, schoolwork, hurdle. If I closed my eyes I could see the runner's back, the movement of her sinewy muscles, glistening with sweat, bounding over the hurdles, one by one. On mornings when I did not want to get out of bed, I saw another hurdle to leap over. This way, obstacles became a natural part of the course, an indication that I was right where I needed to be, running the track, which was entirely different from letting obstacles make me believe I was off it. On a racing track, why wouldn't there be hurdles? With this picture in mind—using the hurdles to leap forward toward my diploma—I shrugged the blanket off, went through the door, and got myself to school. That was at least half of my motivation on those tough mornings, and the other half was thinking about my teachers. In my weaker moments of blanket versus door, I knew Perry was waiting for me at school, and so were the other teachers that, much to my surprise, I came to love during my time at Prep.[8]

She did not let obstacles or discouragement get the best of her. Instead, she jumped over the hurdles and fought through discouragement. Liz had more than her share of obstacles. If the school ever discovered that she was homeless, they would have had to notify the authorities. So she had find a place to stay. Sometimes it was at a friend's house for part of the night, but she would have to leave before the parents woke up, sometimes it was under a stairway, and sometimes she rode the subway all night, getting what sleep she could. She needed her rest, since her strategy required that she do four years of school in two years.

She had obstacles, but she also had a compelling vision of a preferred future and a strategic change plan to leave her current reality. The difference between a dreamer and a visionary is the strategic change plan and the willingness to implement it no matter what.

In the end, every vision requires hard work. Murray writes, "For the first time I could really see there was no difference between myself and others; we were all just people. Just as there was no real difference between people who accomplished their goals and me, as long as I was willing to do the work and able to have some help along the way."[9]

---

8   Ibid., 282–83.
9   Ibid., 314.

Organizational Change

While leading a group to change involves more than undergoing personal change, the three steps of Murray's transformation illustrate the necessary elements for group change. Instead of simply defining reality, pastors need to define and communicate the reality to those they serve. The same is true of strategy and vision. They need to discover and communicate a vision of a preferred future that the congregation can work to achieve, and they must develop and implement a strategy that is congruent with their biblical mission and the church's core values.

LEADING A CHANGE PROCESS

Define and Communicate Reality

Max Dupree writes, "The first responsibility of a leader is to define reality."[10] Defining reality is not for the faint of heart. It requires a willingness to compare the current situation with what it could and should be. To some degree, defining reality is the first step in discovering a vision,[11] because it sees what is with a view to what it can be.[12] It requires discipline not to gloss over the way things really are.

Defining Reality

A starting point in defining reality is to lead influencers in discovering if the current structures and strategies are helping or hampering the organization from achieving its mission.[13] Is there something necessary to achieve the mission that is not present? Is there something present that is not

---

10   Dupree, *Leadership Is an Art*, 11.

11   Malphurs, *Ministry Nuts and Bolts*, 100: "[Vision is] a clear, challenging picture of . . . the ministry as it can and must be."

12   Earley, *Pastoral Leadership Is . . .* , 228: "*See the need*: A great need inspires a great leader. Nehemiah purposed to rebuild the walls after being deeply affected by the need to do so (Neh. 1:2–11). Jesus was inspired to reach the multitudes by witnessing the needs of people who were weary and scattered, like sheep with no shepherd (Matt. 9:35–38)."

13   Malphurs, *Ministry Nuts and Bolts*, 61: "[Mission is] a broad, brief, biblical statement of what the organization is supposed to be doing."

necessary or is hindering the church from accomplishing the mission? The mission is central in the strategic change process. Everything else revolves around it. Without a clear understanding of and commitment to the mission, it is impossible to define reality and lead an organization to change.

After analyzing how well the organization is accomplishing its mission, the second step is to ascertain whether the current structures and strategies (intentional or unintentional) are helping or hindering the church in accomplishing its mission. This work requires a brutal analysis of ministry effectiveness, with no sacred cows allowed. Later in the strategic change process, the church can decide what to change, but at this stage it cannot afford to shield anything from the light. Just as a person with a nagging cough and a history of hay fever would not ask a doctor to check for everything except allergies, leaders must examine everything if they hope to define reality with accuracy.

The third step is to anticipate what crises are inevitable if the church decides not to engage in a positive change process. Peter Drucker says, "The most important task of an organization's leader is to anticipate crisis."[14] Pastors must look into the future and anticipate what will happen if they fail to lead the church into a picture of their preferred future.

Communicating Reality

It is not enough to define reality; pastors must also foster discontent with the status quo among the people by communicating their assessment to the congregation. Because of homeostasis, people will not embrace proposed changes without being discontent with the current reality. The discomfort of not changing must be greater than the discomfort of going through the change process.[15] Facts are not enough. People do not change just because they know something to be true. For instance, 90 percent of heart patients do not change their poor lifestyle habits even when a doctor tells them that if they do not change they will die a premature death.[16] There must be a sense of urgency about the proposed change.

---

14   Drucker, *Managing the Non-Profit Organization*, 9.

15   Poole and Robinson, *Lessons from Empowering Leaders*, 3.

16   Deutschman, *Change or Die*, 10–11: "We like to think that the facts can convince people to change. We like to think that people are essentially 'rational'—that is, they'll act in their self-interest if they have accurate information. We believe that 'knowledge is power' and that 'the truth will set you free.' But nine out of ten heart

People will do almost anything to survive during a crisis, which makes an atmosphere of crisis a prime environment for introducing change.[17] People are motivated to do things, even risky things, if there is a crisis. Employers tell those who work on offshore oil platforms not to jump off the oilrig platform into the water. It is just too dangerous. Even if they could avoid the sharks, they likely could not avoid the inevitable hypothermia that accompanies the freezing water. "Never jump into the water," they say, "unless the platform is on fire." With the volatile nature of an oilrig, workers have a better chance of survival if they jump into the shark-infested, freezing water than if they remain on a burning platform.[18]

As they define their current reality, pastors also must see the direction the church is drifting and where it will be without their intervention. (Remember, negative change occurs without effort.) In effect, through their communication process they create the atmosphere of crisis,[19] which emerges from critical issues by showing the members of the church the inevitable future reality if the church does not change.[20] This is not to say they manufacture a crisis with a false sense of urgency. Over time, followers' willingness to change in a real genuine crisis wanes if they have a leader who manufactures them and creates false urgency. If the crisis descriptions are inaccurate, the followers will become more change adverse, emboldening their resolve not to change.[21] However, if pastors can show the direction of the drift and help the people to see the inevitable deteriorated future, based on the critical issues involved, they can create a change friendly environment where the risk of changing is less than the perceived

---

patients didn't change even when their doctors informed them about what they had to do to prolong their lives."

17   Hannity, *Conservative Victory*, 86. Rahm Emanuel, President Obama's former chief of staff said, "You don't ever want a crisis to go to waste; it's an opportunity to do important things that you would otherwise avoid."

18   Deutschman, *Change or Die*, 213.

19   Kotter, *A Sense of Urgency*, 132: "Within the logic of burning platforms, if natural events do not create a crisis, you must. You don't wait. You don't hope. You develop a change strategy and act. Employed with blind enthusiasm, this idea is not sensible. Used in a judicious way, it can be exceptionally important."

20   Ibid., 6–7: "True urgency focuses on critical issues, not agendas overstuffed with the important and the trivial. True urgency is driven by a deep determination to win, not anxiety about losing."

21   Gladwell, *David and Goliath*, 114. Surviving "remote misses" does not leave people traumatized; instead, it tends to embolden those in war zones.

risk of not changing.[22] When there is discontent with the status quo and the inevitable future, people are ready to consider a change for the better. They are ready to hear how things could and should be.

People will be more willing to change if there is a true sense of urgency created by the leaders, not if the leaders create a false sense of urgency through appeals to anxiety, fear, or anger.[23] If fear could lead to real change, then 90 percent of heart patients would not ignore their doctor's advice to change their lifestyle.[24] Fear and faith are incompatible (Mark 5:36). Instead of encouraging the people to fear the future, wise pastors encourage them to have faith that God will empower them to fulfill the mission, regardless of the obstacles they currently are facing and will face in the future. Remember from Murray's story: obstacles let you know you are still on track. They are to be expected.

Discover and Communicate a Vision of a Preferred Future

Discovering a Vision of a Preferred Future

The vision emerges at the intersection of the current reality and God's will for the church. The picture of the preferred future does not come from brainstorming sessions with colleagues, attending best practices conferences, or observing successful churches. Rather, it comes from knowing the mind of the Lord (1 Cor. 2:16), submission to the ways of God (Micah 6:8), and conforming to the will of God (Prov. 16:1–4). Something Billy Graham models well.

Few men have cast a shadow of influence on the world like Billy Graham. In his autobiography, *Just as I Am*, Graham mentions a difficult time in his life when Stephen Olford influenced him. Graham writes,

> I returned home from our European tour at the beginning of April,
> 1947, having been gone for six months and knowing that Ruth and I had

---

22   Perkins, *Leading at the Edge*, 126: "There are also times in which taking what appears to be a safe course is actually a dangerous move."

23   Kotter, *A Sense of Urgency*, 2: "While complacency is built on a feeling that the status quo is basically fine, false urgency is built on a platform of anxiety and anger."

24   Duetschman, *Change or Die*, 11: "We like to think that change is motivated by fear and that the strongest force for change is crisis, which creates the greatest fear. There are few crises as threatening as heart disease, and no fear as intense as the fear of death, but even those don't motivate heart patients to change."

weathered the slight tension in our relationship. Those months had also been a time of spiritual challenge and growth. My contact with British evangelical leaders during this and subsequent trips, especially with Stephen Olford, deepened my personal spiritual life. I was beginning to understand that Jesus Himself was our victory, through the Holy Spirit's power.[25]

Graham does not say what happened in that encounter, just that it "deepened his personal spiritual life." Olford told the writers of the *Leadership Secrets of Billy Graham* what happened. "In the small, stone hotel, Olford led Billy step-by-step through the Bible verses on the Spirit's power, which had produced Olford's profound spiritual renewal a few months earlier."[26]

Olford's crucible preceded Graham's. Because he had been there, Olford could guide Graham on his search. A tribute to Olford's life on the Olford Institute website says that Olford had "a crisis experience [that] led to his full surrender to the Lord and his call into the ministry."[27]

Olford's crucible led to full surrender and so did Graham's. The next night Graham and Olford met again for prayer. "I can still hear Billy pouring out his heart in a prayer of total dedication to the Lord," said Olford. With time, the breakthrough he was praying for came. "We were laughing and praising God and Billy was walking back and forth across the room, crying out, 'I have it! I'm filled. This is a turning point in my life.' And he was a new man."[28]

Graham left that encounter knowing the mind of the Lord, in submission to the ways of God and conformed to the will of God. He left with a focus that allowed him to turn down NBC's offer of a million dollars to co-host a TV show and Hollywood's offer to star in two movies.[29] He had laser focus to his life – he was to preach a simple gospel message and invite the multitudes to accept Jesus as their Savior.

This is not to say that the visioning process should not include a realistic analysis, empowered by outside-the-box thinking, restrained by a reasonable probability of success analysis, and enlightened by a comparison of current practices with acceptable standards of best practices. While all of

---

25   Graham, *Just as I Am*, 111.

26   Myra and Shelley, *Leadership Secrets of Billy Graham*, 22.

27   http://www.olford.org/CC_Content_Page/0,,PTID314886%7CCHID702174%7CCIID,00.html (accessed June 4, 2007).

28   Myra and Shelley, *Leadership Secrets of Billy Graham*, 23.

29   Ibid., 68–69.

these are good processes, they are not enough. The visioning process must be soaked in prayer, prompted by the Spirit, and propelled forward by consensus among the Spirit-filled influencers.

The preferred future requires an informed understanding of what could and should be,[30] not a desire to use a preferred, new, or trending methodology. Yet nothing substitutes for knowing the mind of the Lord, submitting to His ways, and being conformed to His will. While pastors must discover a vision (the church does not discover it, the elders do not discover it, the deacons do not discover it), actually it is not their vision, but God's. After all, it is God's church (1 Cor. 12:27), redeemed by Christ's blood (Eph. 1:7) to accomplish God's purpose (Eph. 3:10–11).

Before creating a volatile environment of change, pastors must be certain that the change they seek is worth the risk, pain, and effort that the church will experience to make the change. Before implementing change, pastors should ask themselves the following questions to ascertain if the vision is from the Lord and the timing is right.

Is the New End-State I Desire Mission-Critical?

If the change does not further the mission of the church there is no reason to endure the pain of the change process. Churches suffer when pastors lead them to change to keep up with trends or be like another church the pastor admires. If the change does not help the church accomplish its mission, it is not worth the energy it will take to implement the change.

Is the New End-State I Desire Compatible with Our Core Values?

Violating a strongly held core value will blow up in the volatile environment of change. Values, especially core values, are hard to change without destroying the church's identity. Core values are "deep-seated understandings about who we are."[31] They are not the same as aspirational values (who we wish we were) or common values (how we are like every other church). They are the church's core identity, their DNA, the shared values that bind the many into one.

During a building renovation, contractors do not destroy a solid

---

30   Earley, *Pastoral Leadership Is . . .*, 228: "Vision is a picture of a preferred future told in the present. It is what *could* and *should* happen."

31   Ford, *Transforming Church*, 87.

foundation; instead, they build on it. Core values are foundational in nature and they are what pastors build on, not prime targets for change.[32]

Pastors who accept the call of a church, hoping to reshape it into their image are committing ministerial suicide. Their change efforts will splinter the church and lessen its effectiveness. A church cannot be fighting for identity survival and work its mission at the same time.

Are the Key Influencers Open to This Change?

If the change will be dead on arrival, there is no need to attempt it. It will just cause division and erode trust. However, initial resistance to an idea is common. Though it can vary, depending on the social system, one study illustrates that it can take from .4 of a year to 4.65 years for those who will eventually accept an innovation to adopt it, and 1.14 years to reach an early majority.[33] Change, especially significant change, takes time.

Because of erosion, the historic Cape Hatteras Lighthouse was in peril of washing into the Atlantic Ocean. Congress appropriated $12 million for the National Park Service to move it twenty-nine hundred feet to safety.

With a combination of care, expertise, patience, and raw power, The Expert House Movers of Sharptown, Maryland, moved the 208-foot tall structure to its current home. The option of moving the lighthouse was first proposed in April of 1982, but the light was not lit at its new location until November 13, 1999. Small things move quickly, but big things take time. In this case, it took seventeen years of study and twenty-three days of moving.[34]

Just as it takes time for pastors to define reality and discover a preferred future, it will take key influencers and the rest of the church time to see the current reality and prefer the same future as the pastor. Likely, they will not embrace it when they first hear it. Some will adopt the idea early and help curry support with an early majority in the church, while others will not come around until long after implementation, if they adopt it at all. Leaders tend to overestimate what they can accomplish in a short amount of time, but underestimate what they can do with a large amount

---

32 I am not speaking of a church with unchristian core values. If a church has a core value that is keeping it from fulfilling its mission, of course, it needs to change.

33 Rogers, *Diffusion of Innovations*, 214.

34 Clarke, "Moving Big Stuff," 48–59.

of time.[35] There is a difference between urgency and impatience. Pastors must be patient as they place their hope in God (Rom. 8:25) and trust in God's timing (Hab. 2:3).

Do We Have the Resources to Make It Happen?

Changing Bible study curriculum likely will not cost much; however, constructing a new educational building will. Pastors need to count the cost (Luke 14:28) before casting a vision for a preferred future. This is not to say that God will not provide for the needs of His people (Phil. 4:19). God provides for needs, but He does not always fund unwise projects. Sometimes, He frustrates them (cf. Gen. 11).

Resources are not limited to finances – time and energy are also valuable resources. Time spent on one thing is unavailable for another. The same is true of energy. Change (especially big change) requires time, money, and energy.

Do the People Trust Me Enough to Risk What They Will Need to Risk?

Another way to put this is, Do I have enough change in my pocket[36] to pay the price of the change? Sometimes you will answer yes, and you will press on with the change. But what about when you don't have the credibility yet, does that mean you can't lead the change effort?

No, it just means that you cannot lead the change process now. People have to trust pastors before they will go through the pain of change with them. Pastors need time to develop those trusting relationships by marrying, burying, and caring for the people they serve (see part 2).[37] It also may mean that if you do attempt to lead the change process now, you cannot lead it alone (chap. 13).

---

35   Schriever, *Reflections on Research*, 90.

36   Maxwell, *360 Degree Leader*, 124: "When you do things that add to the relationship, you increase the change in your pocket. When you do negative things, you spend that change. If you keep dropping the hall – professionally or personally – you harm the relationship, and you can eventually spend all the change and bankrupt the relationship."

37   Iorg, *Painful Side of Leadership*, 212–13.

Communicating the Preferred Future

After pastors clearly see how things are (they have defined reality and communicated it to the people) and how things could and should be (discovered a preferred future), they must communicate that vision to the people and begin developing a strategy with them to accomplish it. The communication process will vary by the ministry context; however, it will likely include many private conversations with influencers (chap. 13) along with public sermons (chap. 7).

Some of the visionary members (2.5%) of the congregation will be quick to adopt the idea. Those who are ready for this kind of change (13.5%) will follow quickly, but to get to an early majority, the pastor will also have to communicate the value of the idea to those who are more cautious (34%) about changing things. They will have to believe the proposed future is a preferred future and the pain of not changing is greater than the pain they will experience if they change. Getting to an early majority is not sufficient. Even after the majority of the people are on board, there will still be skeptical people (34%) to convince and resistant people (16 percent) to challenge.[38]

Because not all of the people will prefer the future the pastor does, the communication process is ongoing. During seasons of change, leaders must "give people information, and do it again and again."[39] Telling is not the same as communicating. Use early successes[40] and stories[41] to communicate, do not just tell people what the future will be like — *show them*. Show the future as it arrives. Show them why it is preferred.

---

38   Rogers, *Diffusion of Innovations*, 281. Percentages allocated in this paragraph are taken from Rogers' adopter categorizations of innovators (2.5%), early adopters (13.5%), early majority (34%), late majority (34%) and laggards (16%).

39   William Bridges, *Managing Transitions*, 32.

40   Heath and Heath, *Switch*, 141: "When you engineer early successes, what you're really doing is engineering hope. Hope is precious to a change effort."

41   Kotter, *A Sense of Urgency*, 54: "Neurologists say that our brains are programmed much more for stories than for PowerPoint slides and abstract ideas. Stories with a little drama seem to be enjoyed by our feelings and, more importantly, are remembered far longer than any dry slide filled with analytics. Personal stories also create a more intimate atmosphere. Intimacy suggests friends. Friends suggest people who are lot trying to take advantage of one another."

Develop and Implement a Change Strategy

Positive change does not happen just because the people adopt it as their preferred future—all good ideas "degenerate into hard work."[42] As momentum builds for the vision, pastors need to lead a group of influencers to develop a change strategy to move the church from the current reality into the preferred future.

Identify Key Behaviors That Will Achieve the Vision

Pastors can identify a handful of satisfying[43] behavioral changes[44] in the people, which, if done consistently over time, will have a high probability of accomplishing the clear and compelling vision of a preferred future.[45] The key is to identify the behavior people will embrace that will most greatly influence vision realization.[46] Doing more of the same will not provide the desired results—a change must happen.[47] Just as the transformational truth of the sermon is at the intersection of God's glory as revealed in the text and the listener's response to it (chap. 7), the key behaviors are at the intersection of the preferred future and the follower's response to it. If the preferred future is to become an outwardly focused church, then the key behaviors might be reading the Bible in a year, praying for unreached

---

42   Edersheim and Drucker, *The Definitive Drucker*, x.

43   McClelland, *Power*, 260: "There has been much discussion of whether the leader's ideas about what will inspire his followers come from God, from himself, or from some intuitive sense of what the people need. Whatever the source of the leader's ideas, he cannot inspire his people unless he expresses vivid goals which in some sense they want."

44   Patterson et al., *Influencer*, 43: "Take care to ensure that you're searching for strategies that focus on *behavior*."

45   Covey, McChesney, and Huling, *Four Disciplines of Execution*, 44. The authors refer to these behaviors as "the measures of the activities most connected to achieving the goal."

46   Bennis and Thomas, *Geeks and Geezers*, 137: "Stripped to its essentials, leadership involves just three things—a leader, followers, and a common goal."

47   Deutschman, *Change or Die*, 150: "Why do people persist in their self-destructive behaviors, ignoring the blatant fact that what they've been doing for many years hasn't solved their problems? They think that they need to do it even more fervently or frequently as if they were doing the right thing but simply had to try even harder. They continue to do 'more of the same.'"

people groups on a regular basis, sacrificial giving, and committing to invest one week of annual vacation time in a face-to-face service project. Those people who engage in these key behaviors have a greater possibility of becoming more outwardly focused and, since the people are the church, it will ultimately change the church itself.

Make the Change Appealing

To Calvin Miller, vision is "the photographic image";[48] to George Barna, it is a "mental image";[49] and to Andy Stanley, it is a "clear mental picture."[50] A vision of a preferred future is not something people absorb in a quick hallway conversation or adopt in a PowerPoint presentation. It has a gestation period.

If you want people to give their lives to accomplishing a vision, they have to see it clearly and embrace personal behavioral with their heart, soul, and mind.[51] Kotter says, "Plans and actions should always focus on others hearts as much or more than their minds. Behaving with passion, conviction, optimism, urgency, and a steely determination will trump an analytically brilliant memo every time."[52]

Chip and Dan Heath promote the importance of the emotional elements of change by using the metaphor of a rider for the mind and an elephant for the heart.[53] Just as elephants have more mass and sheer power than riders do, the heart wins over struggles with the head. If leaders do not align the heart with the head, change will not occur

Social structures in the church can reinforce change. Personal, social,[54] and structural sources can influence the motivation and ability to change

---

48   Miller, *The Empowered Leader*, 63: "Vision is the photographic image that guides a pilgrimage to the goal it depicts."

49   Barna, *The Power of Vision*, 28: "Vision for ministry is a clear mental image of a preferable future imparted by God to His chosen servants and is based upon an accurate understanding of God, self and circumstances."

50   Stanley, *Visioneering*, 18: "Vision is a clear mental picture of what could be, fueled by the conviction that it should be."

51   Heath and Heath, *Made to Stick*, 203: "We appeal to their self-interest, but we also appeal to their identities—not only to the people they are right now but also to the people they would like to be."

52   Kotter, *A Sense of Urgency*, 142-43.

53   Heath and Heath, *Switch*.

54   Ibid., 255: "Although inertia may be a formidable opponent in the early goings

the vital behavior.[55] So if the key behavior is for church members to invest one week of vacation time in a face-to-face service project per year, pastors could form an action team, have them design a uniform T-shirt to wear while doing the project they choose in the community. As a group, they will experience esprit de corps, self-regulate, and form a positive peer pressure among themselves to accomplish the self-sacrificing behavior.

Make the Behavior Easier to Change

Wise leaders work out the logistics of complying with key behavioral changes by shaping a path for change.[56] If the key behavior is reading the Bible in a year, then the pastor will provide a reading plan with the commitment card. If it is praying for unreached people groups, then the pastor can give the congregation resources from organizations like the Joshua Project so the people can pray strategically.[57]

Pastors can lead their churches to change, but it requires that they define reality, discover a preferred future, and develop a change strategy. They are responsible to lead the church into positive change. To increase their probability of success, they will not attempt to do it alone.

---

of your switch, at some point inertia will shift from resisting change to supporting it. Small changes can snowball to big changes."

55   Patterson, *Influencer.*

56   Heath and Heath, *Switch,* 179–249.

57   "The Joshua Project: Bringing Definition to the Unfinished Task," The Joshua Project, accessed January 1, 2015, http://joshuaproject.net.

Chapter 13   Leading as a Powerful Servant Leader

As a ministry, leadership includes serving others. Remember that ministry *is participating with God and cooperating with His people in serving others to meet their needs, fulfill our calling, and bring glory to God* (see chap. 2). Service is at the heart of all ministries, including the leadership aspect of pastoral ministry.

The words "power" and "servant" do not seem to go together. Those people who are servants in society tend to be disenfranchised and powerless. The assumption is, they work in the service industry only because they cannot find more prestigious and financially rewarding employment. Jesus saw service differently. He saw service as something great people did (Matt. 20:25–27).[1] Power is necessary for pastors to be servant leaders who lead the church to fulfill its mission. The Great Commission, which is foundational to the church's mission, is to make disciples by going, teaching, and baptizing people from all nations (Matt. 28:19–20). The only reason the church can carry out that mission is Jesus has all power (Matt. 28:18). Without His power, they could do nothing (John 15:5).

---

1   White, *Becoming a Christian Leader*, 11: "Jesus taught of kingdom leadership that turned current leadership ideas upside down. He revolutionized leadership for this day and ours by teaching that leadership comes from serving."

SERVANT LEADERSHIP

Servant leaders are secure in their identity in Christ,[2] desiring to serve and not necessarily to lead[3] so that others can know, love, and submit to God.[4] Servant leadership is not a leadership style[5] as much as it is an attitude and the essence of who leaders are and how they view others.[6] To servant leaders, the people do not belong to them – they are not "my people"[7]–they are God's people (cf. 2 Chron. 7:14) whom they serve in Jesus' name and whom they serve beside (cf. 1 Cor. 3:9) for the cause of Christ.

---

2   Warren, *Ministry: How Real Servants Think*, http://www.cbn.com/spirituallife/ biblestudyandtheology/discipleship/warren_purposedrivenlife.aspx (accessed 22 June 2015): "If you're going to be a servant you must settle your identity in Christ. Only secure people can serve. The more insecure you are, the more you'll want people to serve you, and the more you'll need their approval. On the other hand, when you base your worth and identity on your relationship to Christ, you are freed from the expectation of others. You are freed to serve."

3   Greenleaf, *Servant Leadership*, 27: "The servant-leader *is* servant first.... It begins with the natural feeling that one wants to serve, to serve *first*. Then conscious choice brings one to aspire to lead. That person is sharply different from one who is *leader* first, perhaps because of the need to assuage an unusual power drive or to acquire material possessions. For such, it will be a later choice to serve – after leadership is established."

4   Claude Cone, retired Executive Director of the Baptist Convention of New Mexico, interview conducted by Carl Russell, transcribed November 3, 2007: "I like to picture myself with a towel in one hand and a wash basin in the other hand, looking for dirty feet to wash, just trying to find people to serve and minster to and help them to know God, help them to love God, and help them to let God control their lives."

5   McNeal, *Practicing Greatness*, 4: "Servant leadership is an attitude, not a genre of narrowly circumscribed actions. Service is about a desired outcome, not just the type of action a leader takes on behalf of others."

6   Iorg, *Character of Leadership*, 117: "Servant leadership is defined more by who you are than what you do."

7   De Pree, *Leading without Power*, 71: "I've often noticed the manager of a professional sports team or a member of Congress or a pastor using the phrase 'my people.' Even though such an expression may rise from the best of motivations and real concern, to the ear of a follower this language reveals perception 180 degrees from reality. Leaders belong to their followers. A director should refer to employees as 'the people I serve.' What a different reality that is! And what a different effect on followers."

POWER

Paul Hersey defines power as "the things I have going for me as a manager that allow me to influence other people."[8] Power is a combination of positional authority[9] and personal influence. It is a tool to accomplish the vision,[10] not a status or achievement.[11] Servant leaders do not seek to have power for personal reasons. They see themselves as stewards of their positional authority and personal influence so they can better serve others.

Positional Authority

Positional authority is formal in nature. It is established by official documents[12] and exercised through accepted procedures.[13] By the nature of their work, pastors have authority. Those they serve should observe, imitate (Heb. 13:7), and submit to them (Heb. 13:17). Endemic in that authority is the responsibility pastors have to keep watch over the souls of God's people and give account to God for their work (Heb. 13:17). God sends pastors to a church (Eph. 4:11) and the church's ecclesiastical authority affirms the pastors' calling to ministry in general[14] and specifically to a local church.[15] Pastors' positional authority comes from God, who sends them, and the church that receives them.[16] While pastoral authority is a significant source

---

8 Hersey, *The Situational Leader*, 73.

9 In the context of Hersey's definition, the positional authority was being the manager; for our use, it is being the pastor.

10 Blanchard and Hodges, *The Servant Leader*, 56: "Leadership is not about power, it's not about control. It's about helping people live according to the vision. It's the vision – the purpose, picture of the future and values – that everyone should serve."

11 Carlson, "How Pure," 8: "A lust for power and wealth would, in my mind, be a disqualifier for ministry, because it inevitably leads to a lack of integrity."

12 By official documents, I mean things like the articles of incorporation, constitution, bylaws, job descriptions, etc.

13 By procedures, I mean, congregational votes, Robert's Rules of Order, procedures manuals, etc.

14 Churches will typically grant a license and/or ordination certificate to credential a pastor to minister.

15 Different traditions place the authority in different places. Some place it with the congregation, while other traditions give it to a board of elders, bishop or presbytery.

16 Allender, *Leading with a Limp*, 110: "The moment we take on the mantle of

of power,[17] it is not the only necessary one.[18] People may rebel against authority or they may follow it.[19] Pastors need more than positional authority; they also need personal influence.[20]

Personal Influence

Personal influence is less formal than positional authority. It is relational[21] in nature and driven by people's perceptions,[22] which can change over time. Personal influence grows as leaders give themselves to the mission and live the vision in a consistent[23] and visible way.

Lee Iacocca, the former chair of Chrysler Corporation, turned the failing automaker around by encouraging equal sacrifice among everyone. He set the example by reducing his salary to a dollar a year. Others in the corporation followed his sacrificial example. Members of the United

---

leadership, other people assign us a power that can do them harm or good. Most leaders don't ask for such power over others; the power is simply given."

17   Ibid., 151: "A leader—whether in the home, church, business, community, or government—has authority due to her role, but her positional power will not bring about good for individuals or organizations unless it is backed up by the capital of character. You may obey a leader who has power and authority, but you will not strive to serve her or the cause of the organization unless you respect and care for her in addition to the ones with whom you serve."

18   Hersey, *Situational Leader*, 81: "Effective leaders do not rely exclusively on either power base. They build and sustain both."

19   Aubrey Malphurs, *Being Leaders*, 49: "Leadership can take place only when people make a conscious decision to follow."

20   Maxwell, *360 Degree Leader*, 13: "In leadership—no matter where you are in an organization—the bottom line is always influence."

21   Ibid., 213: "Relationship building is always the foundation of effective leadership. Leaders who ignore the relational aspect of leadership tend to rely on their position instead. Or they expect competence to do 'all the talking' for them. True, good leaders are competent, but they are also intentionally connected to the people they lead."

22   McNeal, *Practicing Greatness*, 64: "Spiritual leaders who have trained for institutional leadership, who anchor their leadership in positional authority, and who rely on educational credentialing don't understand the new expectations for leadership rooted in personal credibility, legitimized by followers, not external agencies."

23   Kotter, *Leading Change*, 97: "Nothing undermines the communication of a change vision more than behavior on the part of key players that seems inconsistent with the vision."

Auto Workers followed, making their own concessions. The wildfire of enthusiasm for the recovery effort went to the extent that even celebrities pitched in to help.[24] Iacocca's dedication to the turnaround, as evidenced by his visible personal sacrifice, helped influence co-workers to do things he did not have the authority to make them do.

Personal influence grows as pastors build their credibility by loving and teaching God's people with integrity and consistency.[25] That is why "Leading God's People" is the final section of this book and this discussion is in the final chapter. Pastors cannot lead people they have not loved nor taught. Pastors who are not faithful to love God's people and teach them will not have the necessary influence it takes to lead them through difficult days or when change is necessary. Building strong relationships is the key.[26] Pastors will grow in their personal influence as they live life with their people. Personal influence grows as pastors weep, laugh, share a meal, or drink coffee with the people. Influence is personal in nature.

Competence and impressive credentials are never a substitute for garden-variety likability developed over time by treating others with respect.[27] People are more likely to follow Golden Rule (Matt. 7:12) leaders[28] who treat people like they matter to them.[29] The converse is also true. In the medical profession, doctors who evidence poor bedside manners and

---

24 Iacocca and Novak, *Iacocca*, 229.

25 Larson, *Persuasion Reception and Responsibility*, 121: "Current research shows three key factors that account for most of one's credibility. They are trustworthiness (goodwill and high character), expertise (wisdom and experience), and dynamism (an active, artful style and delivery)."

26 De Pree, *Leading without Power*, 167: "The longer I live and the more I see of organizations, the more I'm forced to the conclusion that at the heart of our organizations is always this matter of competence in relationships. While technical skill and lifetime learning are essential, I'm convinced that competence in relationships remains most important in making organizations places of realized potential."

27 Neither is likability a substitute for competence. My argument is not one over the other, but the need for both.

28 Kouzes and Posner, *Credibility*, 218: "Constituents look for leaders who demonstrate an enthusiastic and genuine belief in the capacity of others, who strengthen people's will, who supply the means to achieve and who express optimism for the future."

29 Wooden and Jamison, *Wooden on Leadership*, 122: "Individuals who feel they don't matter will perform their jobs as if they don't count."

make mistakes are more likely to face malpractice lawsuits than their more likable peers making similar mistakes.[30]

Most of the characteristics listed in 1 Timothy 3:2–7 and Titus 1:6–9 (chap. 1) are character traits of a Golden Rule Christian leader with strong relationship skills. Regardless of the positional authority that pastors possess, if they are unlikable, hot-tempered, self-righteous bullies who are quick to quarrel, and lack a good reputation the people will not follow them.[31] Their title will not help them. Demanding respect of their office will not help them. Reminding people of their title, position in the organization[32] or number of educational credentials they have earned will not help them. Authority is no substitute for influence. Pastors need both.

While power is necessary,[33] power struggles are not. Pastors can co-exist and collaborate with other powerful people for the cause of Christ. This is a preferred approach over abusing their power for personal gain,[34] or suffering from leadership paralysis due to feeling threatened by other powerful people.[35]

Power Levels

While not an exact science, leaders should know what level of power they and other key leaders have at any given time.[36]

---

30   Gladwell, *Blink*, 40: "What comes up again and again in malpractice cases is that patients say they were rushed or ignored or treated poorly. 'People just don't sue doctors they like,' is how Alice Burkin, a leading medical malpractice lawyer puts it."

31   McKee, Boyatzis, and Johnston, *Becoming a Resonant Leader*, 30: "Studies have shown that lack of emotional self-control is a major impediment to executive success in organizations."

32   Blanchard and Barrett, *Lead with LUV*, 117: "Your power doesn't come from your position; it comes from the people whose lives you touch."

33   Pfeffer, *Power*, 7.

34   Miller, *Leadership*, 86: "Servant leadership is the all-important checkpoint that bridles demonic power."

35   Carter, *Leadership*, 217.

36   Schaller, *The Change Agent*, 143: "One of the most difficult problems encountered by a change agent is to have a current estimate of his own power and that of his organization."

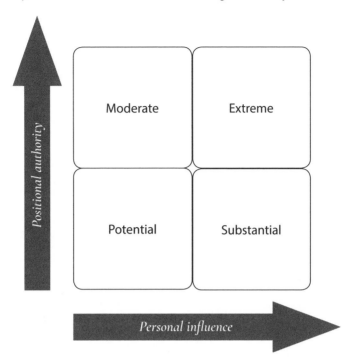

Figure 3. Authority and Influence Matrix

Positional Authority

Positional authority is easy to assess. Where is the leader on the organizational chart? The closer a leader is to the top, the higher their positional authority. Senior pastors have more authority than nursery workers have. Board members have more authority than subcommittee members do. Ministerial staff members (pastors, youth ministers, ministers of education, etc.) have more authority than support staff members (clerks, administrative assistants, janitors, etc.) have. However, that does not mean they have more influence.

Personal Influence

Personal Influence grows with time as people prove themselves credible, accountable, personable, and competent. For that reason, leaders with high influence, but low authority (substantial power), have more power than other leaders with high authority and low influence (moderate power).

While it is more difficult to ascertain personal influence than positional authority, it is possible. Personal influence grows over time, as people are faithful to attend, make positive contributions to the group, and use their spiritual gifts to minister. However, that does not mean that every charter member or founding pastor who has made powerful past contributions to the church's development has personal influence. There is also the "it" factor — intangible things that contribute to personal influence. The following questions will help explore those factors:

- Do most people perceive the person to be sincere?
- Is the person friendly?
- Do most people perceive the person to be personable?
- Do most people perceive the person to be accessible?
- Do most people perceive the person to be credible?
- Do most people perceive the person as approachable?
- How likable is the person?

A more objective way to determine how much influence a person has is by polling key leaders. Ask them to make a top ten list of people in the congregation who have the greatest influence on the culture and direction of the church. Next, ask them which word best describes each listed person's leadership style: "easygoing," "strong," or "overbearing." Now ask them to circle the names of the three people they consider the "most trustworthy."[37] After excluding the overbearing people, count the number of times the key leaders circled a person's name — those people with the most circles have the most personal influence.

Potential Power

Leaders with low authority and influence have potential power. They will need permission from a higher authority and support from those with more influence to lead. Good examples of leaders with potential power are student interns or summer missionaries. They should not be at the spear's point in leadership, but should seek permission, support, and guidance as they learn and lead. Their work is significant, but their primary responsibility is to learn, grow, minister — not lead.

---

37   Bullard, *Every Congregation*, 132-33.

Moderate Power

Leaders with high authority and low influence have moderate power. As long as they operate within the boundaries set by the governing body of the church, they have permission to lead the church to carry out its mission.[38] However, they may not have sufficient *influence* to convince the people to adopt their vision, strategies or plans (chap. 12). An example of leaders with moderate power is senior pastors who are relatively new to the role.[39] While few would question their authority, the people may not be ready to follow inexperienced, new pastors their first day on the job. To lead effectively, they must borrow power from more influential leaders in the church.

When John Maxwell accepted his first pastorate in a rural church in Indiana, he learned to borrow influence from others. At his first board meeting he noticed that Claude, a local farmer, had tremendous influence with the others. Instead of entering into a power struggle with Claude, Maxwell determined to work with him for the cause of Christ. Maxwell had the positional authority, Claude had the personal influence, and together they had what they needed to lead the church to accomplish its mission.

After that first board meeting, Maxwell met with Claude before subsequent board meetings to discuss the needs of the church and community as he saw them. Maxwell did not take solutions to Claude and ask him to support his plans, he took the needs to Claude and together they arrived at a proposed ministry response.[40] Maxwell writes, "From then on, if I wanted to accomplish anything at that church, I just went out to the farm and did chores with Claude. I could always count on him to bring those things before the people, and whenever Claude spoke, people listened."[41]

Substantial Power

Leaders with low authority, but high influence have substantial power. A good example of this leader is a long-tenured staff member of a church

---

38 By boundaries, I mean governing documents, calendar, budget, procedures, etc.

39 Senior leaders who transfer into a position from a similar position may transfer their credibility into the new position. Though their influence has potential to increase, they will not start with moderate power. They will start with extreme power.

40 Maxwell, *21 Irrefutable Laws*, 43-47.

41 Ibid., 47.

with a new pastor. These staff members, by virtue of their tenure, faithful ministry, and credibility will have more influence with the people than the new pastor will, even though the new pastor is higher on the organizational chart. Those with substantial power still have opportunities to lead,[42] but will need to do so with their pastor's blessing.

Just as Maxwell (moderate power) chose to work with Claude (extreme power), long tenured staff members (substantial power) will need the green light from their new pastor (moderate power) in some leadership decisions.

For instance, a worship pastor who wants the choir to present a seventy-five minute Christmas cantata on Sunday morning needs the green light from the senior pastor before announcing rehearsals. The experienced worship pastor does this because senior pastors typically approve the time allocation of the Sunday morning service in most churches. They have authority over the worship hour.

In this instance, the worship pastor (substantial power) defers to the new senior (moderate power) about when the cantata takes place; however, that does not mean the senior pastor selects the songs for the cantata. The worship pastor retains jurisdiction in that decision.

Extreme Power

Leaders with high authority and influence have extreme power. A good example of this leader is founding pastors of thriving churches. Even when pastors have extreme power, they still need others to lead the church to accomplish its mission. They empower those with potential power, include those with moderate power, consult with those with substantial power, and have a shared relationship with others with extreme power.[43]

The shared leadership model remains effective long after pastors attain extreme power. Instead of borrowing power (like Maxwell did from Claude), they are now in the position to lend it to others.

There are crucial moments when influential leaders loan their credibility to others. Barnabas loaned credibility to Saul of Tarsus when he

---

42   Maxwell, *360 Degree Leader*, 7: "Leadership is a choice you make, not a place you sit. Anyone can choose to become a leader wherever he is. You can make a difference no matter where you are."

43   Greenleaf, *Servant Leadership*, 76: "To be a lone chief atop a pyramid is abnormal and corrupting. None of us is perfect by ourselves, and all of us need the help of correcting influence of close colleagues."

vouched for him with the apostles (Acts 9:26–28). Pee Wee Reese loaned his credibility to Jackie Robinson in 1947 when they stood together as the crowd booed, heckled, and yelled death threats at the first man to break the color barrier in Major League Baseball (depicted in a statue at KeySpan Park by sculptor William Behrends, unveiled Nov. 1, 2005).[44] In both cases, men with influence transferred their blessing to men who needed it. They were stewards of their power.

Powerful servant leaders lend their power to others by endorsing projects, recommending people for positions, writing letters of support, or introducing a speaker. People notice when an influential pastor endorses something or someone. Pastors with extreme power must use it with care so as not to crush those they oppose. They also must lend it judiciously so as not to empower others to do harm.

Using Power to Accomplish the Mission

In churches where above-reproach pastors (cf. 1 Tim. 3:2) are powerful servant leaders following the Be-the-Minister model (chap. 2), other staff members and key church members will have opportunity to lead. Because these pastors are secure leaders, who are willing to share the spotlight and their power (sharing power with others does not diminish personal power reserves),[45] the staff and congregation they serve thrives.

Instead of viewing themselves as orchestra directors who remain in control of every played note, they see themselves more like jazz bandleaders who allow their colleagues to control the direction of the piece within set boundaries.[46] This is a flattened leadership structure[47] where powerful servant leaders see themselves as "first among equals."[48]

People can do so much more together than they can alone. On Thursday,

---

44   Ira Berkow, "Two Men Who Did the Right Thing," New York Times, Nov 2, 2005, http://www.nytimes.com/2005/11/02/sports/baseball/02robinson.html?_r=0.

45   Kouzes and Posner, *The Leadership Challenge*, 1984: "The intriguing paradox of power is that the more you give away to others, the more you get for yourself."

46   Allender, *Leading with a Limp*, 92: "Jazz musicians are not merely playing any note they wish. They do not abandon logic, structure, or rationality. The art lies in the musicians' fundamental playing skills that push them to engage not just a musical score but one another."

47   Bennis and Thomas, *Geeks and Geezers*, 11: "The digital world is nonlinear and has ditched the corporate pyramid for the flat organization."

48   Greenleaf, *Servant Leadership*, 75.

23 July 2009, Chicago White Sox pitcher Mark Buehrle threw a perfect game against the Tampa Bay Devil Rays. It was the first time a White Sox pitcher had accomplished such a feat in eighty-seven years. A perfect game means Buehrle did not allow a hit nor did anyone reach base in any inning. At the time, there were only eighteen perfect games in the history of Major League baseball.

However, Buehrle did not do it alone. Eight players stood behind him to make it possible. In one dramatic play in the ninth inning, DeWayne Wise sprinted and leaped to catch a ball that would have gone over the wall. It was a spectacular play. Afterwards, Buehrle said Wise's catch should be the play of the year. He recognized the importance of having a teammate that made his success possible.[49]

In the decisive moment, Buehrle was not in charge – Wise was – and Wise came through. Great accomplishments happen when the team functions well. In the same way, catastrophic failures occur when teamwork breaks down.[50]

THE REWARDS OF PASTORAL MINISTRY

The work of pastoral ministry is a good thing (1 Tim. 3:1), but not an easy thing. Things of real value rarely are easy. Ministers experience persecution (John 15:20), hardships (Luke 9:58), and the work is never done (Matt. 25:14-30). While the work itself is rewarding, the satisfaction does not last (Eccl. 2:9-11) and the fruit of the hard work can be destroyed by the person who follows (Eccl. 2:17-19). Some people will show appreciation, but pastors will rarely know if it was sincere or merely flattery (Prov. 28:23).

Then what are the lasting rewards of ministry? Years ago, one of the students I serve made a report in class on his philosophy of ministry. He said that his goal was to help his congregation integrate the Bible into their daily life – a worthy goal. He said, "I don't remember anything my Sunday school teachers taught me when I was a youth and I want to do a better job teaching than my teachers did." At first, his comment made me a bit defensive, but then I started thinking about it and decided he

---

49 "Mark Buehrle Perfect Game," MLB. Advanced Media, updated June 30, 2014, http://chicago.whitesox.mlb.com/mlb/news/buehrle_perfectgame/index.jsp.

50 Gladwell, *Outliers*, 184: "The kinds of errors that cause plane crashes are invariably errors of teamwork and communication."

was right. I do not specifically remember anything my teachers taught me either. About the time that I was ready to agree with the student, one of his classmates spoke up. "I agree with you," he said. "I can't remember any specific thing my teachers taught me either, but I do remember how much they loved me and that's made a difference in my life."

The student taught the professor that day. Our reward is not in the results of our work, but is relationships we form doing our work. Love is the greatest of all the things that endure (1 Cor. 13:13). Love is our reward. The reward is not just the love received, but also the love given.

God rewards us with the ability to love hurtful people (chap. 4). God rewards us with strong relationships that form over time from working side-by-side during difficult days and against all odds to make disciples (Matt. 28:18–20).[51] God rewards us with His loving presence as we walk through those difficult days (Ps. 23:4).

The love God gives us for the people we serve (and serve beside) is our greatest reward in this life, and second only to having the opportunity to hearing these words in the life to come: "Well *done*, good and faithful servant" (Matt. 25:21, emphasis mine). Until that day, give your life to loving, teaching and leading God's people.

---

51   Finzel, *Top Ten Mistakes*, 52: "When all is said and done, the crowns of my achievements will not be the systems I managed, the things I wrote, the structures I built, but the people I personally permanently influenced through direct contact."

Appendix: One-Point Sermons

SERMON 1: IMPACTING ETERNITY

Genesis 41:34–42

> Let Pharaoh do this: Let him appoint overseers over the land and take a fifth [of the harvest] of the land of Egypt during the seven years of abundance. Let them gather all the [excess] food during these good years that are coming. Under Pharaoh's authority, store the grain in the cities, so they may preserve [it] as food. The food will be a reserve for the land during the seven years of famine that will take place in the land of Egypt. Then the country will not be wiped out by the famine." The proposal pleased Pharaoh and all his servants. Then Pharaoh said to his servants, "Can we find anyone like this, a man who has God's spirit in him?" So Pharaoh said to Joseph, "Since God has made all this known to you, there is no one as intelligent and wise as you are. You will be over my house, and all my people will obey your commands. Only with regard to the throne will I be greater than you." Pharaoh also said to Joseph, "See, I am placing you over all the land of Egypt." Pharaoh removed his signet ring from his hand and put it on Joseph's hand, clothed him with fine linen garments, and placed a gold chain around his neck.

The events unraveled just as Joseph said they would. There were seven years of plenty, followed by seven years of famine. During the years of plenty, Joseph had two sons by the wife Pharaoh gave him and oversaw the storage of grain for the famine. Genesis 41:55 (NASB) says, "So when all the land of Egypt was famished, the people cried out to Pharaoh for bread; and Pharaoh said to all the Egyptians, 'Go to Joseph; whatever he says to you, you shall do.'"

Verse 55 says it vividly: Joseph had absolute power. As the famine progressed, people from everywhere came to Egypt to get food. One of the groups of visitors who knelt before Joseph asking for help was Joseph's brothers. Just as Joseph had dreamed when he was a child, his brothers bowed down before him. Joseph recognized them, but they did not recognize him. They told Joseph that they were ten of twelve sons from the land of Canaan wanting to buy food according to the brothers, their youngest brother was still at home and the other brother was dead. Joseph pretended not to believe their story, accused them of being spies, and he threw them into jail for three days. Was Joseph taking revenge?

When three days passed, Joseph released all but one of them and told them to take some grain home with them, but to return with their youngest brother to prove their story and show they were who they said they were.

The brothers spoke to one another in their language, not knowing that Joseph could understand them. They grieved over what they'd done to Joseph years ago, believing that God was punishing them for that sin. When Joseph heard them, he went into another room and wept.

Joseph returned and sent the brothers away with the grain they bought with a special package inside the bag—the money they'd given for the grain. When the brothers made it home, they told their father what happened and told him they had to take Benjamin back with them to verify their story and redeem Simeon. Here's his reply: "But Jacob said, 'My son shall not go down with you; for his brother is dead, and he alone is left. If harm should befall him on the journey you are taking, then you will bring my gray hair down to Sheol in sorrow'" (Gen. 42:38 NASB).

But when the food ran out, Israel had a change of mind and sent gifts with Benjamin. When they stood before Joseph, he instructed his servants to prepare a feast and invite the brothers to his house for dinner. When he saw Benjamin with his brothers, he went into a private room and wept again.

After dinner, the steward filled their sacks with grain and the money they brought, but that's not all, he also put Joseph's cup in Benjamin's sacks. The trap was set and now Joseph was ready to spring it. Genesis 44:4-5 (NASB) says, "They had just gone out of the city, and were not far off, when Joseph said to his house steward, 'Up, follow the men; and when you overtake them, say to them, 'Why have you repaid evil for good? Is not this the one from which my lord drinks, and which he indeed uses for divination? You have done wrong in doing this.'"

Why is Joseph doing this? Is he being spiteful and exacting revenge? This was a perfect opportunity for Joseph to take vengeance on his brothers for throwing him a pit, threatening to kill him and then selling him to slave traders. This is a turning point in the story. Will Joseph rise above his pain to remain focused on his assignment of preserving life? Or will he forego his purpose to exact revenge for the pain his brothers inflicted on him when he was young?

While these actions appear vengeful, they are not. Joseph was leveraging Israel's love for Benjamin to force him to travel to Egypt. However, Joseph could not have anticipated what happened next. When the brothers returned, Judah made a passionate plea to imprison him and let the other brothers, especially Benjamin, go free. (Please remember the name Judah since it will be very important in about ten minutes that you remember it was he who made this offer.) Judah made it clear that if his father suffered any more sorrow that it would kill him.

Let's rejoin the text to see what happens next (Gen. 45:1–15 NIV):

> Then Joseph could no longer control himself before all his attendants and he cried out, "Have everyone leave my presence!" So there was no one with Joseph when he made himself known to his brothers. And he wept so loudly that the Egyptians heard him, and Pharaoh's household heard about it.
>
> Joseph said to his brothers, "I am Joseph! Is my father still living?" But his brothers were not able to answer him, because they were terrified at his presence.
>
> Then Joseph said to his brothers, "Come close to me." When they had done so, he said, "I am your brother Joseph, the one you sold into Egypt! And now, do not be distressed and do not be angry with yourselves for selling me here, because it was to save lives that God sent me ahead of you. For two years now there has been famine in the land, and for the next five years there will not be plowing and reaping. But God sent me ahead of you to preserve for you a remnant on earth and to save your lives by a great deliverance. So then, it was not you who sent me here, but God. He made me father to Pharaoh, lord of his entire household and ruler of all Egypt. Now hurry back to my father and say to him, 'This is what your son Joseph says: God has made me lord of all Egypt. Come down to me; don't delay. You shall live in the region of Goshen and be near me you, your children and grandchildren, your flocks and herds, and all you have. I will provide for you there, because five years of famine are still to come. Otherwise you and your household and all who belong to you will become destitute.'
>
> "You can see for yourselves, and so can my brother Benjamin, that it is really I who am speaking to you. Tell my father about all the honor accorded me in Egypt and about everything you have seen. And bring my father down here quickly."

Then he threw his arms around his brother Benjamin and wept, and Benjamin embraced him, weeping. And he kissed all his brothers and wept over them. Afterward his brothers talked with him.

Few people have suffered more injustice in life than Joseph did. His own flesh and blood—his brothers—sold him to slave traders. His brothers betrayed him. When he refused to sleep with his owner's wife, she had him thrown into prison. His owner's wife betrayed him. In prison, he helped some prison mates through some troubling times by interpreting their dreams. One of them promised to put in a good word to Pharaoh for Joseph when he got out, but he didn't. One again, Joseph was betrayed. It would have been easy for Joseph to be vengeful and get even with everyone who had betrayed him, but he didn't. Why? He understood that all of the pain he suffered was collateral damage in God's great plan to use him to preserve Israel. Genesis 45:7 (NIV) says, "But God sent me ahead of you to preserve for you a remnant on earth and to save your lives by a great deliverance." What was at stake was not just the well-being of his family. I asked you to remember a name a few minutes ago: Who was it that offered himself as a substitute for Benjamin? What tribe was Jesus descended from? Out of Judah's family linage a Savor would be born—his decision not to sabotage God's plan for a moment of personal revenge had great impact. God had devised a way for the ancestors of Jesus to live through a terrible life-threatening famine and it included some personal suffering on Joseph's part.

We don't just extend grace to benefit people in the moment, it impacts eternity. It is God's great plan for you.

The Bible says, "And be kind and compassionate to one another, forgiving one another, just as God also forgave you in Christ" (Eph. 4:32). Is there someone you need to forgive today? If so, begin that process right now by asking God for the strength to forgive. Forgiveness will benefit you. It will benefit the person who harmed you, and who knows, it may just impact eternity.

SERMON 2: CELEBRATE!

Luke 15:3–24

[Jesus] told them this parable: "What man among you, who has 100 sheep and loses one of them, does not leave the 99 in the open field and go after the lost one until he finds it? When he has found it, he joyfully puts it on his shoulders, and coming home, he calls his friends and neighbors together, saying to them, 'Rejoice with me, because I have found my lost sheep!' I tell you, in the same way, there will be more joy in heaven over one sinner who repents than over 99 righteous people who don't need repentance.

"Or what woman who has 10 silver coins, denarius. if she loses one coin, does not light a lamp, sweep the house, and search carefully until she finds it? When she finds it, she calls her women friends and neighbors together, saying, 'Rejoice with me, because I have found the silver coin I lost!' I tell you, in the same way, there is joy in the presence of God's angels over one sinner who repents."

He also said: "A man had two sons. The younger of them said to his father, 'Father, give me the share of the estate I have coming to me.' So he distributed the assets to them. Not many days later, the younger son gathered together all he had and traveled to a distant country, where he squandered his estate in foolish living. After he had spent everything, a severe famine struck that country, and he had nothing. Then he went to work for one of the citizens of that country, who sent him into his fields to feed pigs. He longed to eat his fill from the carob pods the pigs were eating, but no one would give him any. When he came to his senses, he said, 'How many of my father's hired hands have more than enough food, and here I am dying of hunger! I'll get up, go to my father, and say to him, Father, I have sinned against heaven and in your sight. I'm no longer worthy to be called your son. Make me like one of your hired hands.' So he got up and went to his father. But while the son was still a long way off, his father saw him and was filled with compassion. He ran, threw his arms around his neck, and kissed him. The son said to him, 'Father, I have sinned against heaven and in your sight. I'm no longer worthy to be called your son.'

"But the father told his slaves, 'Quick! Bring out the best robe and put it on him; put a ring on his finger and sandals on his feet. Then bring the fattened calf and slaughter it, and let's celebrate with a feast, because this son of mine was dead and is alive again; he was lost and is found!' So they began to celebrate."

When was the last time something really good happened to you? What did you do to celebrate it?

In our text today, we see three people who have something very good happen to them. I want you to notice what they did to celebrate.

There was a shepherd with hundred sheep that lost one of them. He cared so much for the lost sheep that he left the other ninety-nine behind to go find the sheep. When found the lost sheep, he called his friends and neighbors together to celebrate his good fortune. I want you to notice the pattern here: lost – found – celebrate. The sheep was lost, then it was found, which was reason to celebrate.

There was a woman with ten coins that lost one of them. She searched her house until she found the lost coin and when she found it, she called her friends and neighbors together and they celebrated her good fortune. I want you to notice the pattern here: lost – found – celebrate. The coin was lost, and then it was found, which was reason to celebrate.

Then Jesus raised the stakes – it wasn't an animal or a coin that was lost this time. It was a son. The father lost one of his sons, who asked for his inheritance early and left home and squandered it in a foreign land. This father didn't leave his older son at home to search for the prodigal, he just waited and hoped that his son would return. When he did, the father was ready to celebrate. Notice the pattern: lost – found – celebrate. The son was lost, and then he was found, which was reason to celebrate.

Is the message of these parables that we are to celebrate when something good happens to us? I don't think so, mainly because we don't need guidance to do that. It is what comes natural.

Let's dig a little deeper to see if we can discover the meaning. A parable is a story that Jesus "throws alongside" (literal meaning of the word "parable") of a truth to help define it. It provides a contextual "a-ha" moment for the listener. Jesus uses common, earthy things to illustrate the truths he taught.

Prior to the twentieth century, interpreters viewed the parables allegorically, assigning a meaning to every element of the story and drawing conclusions. Sometimes this process yielded wild conclusions based upon the most inconsequential detail.

Near the end of the nineteenth century, Adolf Jülicher point out the inconsistency of the allegorical interpretations and argued that instead of assigning an allegorical meaning to every detail, Bible students should look for one main point per parable. Recently, Blomberg has argued that there is one main point per character in the parable.[1] In my view, Klyne Snodgrass gives a helpful perspective when he writes, "In short, some parables make one point, and some make several points. A formulaic approach to parable interpretation, as for all biblical studies, just does not work. One must discern from context the intent of the analogy."[2]

To find the heart of this parable cluster, you have to look at two things. First, you look at the patterns in the text, and then you look at the situational context of the parable.

Following Snodgrass's advice, I believe there is one point in the parable cluster, not a different point in each parable. Thus far, we've looked at two parables and a part of the third: the parable of the lost sheep, the lost coin, and the lost son. In each instance, we've seen the unmistakable pattern of lost — found — celebrate, and it would be easy draw the conclusion that Jesus' teaching is that we should celebrate when good things happen to us. However, we've failed to look at the end of this parable cluster — the portion of the third parable that speaks of the older brother.

Stein adds to our understanding of interpreting parables with his "end stress."[3] He points out that in most stories the climax comes at the end, so if you want to really know the point of the parable look at the concluding words. So let's look at the end of the parable cluster Luke 15:25–32:

> "Now his older son was in the field; as he came near the house, he heard music and dancing. So he summoned one of the servants and asked what these things meant. 'Your brother is here,' he told him, 'and your father has slaughtered the fattened calf because he has him back safe and sound.'
>
> "Then he became angry and didn't want to go in. So his father came out and pleaded with him. But he replied to his father, 'Look, I have been slaving many years for you, and I have never disobeyed your orders, yet you never gave me a young goat so I could celebrate with my friends. But when this son of yours came, who has devoured your assets with prostitutes, you slaughtered the fattened calf for him.'

---

1   Blomberg, *Preaching the Parables*, chap. 1.
2   Snodgrass, Stories with Intent, 29.
3   Stein, Parables of Jesus.

> "'Son,' he said to him, 'you are always with me, and everything I have is yours. But we had to celebrate and rejoice, because this brother of yours was dead and is alive again; he was lost and is found.'"

With this final parable, the older son breaks the patterned response to lost and found that we've noticed. With the shepherd, when he found his lost sheep he called his friends and neighbors together and they celebrated. When the woman found her lost coin, she brought her friends and neighbors together and they celebrated. When the father found his lost son, he killed the fatted calf and wanted to celebrate. But when the brother found his lost little brother, he didn't celebrate — he became angry. Parable 1: lost — found — celebrate. Parable 2: lost — found — celebrate. Parable 3: lost — found — celebrate; second half of parable 3: lost — found — ANGER.

There is one more place where the pattern breaks down. In the case of the lost sheep, the shepherd left the ninety-nine to seek for it. In the case of the lost coin, the woman of the house set aside all other duties to focus on finding the coin. But when the prodigal was lost, the father did not leave his older son to search for the prodigal. He stayed home.

However, when the older brother did not come to the celebration, the father left the party to find the older brother. This leads me to believe that the main point in this parable cluster does not have to do with the younger son, but the older one. The shepherd searched for the sheep, the woman of the house searched for the coin and the father searched for the older brother.

We've explored the patterns, now let's look at the context. Luke writes in 15:1-3, "All the tax collectors and sinners were approaching to listen to Him. And the Pharisees and scribes were complaining, 'This man welcomes sinners and eats with them!' So He told them this parable." The Pharisees were grieved because Jesus was being gracious to sinners just as the older brother was grieved because the father was being gracious to the prodigal.

This parable cluster isn't about celebrating when something good happens to you, but celebrating God's grace when something good happens to someone else — even your rival brother that doesn't deserve grace.

I've spent the first half of my ministry preaching against Pharisees. Now I've come to understand I am one. I am the older brother who dutifully does the right thing and takes notice of others who do the wrong thing. Having come face to face with the teachings of Jesus in these parables, I know I need God's grace in my life as desperately as the prodigal son. I'm learning the issue isn't who is better, but that we're brothers. And brothers celebrate when something good happens in the other's life—especially when it isn't deserved.

Do you love God's grace? The real test of how much you love the grace of God isn't how you respond to it when you receive it, but whether you can celebrate at someone who doesn't deserve it receives it. And whether you can acknowledge that you don't deserve it when you get it either.

Sermon 3: The Reward for Faithfulness

Matthew 25:14-30 (NASB)

"For it is just like a man about to go on a journey, who called his own slaves, and entrusted his possessions to them. And to one he gave five talents, to another, two, and to another, one, each according to his own ability; and he went on his journey. Immediately the one who had received the five talents went and traded with them, and gained five more talents. In the same manner the one who had received the two talents gained two more. But he who received the one talent went away and dug in the ground, and hid his master's money. Now after a long time the master of those slaves came and settled accounts with them. And the one who had received the five talents came up and brought five more talents, saying, 'Master, you entrusted five talents to me; see, I have gained five more talents.' His master said to him, 'Well done, good and faithful slave; you were faithful with a few things, I will put you in charge of many things, enter into the joy of your master.' The one also who had received the two talents came up and said, 'Master, you entrusted to me two talents; see, I have gained two more talents.' His master said to him, 'Well done, good and faithful slave; you were faithful with a few things, I will put you in charge of many things; enter into the joy of your master.' And the one also who had received the one talent came up and said, 'Master, I knew you to be a hard man, reaping where you did not sow, and gathering where you scattered no seed. And I was afraid, and went away and hid your talent in the ground; see, you have what is yours.' But his master answered and said to him, 'You wicked, lazy slave, you knew that I reap where I did not sow, and gather where I scattered no seed. Then you ought to have put my money in the bank, and on my arrival I would have received my money back with interest. Therefore take away the talent from him, and give it to the one who has the ten talents.' For to everyone who has shall more be given, and he shall have an abundance; but from the one who does not have, even what he does have shall be taken away. And throw out the worthless slave into the outer darkness; in that place there shall be weeping and gnashing of teeth.'"

In this parable, Jesus gives three different people differing numbers of talents. What is a talent? In the church, we often make a distinction between a talent and a spiritual gift. We usually define a talent as something we come by naturally, something we're born with. A spiritual gift, however, is something mystically given to us by God when He saves us. In other words, something we're "born again" with.

Certainly, there needs to be a distinction between talents and spiritual gifts, but part of that distinction does not need to be the source of the ability. Whether we're born with it or God mystically bestows us with it after our conversion, the source is the same — God. James 1:17 says, "Every good gift and every perfect gift is from above, and cometh down from the Father of lights, with whom is no variableness, neither shadow of turning" (KJV). So whatever the "talent" is that the master gives his servants we must note that the source of the gift is the master, the servants would not have it without his act of giving.

As I've said, when we use the word "talent," we immediately think of it as a special ability that someone has; therefore, we interpret this parable in that light. We condense the teaching by saying that if God gives you a talent — meaning a special ability — you'd better develop it or He will take it away. This sounds good on the surface, except the word "talent" in this usage doesn't mean a special ability.

In Palestine, a talent was a weight of money. The master in this parable isn't giving special abilities to his servants (something a man couldn't do anyway). He was giving money. How much? Likely it was worth around sixty days wages of a worker. With the California minimum wage at $8.00 an hour, it would be worth close to $4,000 in our current context. Regardless of the details, it was enough money that the master cared what they did with it.

God Doesn't Operate by Our Sense of Fairness

Beyond the linguistics involved, there is another issue that we have to deal with in this text: the master didn't distribute the talents fairly. To one he gave five, to another he gave two and the other he gave only one. In a day where it doesn't matter whether you win or lose, it just matters if everybody gets to play and has a good time, this seems inequitable. Is it fair for the master to give more to one and less to another? Doesn't that give one an unfair advantage?

Okay, let's stop here for a moment — let's leave the parable to talk about God (not a bad thing to do since the parable is teaching us about God's kingdom). In a cartoon strip of Calvin and Hobbes, the mischievous imp Calvin is climbing on a rock when he says: "This whole Santa Claus thing just doesn't make sense." In the next frame, he continues, "Why all the secrecy? Why all the mystery? If the guy exists, why doesn't he ever show himself and prove it." Then, jumping off the rock, he says, "And if he doesn't exist, what's the meaning of all this?" Hobbs responds, "I dunno — isn't this a religious holiday." Calvin quips, "Yeah, but actually, I've got the same questions about God."

Like cartoon characters, people often try to fit God in their mold and get Him to show and explain Himself. They don't just want Him to be just; they want Him to be fair.

God is just. He judges each man based on the opportunities and responsibilities He's given him. But He isn't fair. He doesn't give every man the same opportunities and responsibilities. I like the attitude of Captain David Fortune of the Monterey Police Department. Captain Fortune has had three different types of cancer. His first round was with cancer of the larynx in 1979. That cancer led to surgery, radiation, and an artificial voice box. Later, in 1988, he got cancer again but in his left kidney, and then skin cancer in 1993. The odds of getting two types of cancer is great, but the odds of getting three types is astronomical. What was his response? "I don't feel picked on. I don't feel I'm a marked man," he said. "I feel blessed to be able to handle the challenges and keep going."[4] Instead of bellyaching over the hardships we face in life, perhaps we need to develop an attitude of gratitude, like Captain Fortune has.

God Gives People Opportunities according to Their Abilities

Why would the master distribute the talents unfairly? He gave them to the people according to their ability. Wouldn't you do the same? Aren't you doing the same? Those of you who are in the age group investing for your retirement, think about how you are allocating your resources. Do you

---

4 *Monterey County Herald,* June 19, 2002.

put the same amount of money in every stock there is so you can be fair? Or do you put the greater amount of money in funds that you believe will perform well and lesser amounts in funds that you are uncertain about? That's exactly what the master did. He placed the greater amount of his wealth in the person he believed would give him the greatest return on his investment.

God Expects His People to Fulfill Their Potential

When he returned, he found what he'd expected. The one he gave five talents to and the one he gave two talents doubled his money, but the one he gave only one talent did not earn a return at all. As it turns out, he took the money and buried it in the ground so it would be safe. His concern was with keeping things the way they are instead of achieving his potential. The master was livid with him and called him lazy. Okay, no argument here. Obviously, the man was lazy—he didn't do anything except bury the money and dig it back up. The other two were wheeling and dealing—working hard to make a profit, but not this one. He was lazy. But the master called him more than lazy, he called him wicked. Wait a minute, that's a strong word: WICKED. The punishment was as startling—the useless servant was cast into darkness where there is weeping and gnashing of teeth.

God Rewards the Faithful with More Responsibilities

The rewards to the faithful are just as surprising. I'd expect him to give them a cut of the profit and send them away on vacation, instead he gives them more responsibility.

Why do the rewards and punishments seem strange to us? Because we usually view the world through the eyes of the leading man and woman and think of God as playing a supporting role. He isn't! It isn't about us, it is about God! *He does not exist to make our life easier. We exist to serve and worship Him and the greatest reward we can ever receive is to have the honor of having more responsibility, and the greatest thing we can ever do in life, is to fulfill the potential that God has given us.*

Bibliography

Allender, Dan B. *Leading with a Limp: Turning Your Struggles into Strengths*. Colorado Springs, CO: Waterbrook, 2006.

American Counseling Association, "*ACA Code of Ethics*." Accessed September 18, 2014, www.ncblpc.org/Laws_and_Codes/ACA_Code_of_Ethics.pdf.

Andersen, Hans Christian. *The Emperor's New Clothes*. Edited and adapted by Stephen Corrin. London, 1964. http://www.mindfully.org/Reform/Emperors-New-Clothes.htm.

Arichea, Daniel C., and Eugene Albert Nida. *A Handbook on the First Letter from Peter*. UBS Handbook Series: Helps for Translators. New York: United Bible Societies, 1980.

Aristotle. *Rhetoric*. Stilwell: Digireads.com, 2005.

Arthurs, Jeffrey D. "Preaching the Old Testament Narratives." In *Preaching the Old Testament*, edited by Scott M. Gibson, 73–86. Grand Rapids: Baker, 2006.

Bailey, Sarah Pulliam. "Exclusive: Mark Driscoll's Resignation Letter to Mars Hill Church." In *Religion News Service*. online, October 14, 2014. http://www.religionnews.com/2014/10/15/exclusive-mark-driscolls-resignation-letter-to-mars-hill-church.

Barna, George. *The Power of Vision: How You Can Capture and Apply God's Vision for Your Ministry*. Ventura, CA: Regal, 1992.

Bayley, Peter. *French Pulpit Oratory, 1598–1650: A Study in Themes and Styles, with a Descriptive Catalogue of Printed Texts*. Cambridge: Cambridge University Press, 1980.

Behm, J. "ορφοω." In *Theological Dictionary of the New Testament*: L-N. Vol. 4. Edited by Gerhard Kittel, Geoffrey W. Bromiley, and Gerhard Friedrich. Grand Rapids: Eerdmans, 1964.

Bennis, Warren G., and Robert J. Thomas. *Geeks and Geezers: How Era, Values, and Defining Moments Shape Leaders*. Boston: Harvard Business School Press, 2002.

Berkow, Ira. "Two Men Who Did the Right Thing." In *The New York Times*, 2005.

Berne, Eric. *Games People Play: The Psychology of Human Relationships*. New York: Ballantine, 1996.

Bibliography

Blackaby, Henry, Henry T. Blackaby, and Richard Blackaby. *Spiritual Leadership: Moving People on to God's Agenda*. Nashville: B & H, 2001.

Blackaby, Henry T., Richard Blackaby, and Claude V. King. *Experiencing God: Knowing and Doing the Will of God*. Revised and Expanded ed. Nashville: B & H, 2008.

Blackwood, Andrew W. *Preaching from the Bible*. Grand Rapids: Baker, 1974.

Blanchard, Ken, and Colleen Barrett. *Lead with LUV: A Different Way to Create Real Success*. Upper Saddle River, NJ: FT Press, 2010.

Blanchard, Kenneth H., and Phil Hodges. *The Servant Leader: Transforming Your Heart, Head, Hands, and Habits*. Nashville: J. Countryman, 2003.

Blomberg, Craig L. *Matthew: An Exegetical and Theological Exposition of Holy Scripture*. New American Commentary, edited by David Dockery, vol. 22. Nashville: B & H, 1992.

———. *Preaching the Parables: From Responsible Interpretation to Powerful Proclamation*. Grand Rapids: Baker, 2004.

Bridges, William. *Managing Transitions: Making the Most of Change*. Philadelphia: Da Capo Press, 2009.

Brooks, James A. *Mark*. The New American Commentary, edited by David S. Dockery, vol. 23. Nashville: B & H, 1991.

Bryant, James W. *The New Guidebook for Pastors*. Nashville: B & H, 2007.

Bryer, K. J. "Burchard." In *Who's Who in Christian History*, edited by J. D. Douglas, Philip Wesley Comfort, and Donald Mitchell, 119. Wheaton, IL: Tyndale, 1992.

Bullard, George W. *Every Congregation Needs a Little Conflict*. St. Louis: Chalice Press, 2008.

Bullinger, E. W. *How to Enjoy the Bible*. New York: Cosimo Classics, 2008.

Bumpus, Tracey L. "Billy Graham Answers." *HomeLife*. September, 2000.

Bush, George W. *Decision Points*. New York: Broadway, 2011.

Buttrick, David G. *Homiletic: Moves and Structures*. Philadelphia: Fortress Press, 2008.

Callahan, Kennon L. *Twelve Keys to an Effective Church: Strategic Planning for Mission*. San Francisco: Harper & Row, 1983.

Carlson, G. Raymond. "How Pure Must a Pastor Be?" *Leadership Journal* (Spring, 1988): 12–23.

Carr, David M. *An Introduction to the Old Testament: Sacred Texts and Imperial Contexts of the Hebrew Bible*. Malden: Wiley-Blackwell, 2010.

Carson, D. A. *Exegetical Fallacies*. Grand Rapids: Baker, 1984.

Carson, D. A., R. T. France, J. A. Motyer, and G. J. Wenham, eds. *New Bible Commentary: 21st Century Edition*. Leicester, UK: Inter-Varsity Press, 1994.

Carter, Harry R. *Leadership: A View from the Trenches*. Bloomington, IN: Trafford, 2007.

Caruso, David, and Peter Salovey. *The Emotionally Intelligent Manager: How to Develop and Use the Four Key Emotional Skills of Leadership*. San Francisco: Jossey-Bass, 2004.

Cedar, Paul A. "Leading or Responding?" In *Mastering the Pastoral Role*. Mastering Ministry, edited by Paul A. Cedar, R. Kent Hughes, and Ben Patterson, 49-64. Portland: Multnomah, 1991.

Chadwick, Henry. *The Early Church*. The Penguin History of the Church, vol. 1. Middlesex: Penguin, 1967.

Chapell, Bryan. *Christ-Centered Preaching: Redeeming the Expository Sermon*. 2nd ed. Grand Rapids: Baker, 2005.

Clarke, Wendy M. "Moving Big Stuff: If You Can Move a Lighthouse, You Can Move Anything." *Smithsonian*, January 1, 2000, 48-59.

Clement. *On Marriage*. Translated by Henry Chadwick. Philadelphia: Westminster Press, 1955.

Cloud, Henry, and John Sims Townsend. *Boundaries: When to Say Yes, When to Say No to Take Control of Your Life*. Grand Rapids: Zondervan, 1992.

Colson, Charles W., and Ellen Santilli Vaughn. *Being the Body*. Nashville: Nelson, 2004.

Cooper, Owen. "The Need." In *Laos: All the People of God*, edited by F. Humphreys and T. A. Kinchen, 5-19. New Orleans: New Orleans Baptist Theological Seminary, 1984.

Cornes, Andrew. *Divorce and Remarriage: Biblical Principle and Pastoral Practice*. Fearn: Christian Focus, 2002.

Cott, Nancy F. *Public Vows: A History of Marriage and the Nation*. Cambridge, MA: Harvard University Press, 2000.

Craddock, Fred B. *As One without Authority: Fourth Edition Revised and with New Sermons*. St. Louis: Chalice Press, 2001.

——. *Preaching*. Nashville: Abingdon, 1985.

Dahan, Gilbert. "Genres, Forms, and Various Methods in Christian Exegesis of the Middle Ages." In *Hebrew Bible, Old Testament: The History of Its Interpretation, Vol. 1; from the Beginnings to the Middle Ages (until 1300), Part 1, Antiquity*, edited by Chris Brekelmans and Magne Saebø, 196-236. Göttingen: Vandenhoeck and Ruprecht, 1996.

De Pree, Max. *Leadership Is an Art*. New York: Currency, 2004.

——. *Leading without Power: Finding Hope in Serving Community*. San Francisco: Jossey-Bass, 1997.

de Villiers, J. L. "Philosophical Trends in the Graeco-Roman World." In *The New*

Testament Milieu. Guide to the New Testament, edited by A. B. du Toit, vol. 2. Johannesburg: Orion, 1998.

DeGroat, Chuck. *Toughest People to Love: How to Understand, Lead, and Love the Difficult People in Your Life — Including Yourself*. Grand Rapids: Eerdmans, 2014.

Demarest, Bruce A. *Soul Guide: Following Jesus as Spiritual Director*. Colorado Springs, CO: NavPress, 2003.

Deutschman, Alan. *Change or Die: The Three Keys to Change at Work and in Life*. New York: Regan, 2007.

DiGiuseppe, Raymond, and Raymond C. Tafrate. *Understanding Anger Disorders*. New York: Oxford University Press, 2006.

Dobson, Ed. "Speaking Truth in a Relativistic Society." In *Standing Fast: Ministry in an Unfriendly World*, edited by Ed Dobson, Wayne Gordon, and Louis McBurney, 29–39. Sisters: Multnomah, 1994.

Dobson, James. "Keys to a Family-Friendly Church." In *Building Your Church through Counsel and Care: 30 Strategies to Transform Your Ministry*. Library of Leadership Development 3, edited by Marshall Shelley,121–30. Minneapolis: Bethany, 1997.

Donahue, John R., and Daniel J. Harrington. *The Gospel of Mark*. Collegeville, MN: The Liturgical Press, 2002.

Driscoll, Mark. *The Radical Reformission: Reaching out without Selling Out*. Grand Rapids: Zondervan, 2004.

Drucker, Peter F. *Managing the Non-Profit Organization: Practices and Principles*. New York: HarperCollins, 1990.

D'souza, Dinesh. *Ronald Reagan: How an Ordinary Man Became an Extraordinary Leader*. New York: Simon & Schuster, 1997.

Dudley, Carl, Theresa Zingery, and David Breeden. "Insights into Congregational Conflict." *Insights Into* 8, 2007. http://faithcommunitiestoday.org/sites/all/themes/factzen4/files/InsightsIntoCongregationalConflict.pdf.

Dufrensne, Ronald L., and Judith A. Chair. "Mind the Gap: Hypocrisy Monitoring and Integrity Striving as a Source of Ethical Leadership." In *Organizational Change, Leadership, and Ethics: Leading Organizations toward Sustainability*, edited by Rune T. By and Bernard Burnes, 97–119. New York: Routledge, 2013.

Dunagan, Ann. *The Mission-Minded Family: Releasing Your Family to God's Destiny*. Milton Kyenes: Authentic Media, 2008.

Earle, Ralph. "1 Timothy." In *The Expositor's Bible Commentary: Ephesians through Philemon*, edited by Frank E. Gaebelein, vol. 11, 341–90. Grand Rapids: Zondervan, 1981.

Earley, Dave. *Pastoral Leadership Is . . . : How to Shepherd God's People with Passion and Confidence*. Nashville: B &H, 2012.

Edersheim, Elizabeth Haas, and Peter F. Drucker. *The Definitive Drucker*. New York: McGraw-Hill, 2007.

Edge, Findley B. *The Doctrine of the Laity*. Nashville: Convention Press, 1985.

Edwards, J. Kent. *Deep Preaching: Creating Sermons That Go Beyond the Superficial*. Nashville: B & H, 2009.

Edwards, O. C. *Elements of Homiletic: A Method for Preparing to Preach*. Collegeville, MN: Liturgical Press, 1990.

———. *A History of Preaching*. Nashville: Abingdon, 2004.

Emmerich, Roland. "The Patriot." Culver City: Columbia Pictures, 2000.

Eyler, Janet, and Dwight Giles. *Where's the Learning in Service-Learning?* San Francisco: Jossey-Bass, 1999.

Fee, Gordon D., and Douglas K. Stuart. *How to Read the Bible for All It's Worth: A Guide to Understanding the Bible*. Grand Rapids: Zondervan, 1993.

Feindler, Eva L., ed. *Anger-Related Disorders: A Practitioner's Guide to Comparative Treatments*. Springer Series on Comparative Treatments for Psychological Disorders. New York: Springer, 2006.

Ferguson, Sinclair B. "Murray, John." In *Biographical Dictionary of Evangelicals*, edited by Timothy Larsen, David Bebbington, and Mark A. Noll, 463–65. Leicester, UK: Inter-Varsity Press, 2003.

Figley, Charles R., ed. *Compassion Fatigue: Coping with Secondary Traumatic Stress Disorder in Those Who Treat the Traumatized*. Brunner Mazel Psychosocial Stress Series 23, New York: Brunner/Mazel, 1995.

Finzel, Hans. *The Top Ten Mistakes Leaders Make*. Colorado Springs, CO: David C. Cook, 2000.

Fisher, Fred L. *Commentary on 1 and 2 Corinthians*. Waco: Word, 1975.

Flanagan, Kelly S., and Sarah E. Hall. *Christianity and Developmental Psychopathology: Foundations and Approaches*. Downers Grove, IL: IVP, 2014.

Ford, Kevin G. *Transforming Church: Bringing out the Good to Get to Great*. Carol Stream, IL: Tyndale, 2007.

France, R. T. *The Gospel of Matthew*. The New International Commentary on the New Testament, edited by Gordon Fee. Grand Rapids: Eerdmans, 2007.

Franklin, Ben, and Richard. Saunders. *Poor Richard's Almanac: For the Year of Christ 1733*. Reprint ed. Bedford: Applewood Books, 2002.

Friedman, Edwin H. *Generation to Generation: Family Process in Church and Synagogue*. New York: Guilford Press, 1985.

Gardner, Howard. *The Disciplined Mind: Beyond Facts and Standardized Tests, the K-12 Education That Every Child Deserves*. New York: Penguin, 2000.

Garland, Dale. "Ordination of Miles Hanson." A Sermon delivered at the Hemet Valley Baptist Church, Hemet, CA. October, 26, 2014.

Garland, David E. *2 Corinthians*. The New American Commentary, edited by E. Ray Clendenen, vol. 29. Nashville: B & H, 1999.

Gerberding, George H. *The Lutheran Pastor*. Philadelphia: Lutheran Publication Society, 1902.

Gerzon, Mark. *Leading through Conflict: How Successful Leaders Transform Differences into Opportunities*. Boston: Harvard Business School, 2006.

Gilbert, Binford W. *The Pastoral Care of Depression: A Guidebook*. Haworth Religion and Mental Health. Philadelphia: Haworth Press, 1998.

Gilbert, Roberta M. *The Eight Concepts of Bowen Theory*. Falls Church, VA: Leading Systems Press, 2006.

Gillette, Abram D., ed. *Minutes of the Philadelphia Baptist Association, from A.D. 1707 to A.D. 1807: Being the First One Hundred Years of Its Existence*. Philadelphia: American Baptist Publication Society, 1851.

Gladwell, Malcolm. *Blink: The Power of Thinking without Thinking*. New York: Little, Brown, 2005.

———. *David and Goliath: Underdogs, Misfits, and the Art of Battling Giants*. New York: Little, Brown, 2013.

———. *Outliers: The Story of Success*. New York: Little, Brown, 2008.

———. *The Tipping Point: How Little Things Can Make a Big Difference*. New York: Back Bay Books, 2002.

Goetz, David L. "How Pastors Practice the Presence of God." *Leadership Journal* 14, no. 4 (Fall, 1993): 28–42.

Goldingay, John. *Old Testament Theology, Volume 1: Israel's Gospel*. Downers Grove, IL: IVP, 2003.

Goleman, Daniel. *Working with Emotional Intelligence*. New York: Bantam Books, 1998.

Gottman, John. *The Seven Principles for Making Marriage Work*. New York: Three Rivers, 1999.

Graham, Billy. *Just as I Am: The Autobiography of Billy Graham*. New York: HarperCollins, 1997.

Greenleaf, Robert K., and Larry C. Spears. *Servant Leadership: A Journey into the Nature of Legitimate Power and Greatness*. Mahwah: Paulist Press, 2002.

Gregory, Sean, "Jim Tressell," *Time* 19, June 13, 2011.

Greidanus, Sidney. *The Modern Preacher and the Ancient Text: Interpreting and Preaching Biblical Literature*. Grand Rapids: Eerdmans, 1988.

———. *Sola Scriptura: Problems and Principles in Preaching Historical Texts*. Kampen: J. H. Kok, 1970.

Grissom, Fred A. "Elder." In *Holman Illustrated Bible Dictionary*, edited by Charles W. Draper, Chad Brand, and Archie England, 472–73. Nashville: Holman, 2003.

Grossman, Dave, and Loren W. Christensen. *On Combat: The Psychology and Physiology of Deadly Conflict in War and in Peace.* 3rd ed. Millstadt: Human Factor Research Group, 2011.

Gula, Richard M. "Ethics in Pastoral Ministry." New York: Paulist Press, 1996.

Hamilton, David R. *The Blog* (blog). http://www.huffingtonpost.com/david -r-hamilton-phd/longevity-_b_1978890.html?utm_hp_ref=healthy-living&i cid=maing-grid7|main5|dl29|sec1_lnk2&pLid=223572.

Hannity, Sean. *Conservative Victory: Defeating Obama's Radical Agenda.* New York: Harper, 2010.

Harris, Murray J. "2 Corinthians." In *The Expositor's Bible Commentary: Romans through Galatians,* edited by Frank E. Gaebelein, Everett F. Harrison, W. Harold Mare, Murray J. Harris, and James Montgomery Boice, vol. 10, 319–405. Grand Rapids: Zondervan, 1976.

Haugk, Kenneth C., and R. Scott Perry. *Antagonists in the Church: How to Identify and Deal with Destructive Conflict.* Minneapolis: Augsburg, 1988.

Hawkins, Greg L., Cally Parkinson, Eric Arnson, and Bill Hybels. *Reveal: Where Are You?* Barrington, IL: Willow Creek Resources, 2007.

Heath, Chip, and Dan Heath. *Made to Stick: Why Some Ideas Survive and Others Die.* New York: Random House, 2007.

———. *Switch: How to Change Things When Change Is Hard.* London: Random House, 2011.

Henry, Jim. *In Remembrance of Me: A Manual on Observing the Lord's Supper.* Nashville: B & H, 1998.

Herrnstein, Richard J., and Charles A. Murray. *The Bell Curve: Intelligence and Class Structure in American Life.* New York: Free Press, 1994.

Hersey, Paul. *The Situational Leader.* New York: Warner Books, 1985.

Hobbs, Herschel H. *The Baptist Faith and Message.* Revised ed. Nashville: Convention Press, 1996.

Hoffman, Martin L. *Empathy and Moral Development: Implications for Caring and Justice.* Cambridge: Cambridge University Press, 2000.

Hopkins, Paul E. *Pursuing Pastoral Excellence: Pathways to Fruitful Leadership.* Herndon, VA: Alban Institute, 2011.

Hopson, Barrie. *Managing for Development.* Lifeskills Management Book. Farnham, UK: Gower, 1999.

Huffman, John A. *The Family You Want.* Fearn: Christian Focus, 2001.

Hughes, Kent. "Going to Your Left." In *Deepening Your Ministry through Prayer and Personal Growth: 30 Strategies to Transform Your Ministry,* edited by Marshall Shelley, vol. 4, 221–29. Nashville: Moorings, 1995.

Hughes, Philip Edgcumbe. *Paul's Second Epistle to the Corinthians; the English Text with Introduction, Exposition and Notes.* Grand Rapids: Eerdmans, 1962.

Hunter, A. M. *Interpreting the Parables.* 2nd revised ed. London: SCM, 2012.

Hurtado, Larry W. *Mark.* Understanding the Bible Commentary, edited by W. Ward Gasque, Robert L. Hubbard Jr., and Robert K. Johnston. Grand Rapids: Baker, 2011.

Hybels, Lynne, and Bill Hybels. *Rediscovering Church: The Story and Vision of Willow Creek Community Church.* Grand Rapids: Zondervan, 1995.

Iacocca, Lee A., and William Novak. *Iacocca: An Autobiography.* Toronto: Bantam, 1986.

Iorg, Jeff. *The Character of Leadership: Nine Qualities That Define Great Leaders.* Nashville: B & H, 2007.

———. *Is God Calling Me? Answering the Question Every Leader Asks.* Nashville: B & H, 2008.

———. *Ministry in the New Marriage Culture.* Nashville: B & H, 2015.

———. *The Painful Side of Leadership: Moving Forward Even When It Hurts.* Nashville: B & H, 2009.

Jackson, Neil E. Jr. *Doing the Impossible: Motivating Yourself and Others for the Maximum* Nashville: Broadman, 1985.

Jacobs, Alan. *A Theology of Reading: The Hermeneutics of Love.* E-Print ed. Boulder, CO: Westview Press, 2001.

Jobes, Karen H. *1 Peter.* Baker Exegetical Commentary on the New Testament. Grand Rapids: Baker, 2005.

Kaiser, Walter C. Jr. *Grief and Pain in the Plan of God: Christian Assurance and the Message of Lamentations.* Fearn: Christian Focus, 2004.

Katz, Laurence, and Harvey M. Chochinov. "The Spectrum of Grief in Palliative Care." In *Topics in Palliative Care*, edited by Eduardo Bruera and Ruth K. Portenoy, vol. 2, 295–310. New York: Oxford University Press, 1998.

Kepcher, Carolyn, and Stephen Fenichell. *Carolyn 101: Business Lessons from the Apprentice's Straight Shooter.* New York: Fireside, 2004.

Kistemaker, Simon J. *Exposition of Hebrews*, vol. 16. Grand Rapids: Baker, 2001.

Knowles, Malcolm S., Elwood F. Holton, and Richard A. Swanson. *The Adult Learner: The Definitive Classic in Adult Education and Human Resource Development.* London: Routledge, 2011.

Koenig, Harold G., Michael E. Mccullough, and David B. Larson. *Handbook of Religion and Health.* Oxford: Oxford University Press, 2000.

Kollack-Walker, S., H. E. W. Day, and H. Akil. "Central Stress Neurocircuits." In *Stress Science: Neuroendocrinology*, edited by George Fink, 340–47. Waltham: Academic Press, 2010.

Konigsberg, Ruth D. *The Truth about Grief: The Myth of Its Five Stages and the New Science of Loss*. New York: Simon & Schuster, 2011.

Köstenberger, Andreas J., and David W. Jones. *God, Marriage, and Family: Rebuilding the Biblical Foundation*. Wheaton, IL: Crossway, 2010.

Kotter, John P. *Leading Change*. Boston: Harvard Business School, 1996.

———. *A Sense of Urgency*. Boston: Harvard Business School, 2008.

Kouzes, James M., and Barry Z. Posner. *Credibility: How Leaders Gain and Lose It, Why People Demand It*. San Francisco: Jossey-Bass, 2003.

———. *Encouraging the Heart: A Leader's Guide to Rewarding and Recognizing Others*. San Francisco: Jossey-Bass, 2009.

———. *The Leadership Challenge: How to Keep Getting Extraordinary Things Done in Organizations*. San Francisco: Jossey-Bass, 1984.

Krejcir, Richard J., "Statistics on Pastors." FASICLD. A PDF accessed October, 24, 2014, www.lifechristiancounseling.com/pastors/Statistics%20on%20Pastors.pdf.

Kübler-Ross, E., and Ira Byock. *On Death and Dying: What the Dying Have to Teach Doctors, Nurses, Clergy and Their Own Families*. Reprint edition. New York: Scribner, 2011.

Lane, Richard D. *Levels of Emotional Awareness: Neurological, Psychological, and Social Perspectives*. The Handbook of Emotional Intelligence: Theory, Development, Assessment, and Application at Home, School, and in the Workplace, edited by Reuven Bar-On and James D. A. Parker. San Francisco: Jossey-Bass, 2000.

Lange, John P., Philip Schaff, and William G. T. Shedd. *Mark*. A Commentary on the Holy Scriptures. Bellingham, WA: Logos Bible Software, 2008.

Larsen, David L. *The Anatomy of Preaching: Identifying the Issues in Preaching Today*. Grand Rapids: Kregel, 1999.

———. *The Company of the Preachers: A History of Biblical Preaching from the Old Testament to the Modern Era*. Grand Rapids: Kregel, 1998.

Larson, Charles U. *Persuasion: Reception and Responsibility*. Belmont: Wadsworth, 1979.

Latourette, Kenneth S. *A History of Christianity, Volume 1: Beginnings to 1500*. New York: HarperCollins, 1953.

———. *A History of Christianity, Volume 2: Reformation to the Present*, Revised Edition. New York: HarperCollins, 1975.

Lazarus, Richard S. *Stress and Emotion: A New Synthesis*. New York: Springer, 2006.

Lea, Thomas D., and Hayne P. Griffin. *1, 2 Timothy, Titus*. The New American Commentary, edited by E. Ray Clendenen, vol. 34. Nashville: B & H, 1992.

Leadership Journal. "How Common Is Pastoral Indiscretion?" *Leadership: A Practical Journal for Church Leaders* vol. 9, no. 110 (Winter 1988): 12–13.

Leas, Speed B. *Leadership and Conflict.* Nashville: Abingdon, 1982.

LeDoux, Joseph E. *The Emotional Brain: The Mysterious Underpinnings of Emotional Life.* New York: Simon & Schuster, 1996.

Lehr, J. Fred. *Clergy Burnout: Recovering from the 70-Hour Work Week and Other Self-Defeating Practices.* Minneapolis: Fortress Press, 2006.

Leonard, B. J. "Barnhouse, Donald Grey." In *Biographical Dictionary of Evangelicals,* edited by Timothy Larsen, David Bebbington, and Mark A. Noll, 34–36. Leicester, UK: Inter-Varsity Press, 2003.

Lewis, D. M. *Dictionary of Evangelical Biography, 1730–1860:* Hendrickson, 2004.

Lingenfelter, Sherwood G., and Marvin Keene Mayers. *Ministering Cross-Culturally: An Incarnational Model for Personal Relationships.* Grand Rapids: Baker, 2003.

London, H. B. *Refresh, Renew, Revive.* Colorado Springs, CO: Focus of the Family, 1996.

London, H. B., and Neil B. Wiseman. *The Shepherd's Covenant for Pastors.* Ventura, CA: Gospel Light, 2005.

Long, Thomas G. *Preaching and the Literary Forms of the Bible.* Philadelphia: Fortress Press, 1989.

———. *The Witness of Preaching.* Louisville: Westminster John Knox Press, 1989.

MacArthur, John. *Called to Lead: 26 Leadership Lessons from the Life of the Apostle Paul.* Nashville: Nelson, 2010.

———. *Pastoral Ministry: How to Shepherd Biblically.* Nashville: Nelson, 2005.

Mackereth, Samara. *Katie's Take* (blog). http://news.yahoo.com/blogs/katies-take -abc-news/friendfluence-friends-shape-us-174534400.html.

Maclean, Paul D. *The Triune Brain in Evolution: Role in Paleocerebral Functions.* New York: Plenum Press, 1990.

Malphurs, Aubrey. *Being Leaders: The Nature of Authentic Christian Leadership.* Grand Rapids: Baker, 2003.

———. *Ministry Nuts and Bolts: What They Don't Teach Pastors in Seminary.* Grand Rapids: Kregel, 2009.

Mare, W. Harold. "1 Corinthians." In *The Expositor's Bible Commentary: Romans through Galatians* edited by Frank E. Gaebelein, D. A. Carson, Walter W. Wessel, and Walter L. Liefeld, vol. 8, 175–318. Grand Rapids: Zondervan, 1984.

Martin, Murilee, "Ten Hours, 800 Rpm, Full Throttle: How Chrysler Used to Test Engines." 2012. http://www.thetruthaboutcars .com/2012/01/ten-hours-800 -rpm-full-throttle-how-chrysler-used-to-test-engines.

Maxwell, John C. *The 21 Irrefutable Laws of Leadership: Follow Them and People Will Follow You.* Nashville: Nelson, 1998.

———. *The 360 Degree Leader: Developing Your Influence from Anywhere in the Organization.* Nashville: Nelson, 2011.

———. *Failing Forward: Turning Mistakes into Stepping Stones for Success.* Nashville: 2007.

———. *Leadership Gold: Lessons Learned from a Lifetime of Leading.* Nashville: Nelson, 2008.

McChesney, Chris, Sean Covey, and Jim Huling. *The 4 Disciplines of Execution: Achieving Your Wildly Important Goals.* New York: Free Press, 2012.

McClelland, David C. *Power: The Inner Experience.* New York: Irvington, 1975.

McDaniel, Antonio L. *The Logic of Faith: A Journey of Understanding.* Bloomington, IN: AuthorHouse, 2011.

McDonough, Reginald M. *Working with Volunteer Leaders in the Church.* Nashville: Broadman Press, 1976.

McKee, Annie, Richard E. Boyatzis, and Frances Johnston. *Becoming a Resonant Leader: Develop Your Emotional Intelligence, Renew Your Relationships, Sustain Your Effectiveness.* Boston: Harvard Business School, 2008.

McKinley, Steve. "Where Does Time Go?" In *The Time Crunch: What to Do When You Can't Do It All.* Mastering Ministry's Pressure Points, edited by Steven L. McKinley, John C. Maxwell, and Greg Asimakoupoulos, 25–33. Sisters, OR: Multnomah, 1993.

McKnight, Scot. *The Blue Parakeet: Rethinking How You Read the Bible.* Grand Rapids: Zondervan, 2008.

McLuhan, Marshall, and W. Terrence Gordon. *Understanding Media: The Extensions of Man.* Corte Madera: Gingko Press, 2003.

McLuhan, Marshall, Eric Mcluhan, and Frank Zingrone. *Essential Mcluhan.* New York: Basic Books, 1995.

McNeal, Reggie, and Network Leadership. *Practicing Greatness: 7 Disciplines of Extraordinary Spiritual Leaders.* San Francisco: Jossey-Bass, 2006.

Melick, Richard R., and Shera Melick. *Teaching That Transforms: Facilitating Life Change through Adult Bible Teaching.* Nashville: B & H, 2010.

Kern, Ronni, "Homeless to Harvard: The Liz Murray Story." Lifetime Television, 1:27:17. 2003. https://www.youtube.com/watch?v=pGe3u5rLGQc.

Mehta, Glenn, *Stolen Treasure.* Dartford, UK: Xlibris Corporation, 2012.

Melrose, Ken. *Making the Grass Greener on Your Side: A CEO's Journey to Leading by Serving.* San Francisco: Berrett-Koehler, 1995.

Merrill, Eugene H. *Deuteronomy.* The New American Commnetary, edited by E. Ray Clendenen, vol. 4. Nashville: B & H, 1994.

Mertens, Jo B. "Incorporating Service-Learning." In *Service-Learning and the Liberal*

Arts: How and Why It Works, edited by Craig A. Rimmerman, 107-36. Lanham, MD: Lexington, 2011.

Metaxas, Eric. *Bonhoeffer: Pastor, Martyr, Prophet, Spy.* Nashville: Nelson, 2011.

Meyer, F. B. *Expository Preaching Plans and Methods.* New York: Hodder & Stoughton, 1912.

Miller, Calvin. *The Empowered Leader: 10 Keys to Servant Leadership.* Nashville: B & H, 1995.

———. *Leadership: An Influencer Discussion Guide.* Colorado Springs, CO: NavPress, 1987.

Miller, Kevin A. *Secrets of Staying Power: Overcomming the Discouragements of Ministry.* Carol Stream, IL: CTi, 1988.

Mittelstaedt, Robert E. *Will Your Next Mistake Be Fatal?: Avoiding the Chain of Mistakes That Can Destroy Your Organization.* Philadelphia: Wharton School, 2005.

Mounce, Robert H. *The Book of Revelation.* The New International Commentary on the New Testament, edited by Gordan Fee. Grand Rapids: Eerdmans, 1997.

———. *Matthew.* Understanding the Bible Commentary, edited by W. Ward Gasque, Robert L. Hubbard Jr., and Robert K. Johnston. Grand Rapids: Baker, 2011.

———. *Romans.* The New American Commentary, edited by E. Ray Clendenen, vol 27. Nashville: Broadman and Holman Publishers, 1995.

Mounce, William D. *Pastoral Epistles.* Word Biblical Commentary, edited by Bruce Metzger, Ralph Martin, and Lyn Allan Losie, vol. 46. Dallas: Word, 2000.

Mulholland, M. Robert. *Invitation to a Journey: A Road Map for Spiritual Formation.* Downers Grove, IL: IVP, 1993.

Murray, Liz. *Breaking Night: A Memoir of Forgiveness, Survival, and My Journey from Homeless to Harvard.* New York: Hyperion, 2010.

Myra, Harold, and Marshall Shelley. *The Leadership Secrets of Billy Graham.* Grand Rapids: Zondervan, 2005.

"Negotiating with God," *The End*, DVD. Directed by Burt Reynolds. Los Angeles, CA: Gordon-Reynolds Productions, 1978.

Nelson-Jones, Richard. *Life Coaching Skills: How to Develop Skilled Clients.* London: SAGE Publications, 2007.

Oates, Wayne E. "The Pastor as Healer." In *Baker's Dictionary of Practical Theology,* edited by Ralph G. Turnbull, 302-305. Grand Rapids: Baker, 1967.

Oden, Thomas C. *Becoming a Minister.* New York: Crossroad, 1987.

Orr, J. Edwin. *My All, His All.* Wheaton, IL: International Awakening, 1989.

Ortberg, John. *The Life You've Always Wanted: Spiritual Disciplines for Ordinary People.* Grand Rapids: Zondervan, 1997.

Osborne, Grant R. *The Hermeneutical Spiral: A Comprehensive Introduction to Biblical Interpretation*. Downers Grove, IL: IVP, 2006.

Parsons, George, and Speed Leas. *Understanding Your Congregation as a System: The Manual*. Bethesda, MD: Alban Institute, 1993.

Patterson, Kerry. *Crucial Conversations: Tools for Talking When Stakes Are High*. New York: McGraw-Hill, 2002.

Paschall, H. Franklin, "The Pastor as Overseer," ed. Ralph G. Turnbull, *Baker's Dictionary of Practical Theology*, 318–19. Grand Rapids: Baker, 1967.

Patterson, Kerry, Joseph Grenny, David Maxfield, Ron Mcmillan, and Al Switzler. *Influencer: The Power to Change Anything*. New York: McGraw-Hill, 2007.

Patzia, Arthur G. *Ephesians, Colossians, Philemon*. Understanding the Bible Commentary, edited by W. Ward Gasque, Robert L. Hubbard Jr., and Robert K. Johnston. Grand Rapids: Baker, 2011.

Pembroke, Neil. *Renewing Pastoral Practice: Trinitarian Perspectives on Pastoral Care and Counselling*. Aldershot, UK: Ashgate, 2006.

Perkins, Dennis N. T. *Leading at the Edge: Leadership Lessons from the Extraordinary Saga of Shackleton's Antarctic Expedition*. New York: AMACOM, 2000.

Peters, Thomas J., and Robert H. Waterman. *In Search of Excellence: Lessons from America's Best-Run Companies*. New York: HarperCollins, 2012.

Pfeffer, Jeffrey. *Power: Why Some People Have It — and Others Don't*. New York: HarperBusiness, 2010.

Polhill, John B. *Acts*. The New American Commentary, edited by David S. Dockery, vol. 26. Nashville: B & H, 1992.

Poole, Ed, and Kathi Robinson. *Lessons from Empowering Leaders: Real Life Stories to Inspire Your Organization toward Greater Success*. New York: Morgan James, 2009.

Potter-Efron, Ronald T. *Handbook of Anger Management: Individual, Couple, Family, and Group Approaches*. The Haworth Handbook Series in Psychotherapy. New York: Haworth Press, 2005.

Pratt, Richard L., Jr. *1 and 2 Corinthians*. Holman New Testament Commentary, edited by Max Anders, vol. 7. Nashville: B & H, 2000.

Rainer, Thom S. *Effective Evangelistic Churches: Successful Churches Reveal What Works and What Doesn't*. Nashville: B & H, 1996.

Rainer, Thom S., and Eric Geiger. *Simple Church: Returning to God's Process for Making Disciples*. Nashville: B & H, 2013.

Rainey, Dennis, Charles R. Swindoll and Roy B. Zuck. *Ministering to Twenty-first Century Families: Eight Big Ideas for Church Leaders*. Nashville: Word, 2001.

Reinke, Tony. *Desiring God* (blog). http://www.desiringgod.org/articles/a-beer-with-jesus.

Robertson, A. T. *Word Pictures in the New Testament*. Nashville: Broadman Press, 1933.

Robinson, Haddon W. *Biblical Preaching: The Development and Delivery of Expository Messages*. Grand Rapids: Baker, 2001.

Rogers, Everett M. *Diffusion of Innovations*. London: Simon & Schuster, 2003.

Romanoff, Bronna D. "Acceptance and Commitment Therapy (Act)." In *Techniques of Grief Therapy: Creative Practices for Counseling the Bereaved*. Series in Death, Dying, and Bereavement, edited by Robert A. Neimeyer, 133-5. New York: Routledge, 2012.

Rumford, Doug. "Untitled Speech." A speech delivered at the Promises Worth Keeping Conference, Alameda, CA. December 15, 1998.

Scazzero, Peter. *Emotionally Healthy Spirituality: Unleash a Revolution in Your Life in Christ*. Nashville: Integrity, 2006.

Schaff, Philip, and David Schley Schaff. *History of the Christian Church, Volume 7: Modern Christianity*. New York: Charles Scribner's Sons, 1910.

Schaller, Lyle E. *The Change Agent*. Nashville: Abingdon, 1972.

Schiltz, Patrick J. "The Future of Sexual Abuse Litigation "*America: The National Catholic Review*, July 7, 2003. http://americamagazine.org/issue/439/article/future-sexual-abuse-litigation.

Schriever, Bernard A., Richard H. Kohn, and Jacob Neufeld. *Reflections on Research and Development in the United States Air Force an Interview with General Bernard A. Schriever, and Generals Samuel C. Phillips, Robert T. Marsh, and James H. Doolittle, and Dr. Ivan A. Getting*. Washington DC: Center for Air Force History, U.S. Air Force, 1992.

Selby, Rosalind M. *The Comical Doctrine: An Epistemology of New Testament Hermeneutics*. Milton Keynes, UK: Paternoster, 2006.

Shelley, Marshall. *Helping Those Who Don't Want Help*. Leadership Library Series, vol. 7. Carol Stream, IL: Christianity Today, 1986.

——. *Ministering to Problem People in Your Church: What to Do with Well-Intentioned Dragons*. Bloomington, MN: Bethany, 2013.

Smart, James D. *The Teaching Ministry of the Church: An Examination of the Basic Principles of Christian Education*. Philadelphia: Westminster Press, 1954.

Smith, Donald P. *Empowering Ministry: Ways to Grow in Effectiveness*. Louisville: Westminster John Knox Press, 1996.

Smyth, Charles H. E. *The Art of Preaching: A Practical Survey of Preaching in the Church of England, 747-1939*. London: SPCK, 1940.

Snodgrass, Klyne. *Stories with Intent: A Comprehensive Guide to the Parables of Jesus*. Grand Rapids: Eerdmans, 2008.

Snowman, Jack, and Rick. R. Mccown. *Psychology Applied to Teaching*. 14th ed. Stamford: Cengage Learning, 2014.

Spicq, Ceslas, and James D. Ernest. "ἑτεροζυγέω." In *Theological Lexicon of the New Testament*. Peabody, MA: Hendrickson, 1994.

Stanley, Andy. *Choosing to Cheat: Who Wins When Family and World Collide*. Portland: Multnomah, 2003.

———. *Visioneering: God's Blueprint for Developing and Maintaining Vision*. Annotated ed. Sisters, OR: Multnomah, 2005.

Stebnicki, Mark A. *Empathy Fatigue Healing the Mind, Body, and Spirit of Professional Counselors*. New York: Springer, 2008.

Stein, Robert H. *A Basic Guide to Interpreting the Bible: Playing by the Rules*. Grand Rapids: Baker, 2011.

Steinke, Peter L. "Addressing Anxiety in Congregations," adobe flash audio, 1:18:00, accessed May 5, 2011, http://my.ekklesia360.com/Clients/mediaaudioplayer.php?CMSCODE=EKK&mediabid=218917&useSkin=skin_plain.xml&CMS_LINK

———. *Congregational Leadership in Anxious Times: Being Calm and Courageous No Matter What*. Herndon, VA: Alban Institute, 2006.

———. *Healthy Congregations: A Systems Approach*. Bethesda, MD: Alban Institute, 1996.

———. *How Your Church Family Works: Understanding Congregations as Emotional Systems*. Washington DC: Alban Institute, 1993.

Steven, Megan S., and Colin Blakemore. "Cortical Plasticity in the Adult Human Brain." In *The Cognitive Neurosciences*, edited by Michael S. Gazzaniga, vol 3, 1243-1254. Cambridge: Bradford Book, 2004.

Stevens, R. Paul, and Phil Collins. *The Equipping Pastor: A Systems Approach to Congregational Leadership*. Lanham: Rowman & Littlefield, 1993.

Stitzinger, James F. "The History of Expository Preaching." In *Rediscovering Expository Preaching*, edited by John MacArthur, 36-62. Dallas: Word, 1992.

Stott, John R. W. *Between Two Worlds: The Art of Preaching in the Twentieth Century*. Grand Rapids: Eerdmans, 1982.

Strathmann, H. "λαός." In *Theological Dictionary of the New Testament*: L-N. The Theological Dictionary of the New Testament, edited by Gerhard Kittel, Geoffrey W. Bromiley, and Gerhard Friedrich, vol. 4, 50-57. Grand Rapids: Eerdmans, 1993.

Stueber, Karsten. "Empathy." In *Stanford Encyclopedia of Philosophy*, edited by Edward N. Zalta. Last updated, Winter, 2014. http://plato.stanford.edu/archives/win2014/entries/empathy.

Sunukjian, Donald R. *Invitation to Biblical Preaching: Proclaiming Truth with Clarity and Relevance*. Grand Rapids: Kregel, 2007.

Susek, Ron. *Firestorm: Preventing and Overcoming Church Conflicts*. Grand Rapids: Baker, 1999.

Sweet, Leonard I., Brian D. Mclaren, and Jerry Haselmayer. *"A" Is for Abductive: The Language of the Emerging Church*. Grand Rapids: Zondervan, 2003.

Swenson, Richard A. *Margin: Restoring Emotional, Physical, Financial, and Time Reserves to Overloaded Lives*. E-book ed. Carol Stream, IL: Tyndale, 2014.

Tabb, Mark A. *Out of the Whirlwind*. Nashville: B & H, 2003.

Tangney, June P., and Ronda L. Dearing. *Shame and Guilt: Emotions and Social Behavior*. New York: Guilford Press, 2003.

Tannehill, Robert C. *The Gospel according to Luke*. Vol. 1 of *The Narrative Unity of Luke-Acts: A Literary Interpretation*. Philadelphia: Fortress Press, 1991.

Taylor, Gardner. "Shaping Sermons by the Shape of Text and Preacher." In *Preaching Biblically: Creating Sermons in the Shape of Scriptures*, edited by Don M. Wardlaw, 60–83. Philadelphia: Westminster Press, 1983.

Thoburn, John, Rob Baker, and Maria Dal Maso. *Clergy Sexual Misconduct: A Systems Approach to Prevention, Intervention, and Oversight*. Carefree, AZ: Gentle Path Press, 2011.

Thomas, James M. *Script Analysis for Actors, Directors, and Designers*. Burlington, MA: Focal Press, 2009.

Tidwell, Charles A. *Educational Ministry of a Church*. Nashville: Broadman Press, 1982.

Titchener, Edward B. *Lectures on the Experimental Psychology of the Thought-Processes*. New York: Macmillan, 1909.

Tov, Emanuel. *Textual Criticism of the Hebrew Bible*. 2nd revised ed. Minneapolis: Fortress Press, 2001.

Towner, Philip. *1–2 Timothy and Titus*, vol. 14. Downers Grove, IL: IVP, 1994.

Towner, Philip H. *The Letters to Timothy and Titus*. Grand Rapids: Eerdmans, 2006.

Trutza, P. "Marriage." In *The Zondervan Pictorial Encyclopedia of the Bible*, edited by Merrill C. Tenney and Steven Barabas, 92–102. Grand Rapids: Zondervan, 1977.

Utley, Robert James. *Paul's Letters to a Troubled Church: 1 and 2 Corinthians*. Study Guide Commentary Series, vol. 6. Marshall, TX: Bible Lessons International, 2002.

Vachon, Mary L. S. "Reflections on Compassion, Suffering and Occupational Stress." In *Perspectives on Human Suffering*, edited by Jeff Malpas and Norelle Lickiss, 317–36. New York: Springer, 2012.

Valent, Paul. "Diagnosis and Treatment of Helper Stresses, Traumas, and Illnesses."

In *Treating Compassion Fatigue*. Brunner-Routledge Psychosocial Stress Series 24, edited by Charles R. Figley, 17–38. Sage Publications, 2002.

Vogel, Robert. "Biblical Genres and the Text-Driven Sermon." In *Text-Driven Preaching: God's Word at the Heart of Every Sermon*, edited by Daniel L. Akin, David Lewis Allen, and Ned Lee Mathews, 163–92. Nashville: B & H, 2010.

Vos, Tineke. *Denial and Quality of Life in Lung Cancer Patients*. Pallas Proefschriften Series. Amsterdam: Amsterdam University Press, 2009.

Waggoner, Brad J. *The Shape of Faith to Come: Spiritual Formation and the Future of Discipleship*. Nashville: B & H, 2008.

Walker, Williston, and Robert T. Handy. *History of the Christian Church*. 3rd rev. ed. New York: Scribner, 1970.

Waltke, Bruce K., and Charles Yu. *An Old Testament Theology: An Exegetical, Canonical, and Thematic Approach*. Grand Rapids: Zondervan, 2007.

Ward, Fenton. *What to Say When They Say I'm Jewish: Sharing the Gospel with the Original Messengers*. San Francisco: Purple Pomegranate Productions, 1999.

White, Ernest O. *Becoming a Christian Leader*. Nashville: Convention Press, 1985.

Wiarda, Timothy. *Interpreting Gospel Narratives: Scenes, People, and Theology*. Nashville: B & H, 2010.

Wickman, Charles A. *Pastors at Risk: Protecting Your Future, Guarding Your Present*. New York: Morgan James, 2014.

Wicks, Robert J., ed. *Handbook of Spirituality for Ministers*, vol. 1. New York: Paulist Press, 1995.

Wiersbe, Warren W. *The Bible Exposition Commentary*. Wheaton, IL: Victor Books, 1996.

Wilder, Christian A. "Establishing and Training a Strategic Church Growth Team at Calvary Baptist Church, Napa, California." D.Min. project, The Southern Baptist Theological Seminary, 2007.

Wilson, Jim L. "A Pastoral Model for Engaging Community" in *Ministry in the New Marriage Culture*, ed. Jeff Iorg, 223–36. Nashville: B & H, 2015.

———. *Future Church: Ministry in a Post-Seeker Age*. Nashville: B & H, 2004.

———. *How to Write Narrative Sermons*. Fresno, CA: Willow City Press, 2002.

———. *Soul Shaping: Disciplines That Conform You to the Image of Christ*. Nashville: LifeWay, 2009.

Wilson, Michael Todd, and Brad Hoffmann. *Preventing Ministry Failure: A Shepherdcare Guide for Pastors, Ministers, and Other Caregivers*. Downers Grove, IL: IVP, 2007.

Wispe, Lauren. "History of the Concept of Empathy." In *Empathy and Its Development*. Cambridge Studies in Social and Emotional Development, edited by Nancy Eisenberg and Janet Strayer, 17–37. Cambridge: Cambridge University Press, 1990.

Witherington, Ben III. *The Gospel of Mark: A Socio-Rhetorical Commentary*. Grand Rapids: Eerdmans, 2001.

Wooden, John, and Steve Jamison. *Wooden on Leadership*. New York: McGraw-Hill, 2005.

Wright, H. Norman. *Helping Those in Grief: A Guide to Help You Care for Others*. Ventura, CA: Gospel Light, 2011.

General Index

Acts, book of: the church's decision-making in, 19; "disciple" as the primary name for a Christian in, 112n23

Aesop, 96n71

agamos (Greek: unmarried one), 77nn34–35

alcohol, 7; and FAA restrictions on pilots, 7n27; and total abstinence, 7n26

Allender, Dan B., 187–88n16, 188n17, 195n46

American Counseling Association, 22n28

anaginoskon (Greek: reading aloud), 100n94

Andersen, Hans Christian, 154

anepilēmptos (Greek: irreproachable), 8n29

Aristotle, 9, 9n32, 93n46; teaching style of, 108

Arthurs, Jeffrey D., 91

Artwohl, Alexis, 52n18

authority: ecclesiastical authority, 187, 187n15; positional authority, 187–88

Baker, Rob, 64n28, 59n50

baptism, 80–82; baby dedications in place of infant baptism, 83; believer's baptism, 83; as a celebration of the gospel's power, 82; importance of, 83; as symbolic in nature, 82

Baptists, standards of for filling the pulpit, 14

baptizō (Greek: to dip or submerge), 82n43

Barna, George, on vision, 183, 183n49

Barnabas, loan of credibility to Saul by, 194–95

Barnhouse, Donald Grey, on divorce, 77n31

Barrett, Colleen, 158, 190n32

Behrends, William, 195

Bennis, Warren G., 195n47

Berna, Gregory, 154

births, 79

Blackwood, Andrew W., 92n28

Blanchard, Kenneth H., 190n32; on servant leadership, 187n10

Blomberg, Craig L., 95, 96, 108n5, 205

Bonhoeffer, Dietrich, 88n4

boundaries: boundaries set by governing bodies of churches, 193, 193n38; emotional boundaries, 70; relational boundaries, 69–70; schedule boundaries, 68–69

Bowen, Murray, 150

Greenleaf, Robert K., 19n24, 20, 114n38, 194n43; on servant leadership, 186n3

Greidanus, Sidney, 89, 94, 94n51, 101

grief ministry, 33; the grieving spectrum, 33–36; listen—and don't repeat clichés, 36–39; remembering anniversaries of death dates, 40. *See also* funerals

Griffin, Hayne P., 8n29

Grossman, Dave, 52n18

groupthink, 154–56; as a survival mechanism in nature, 154–55

Gula, Richard M., 69, 69n51

Hall, Sarah E.: on family homeostasis, 169n1; on homeostasis, 169n1

Haugk, Kenneth C., 144

Hawkins, Greg L., 112n26, 114n37

Heath, Chip, 181n40, 183, 183n51, 183–84n54

Heath, Dan, 181n40, 183, 183n51, 183–84n54

helping others without hurting yourself, 55–61; and the "I feel your pain" attitude, 65–66; and the "whatever it takes" attitude, 62–64. *See also* boundaries; fatigue syndromes; soul hygiene

Henry, Jim, 111

herding. *See* groupthink

Herodians, conflict of with Jesus, 127, 128

Hersey, Paul, 188n18; on power, 187

Hillel, on divorce, 7n30

Hobbs, Herschel H., 22n29

Hodges, Phil, on servant leadership, 187n10

Hoffman, Brad, 132n24

Hoffman, Martin L., on empathy, 65, 65n43

homeostasis, 156, 169, 169n1, 174; family homeostasis, 169n1

hope, 116, 117

Hopkins, Paul E., on resilience, 61n8

Hopson, Barrie, 113n33

hospital visitation, 29–30, 32; be aware of where you are, 30–31; be considerate of the patient's circumstances, 31; listen, 31–32

Huggman, John A., 78n39

Hugo of Saint Cher, 92

Huling, Jim, 182n45

Hunter, A. M., 94n53

Hurtado, Larry W., 120n4, 122n10

Hybels, Bill, 63

Hybels, Lynn, 63

Iacocca, Lee, 188–89

Innocent III, 92

Iorg, Jeff, 60n4, 132–33n25; on a "general call to ministry leadership," 23; on servant leadership, 186n6

Jackson, Neil E., Jr., 19n23

Jacobs, Alan, 89

Jamison, Steve, 189n29

jealousy, morbid, 145, 145n7

Jesus: affirmation of His deity by Jesus Himself, 126n12; appropriate boundaries of, 70; attempts by those close to Him to sabotage Him, 167; compassion of, 65; on divorce, 76–77n30; as fully human, yet without sin, 111n20, 132; as the good shepherd, 4, 131; on His prophetic role, 121; "I am"

101, 101n99; three-point sermons, 93, 96–97; and verse-by-verse preaching, 92. *See also* expository preaching; sermons, and biblical genres

sermons, and biblical genres, 90–91, 97n80. *See also* epistles, the; narratives, biblical; parables; parallelism; proverbs

shama' (Hebrew: to hear), 108–9n8

Shammai, on divorce, 76–77n30

Shedd, William G. T., 120–21n

Shelley, Marshall, 46

Shema, 108, 108–9n8

shepherds, in the ancient world, 4n5

Sidney, Algernon, 96n71

Smart, James D., 109n9

Smith, Donald P., 131n23

Smyth, Charles H. E., 93, 93n43

Snodgrass, Klyne, 95, 205

Snowman, Jack, 113n32

Socrates, 60n7

soul hygiene: give God the first part of your day, 67–68; give God the first part of your energy, 67

Spears, Larry C., 19n24

Spicq, Ceslas, 75n20

splagchnizomai (Greek: to feel compassion), 65n29

Spurgeon, Charles, 111

Stanley, Andy, 64n23; on vision, 183, 183n50

Stebnicki, Mark A., 65n30; on empathy fatigue, 62n16, 66n44

Stein, Robert H., 89, 89n13, 205

Steinke, Peter L., 149–50, 149n2, 152, 157, 160, 165n32, 166n34; on resistance, 168n40; on scapegoating, 156

Stephanus, 92, 92n35

Stott, John R. W., 93, 97; on the

"golden rule for sermon outlines," 91n21

Stuart, Douglas, 89

Sunukjian, Donald R., 87–88, 98

Susek, Ron, 147–48

Sweet, Leonard I., on resistance, 169n3

Swenson, Richard A., 21n26

teaching in conflict situations, 118, 119; conflicts are opportunities to learn as well as teach, 133–34; life and ministry is better with friends, even though pastors will have conflict with them, 131–32; since pastors are sinful, they can expect to have conflicts caused by their failures, 132–33. *See also* Jesus, teaching of in conflict situations

teaching while walking around, 105–7; pastors equip people for ministry, 112–15; pastors teach in times of conflict, 118; pastors teach when people ask questions or engage them in conversations, 115–18; pastors teach when they live what they say they believe, and when they don't, 109–11

teknon (Greek: child, inhabitant), 7n24

Thoburn, John, 64n28, 69n50

Thomas, Walter J., 182n46, 195n47

Tidwell, Charles A., 108n6

Titchener, Edward B., 66

Towner, Philip H., 9n34

Townsend, John, 159, 159n47

Tressell, Jim, 109

tribulations, 116

trust, 116, 117

underfunctioning, 157–58

Scripture Index

OLD TESTAMENT